UNDEFEATED

Terry Marsh

Published by Terry Marsh Publishing
60 Gaynesford Basildon Essex SS16 5SG
www.terrymarsh.info

ISBN 0–9549999-0-8

British Library Cataloguing – in – production Data:
A catalogue record for this book is available from British Library

Printed and bound in Britain

To my children:
Kelly, Karl and Gabrielle
and their Uncle J

Contents

Prologue

"...Ladies and Gentleman of the jury. Let's consider the scene on 30th November 1989, outside the theatre in Barking. The shooting of Frank Warren was a planned assassination attempt. The Crown's case is that Terry Marsh had a powerful motive to wish to dispose of Frank Warren... Marsh had a festering dislike of Warren, whom he saw as standing alone in the way of his re-establishment. That is a very powerful motive. Marsh's swift and severe decline had left him a desperate man. The public pronouncement through the Sun of his epilepsy had ended his boxing career and employment as a fireman. Marsh blamed Warren for his removal as a commentator from the 'Seconds Out' programme.

In January 1989 Warren and Marsh had a meeting at the formers' office in Tavistock Place. Marsh asked for their manager-boxer contract to be rescinded. Warren refused.

Then on the 25th January 1989 Marsh uttered the remarks on Thames TV's 'Midweek Sports Special' that prompted Warren's libel action against him. Warren sued on the third of February. On the twenty first of February the British boxing board of control turned down Marsh's application to box again, thus cutting off another source of income.

The libel case was looming, with the possibility of a large settlement and costs to pay. By the end of November he owed £124,000. He has got a huge mortgage on his house. He had lost his commentary job, lost his fireman's job and he was facing, if he lost the libel action, both costs and damages.

He can't settle the action, as that would mean an apology, it would mean having to admit that what he said on television had been a dreadful lie about Frank Warren. Warren's death would effectively have finished the libel action. Only Frank Warren stood between Marsh and personal vindication.

If at the end of the day...the jigsaw is complete, you will be able to put your hand on your heart and say this case is proved."

Show nothing was the policy from the moment I first entered the dock. Everything you do is with hesitancy. How will the jury interpret your actions or emotions? When you are being demeaned do you show indignation or remain outwardly indifferent? Whatever you do, you see it as the wrong thing. I was even reluctant to look at the jury fearing they may be intimidated by the eye contact. It is a very awkward position to be in. These twelve people are the ultimate arbiters in charge of my destiny and there was now fuck all I could do about it. On hearing the prosecution's summing up I was beginning to have serious doubts. Those matters that she brought to the jury's attention I could have easily explained away I should have addressed them. But now I had to sit in silence and wait. My heart raced not through fear but anger. I should never have listened to my legal team. I ignored my instincts and now I was fucked. How could I go to fucking prison for life? What the fuck am I doing here? How the hell did it happen? Now that is a long story.

CHAPTER ONE
BAD LOSER

I knew from an early age what it was like to be a champion. I was only nine years old when I gained my first title. I will always remember my first words as a champ – checkmate. I was the East London chess champion. East London and Chess some would say was incongruous. Some said I was the best of a bad bunch but I proved the doubters wrong when aged ten years I became the London champion.

The London championships were a cliff-hanger and it was I who was doing the hanging. The final round saw me pitched against Danny Roberts the tournament leader. He had beaten me on a previous occasion. I needed to win; a draw would not have been sufficient. The atmosphere was tense and all were gathered round the small table on which we would do battle. There were too many people trying to occupy too small a space and so the two combatants were moved into a nearby staff room where teachers were the only spectators.

I still don't know whether the change of venue was for the benefit of the contestants or the teachers who also were keen spectators. It was not to my advantage. I was used to playing chess in a noisy environment and the present tranquil surroundings appeared somewhat artificial. The silence was broken when Danny could not stop his tears from subsiding, having recognised finality about his position. As games go the score between us was one each but this was the crucial one for him. As my Dad would say to me, "You're only as good as your last fight."

I'd lost my last fight and I lost my first fight. My record within the ropes was nil wins and 2 losses. Had I won my first fight I don't think there would have been a second fight. The second

fight was a rematch. Had I won the second fight there definitely would not have been a third.
I had joined St Georges not because it was a boxing club but it happened to be near home. It was convenient. Boxing was not a big thing for me but avenging my two losses to Tommy Mooney was.
My matchmaker Kenny Cushway promised me another rematch but in the interim I had a few more fights that met with success. The fight invariably meant a late night and prior to going to bed my Mum would cook something for us to eat while Dad and I went through a post-fight analysis. I was to lose once again to Tommy before finally recording a win. Two weeks later I chalked up another victory. I felt now I had got the measure of him but he proved the better next time around. Had I got to three each I would have hung up my gloves. It was becoming something of an obsession with me and I would find myself dreaming about ways of beating him.
I had the best start in life that any kid could hope for. I'd been given two wonderful parents Maisie and Jimmy Marsh. I was the third of four children. There was Jimmy junior, Billy and my kid brother John.
My eldest brother Jimmy was born a beautiful looking baby some eight years before me. My mother with the benefit of three subsequent births was able to conclude that Jimmy's birth was not an orthodox delivery. As a young lady she had heard the stories of how painful childbirth was and when she endured the pain of her first born she regarded it as par for the course.
Maternal instinct told Maisie that there was something amiss with her, then only, child. These fears grew as Jimmy's development progressed slower than expected. It took more than three years and numerous visits to various Doctors and Consultants before my mother's worst fears were confirmed. Jimmy was mentally retarded, as it was called then, a condition that would ensure Mum and Dad would be looking after Jimmy for the rest of their lives.
Jimmy's condition provoked within me many emotions as a kid, but anger was the most memorable. I often found myself standing up to other kids who had seen my brother as a source of amusement. On some occasions the perpetrators were icons of

hardness within the area and my challenges to them were moments of madness. Yet on such occasions it was they who blinked first. I'm sure had the confrontations reached physical exchanges then I would have suffered. I would not have cared. To do nothing would have hurt much more.

Like everyone else in the East End my father had done a bit of boxing. He had won a schoolboy title, a feat he achieved whilst wearing my grandmother's bloomers. His other claim to fame is the fact he lived in Stepney for forty-eight years and, unlike everyone else of his time, he never knew either of the Kray twins. He worked as a lorry driver for the Port of London Authority (PLA).

Mum seemed to have resigned herself to a life of giving. People would say that she was a typical East Ender. I didn’t know what they meant but it was always articulated with a degree of admiration and affection. Her life revolved around her children. One of her many tasks were the twice weekly visits to Ratcliff baths. It was here that the washing was done. Mum always had a lot of washing in the first twenty years of motherhood. This was mainly due to Jimmy’s bedwetting.

The sleeping arrangements were somewhat cramped. Mum and Dad would sleep in the upstairs front bedroom while we kids were in the rear room. I shared a bed with younger brother John, while the other siblings had their own beds. The lack of space dictated that all the beds were squashed together. This did not make for an easy task when it came to making them. Yet despite this, I never got into a bed that was not clean and neatly made.

The nocturnal toilet was a bucket sited on the small landing. It was either too cold or dark to visit the toilet at the bottom of the yard. The backward sanitation was further highlighted by the absence of a bath. The best we could do was a sink in the kitchen. A gas-fired contraption referred to as the 'geezer' heated the cold water that run from the mains. The gas was on a meter and when the two bobs (10 pence) worth had been extracted the ‘geezer’ would go out. We were in the same position as most down our street but our family was larger and my parents also had the additional problem of Jimmy’s bedwetting along with his poor personal hygiene in general.

A further weekly exercise was our Sunday evening visit to

Nanny Marsh. Very seldom would we have to knock at the door for the key was invariably in the latch. As well as being a social call it served the purpose of us being able to have a bath. At the time it did not appear strange or different and it is only on reflection that I can appreciate the problems my parents had to overcome in rearing their kids. Mum's task was formidable but she never wavered. She badly wanted and more importantly needed a bigger house. The appeals to various agencies achieved little. She was the main obstacle because of the way she was able to get by and cope, despite the problems she faced. The various visitors, who would monitor Jimmy's development, had said this - off the record of course. Mum took pride in this endorsement of her adequacies. Perhaps this is what being a typical East Ender meant.

On leaving primary school I became a pupil of Westminster City Grammar an all boys school. It was one of the top schools in London, with pupils attending from all parts of the Capital but the East London contingent you could count on the fingers of one hand. The initial phase was pleasant enough until the French lesson. "Je m'appelle Madame Bouchee. Comment vous appelez-vous et quel age avez-vous?" Hitherto the only French I had heard was from the song 'Frere Jacque'. Naturally there was no great surprise hearing such sounds in a French lesson but what took me back was that everyone else in the class appeared to be speaking back in French. I thought they might have been to induction classes, during the preceding six weeks holiday, that I had missed, but it was not so. It made me feel very uneasy and obliged to catch up.

The problem was compounded through sitting at the front. On reflection there must have been a fair number of 'francophobes' in the group but with my back to the bulk of the class I was oblivious to such. From where I was sitting I was the only one who did not speak the lingo. The panic I felt only served to erode all objectivity and when the words from Madame Bouchee where directed at me I replied in the only French I knew "We" [sic].

From the moment I got on the tube that evening to the moment I went to bed I had my head in the French textbook. I tried to learn everything and succeeded in learning nothing. The pattern had been set for the remainder of my days at Westminster City

Grammar. I spent my time endeavouring to catch up; I never did.
The homework was never ending and most of my weekends where taken up making up for lost ground. I had lost touch with my former primary school mates, which in some ways was a blessing since it would have been a distraction from my studying. However, it made for a lonely time.
Rising early also exposed me to the problems Mum was having with Jimmy. He now was approaching twenty and still bed-wetting. One occasion, I witnessed, remains with me today. Mum had to cut lumps of shit from Jimmy that must have excreted from him the moment he went to bed. It had dried and meshed to his body hair. It was tragic; a wet bed, shitty pyjamas, and a soiled retarded man resisting his mothers attempts to clean him in a kitchen that did not have enough room to swing a mouse - let alone a cat. I held back the tears that day until I was out the door. I wept for both my Mum and brother. Both my parents deserved medals for the way they cared for my brother Jimmy.

CHAPTER TWO
ESCAPE TO BASILDON

When the opportunity of a change of occupation arrived Dad decided to give it a go. There was a vacancy for a lock keeper at Tilbury dock. He got the job. Working in Essex presented the opportunity of moving to Basildon. I never shed any tears about leaving Westminster City and was full of excitement about moving to, what was then, relative countryside. Our new house had 4 bedrooms, a dining room, a sunroof, a large fitted kitchen and two toilets. We also had a garden instead of a yard.

I had a week's grace before enrolling at the local comprehensive school. My first visit with Mum entailed seeing Mr Suthers who held the title School Counsellor. He paraded a very unconventional beard, which had a resemblance to a television character of the time called Catweazle. "I am sure, Mrs Marsh, that you have had a lot of expense with moving so there is no urgency regarding uniform. Terry can wear his old uniform or whatever for the time being."

I turned up at the school the next morning modestly conforming to the dress requirements, which included my blue surge Crombie overcoat with the compulsory red satin hanky protruding from the left breast pocket. My attire complemented my short haircut. As Catweazle and I approached my new class, a jarring cacophony was emanating from behind the door that displayed the alphanumeric 2C. As Catweazle entered followed by the new boy the noise continued. I was introduced to my class tutor and then Catweazle took the stage, "2C." The noise had ceased but he had not got everybody's attention. There were still groups seated on desks with their own agendas, "This is Terry and he is joining the class. Who would like to show him round?" One caucus volunteered unanimously and so I was pointed in

their direction. Their gang of three was now four. There was I in my Crombie overcoat contrasting against the three anoraks.
The class appeared to have the measure of the teacher. She was young and, from my perspective, appeared as though the present location was the last place she wanted to be. The register was never called she would complete it by sight. There was an air of defeatism about her but no sense of victory from her charges. She was of little consequence to the class and carried as much presence as one of the chairs.
The initial excursions into the playground were times of trepidation. I have never felt such vulnerability before or since. It may have been due to the picture of horror and terror relayed by the anoraks but my first impressions suggested they were accurate.
Of all the various groups positioned in the playground one, mob like, congregation stood out. The anoraks informed me to stay well clear of 'smokers' corner' but curiosity got the better. A meaner bunch I had not seen hitherto. The other members of the school all appeared to have made some effort to conform to the school uniform, like the token tie or an acceptable coloured jumper. Yet the coterie before me had no such concession. The dress suggested no surrender, as did the unconcealed cigarettes.
Despite all this perceived intimidation I was revelling in the new environment. The journey to and from school was measured in metres rather than kilometres. School started later and finished earlier than my former *alma mater*. The lessons were lax, the discipline devoid and the teachers tender.
I had now progressed from the anoraks into a more middle of the road peer group within the class. This, I suspect, was related to the promise I had shown in the playground at football. There was talk of making the second year team. At the trials I played sufficiently well to unease the incumbent left half.
I made the team but did not stay in it for long. I became very aware of the maturity of most of the team who seemed like men to me. I was becoming aware of the advance of puberty in my peers and the dormancy of my own body clock. The after match showers were becoming an embarrassment.

Bikes were a big interest and many hours were spent working on them. John Hevizi, a lad who lived opposite, and I decided, as we had done a number of times before, to visit the local dump in search of bike parts with a view to making our own bikes and selling them. The dump was a couple of miles away and our trek entailed crossing a railway line. It was adjacent to Pitsea marshes and sat beside some tributaries of the river Thames. The dump was always the host to an acrid smell and flocks of sea gulls who were not averse to coming in for a closer look. In our pursuit of spare parts the irritants would be endured.

As well as the gulls the dump had quite a number of human visitors who would unearth all sorts of artefacts. On many occasions I had returned home with items that would look good in the house. To my puzzlement Mum and Dad disagreed. We had been children of Basildon for three months when Colin Smith, a younger but heavier lad who lived next to John, asked us if he could come along.

We walked to the end of the tarmac road that serviced the tipper lorries and began our ascent over the mounds of rubbish. The smell was still present, as were the birds but we were the only representatives of our species. We came across a window frame that contained a number of sections with the glass still in place. The sound of the breaking glass was fun. Colin smashed one with the heel of his shoe but the downward motion of the foot continued. I was squirted with what I first thought was red paint. It was only when Colin screamed that I realised it was blood and that we were in the shit. It was squirting everywhere and we could do nothing about it. We tried to carry him from the dump but were quick to recognise the futility of the task. He was far too heavy. We decided, simultaneously that one of us would stay with him while the other went for help. John stayed while I ran as fast as my legs would carry me. It was about a half a kilometre to the main road.

I was scared for Colin and of the situation. I felt that as much as I was going for help I was also running away from the problem. John had the hardest task in having to sit and wait. I was only too aware that we all possess a finite amount of blood and my clothing was carrying a lot of Colin's. I took off like my journey was a 50-metre dash and after 40 metres began to realise the error of my eagerness. I was gasping for breath and the mounds

of rubbish I had to run through had sapped the strength from my legs. I was running but appeared to be getting nowhere and recognised it as being a theme of dreams that I occasionally endured. I fell on a few occasions due to my desperation and it was certainly a case of more haste and less speed. Eventually I hit the hard standing and was able to make ground but not before falling once again as my legs reacted to the solid surfaces.
I knew I had to keep my concentration and was able to run to a rhythm as I was shouting profanities. I had somehow been able to put Colin from my mind till the moment I hit the main road. My luck was in as a car and a van approached. At this time of the evening it was not a particularly busy period. I jumped into the road waving my hands but to little effect. The railway crossing was a further four hundred metres and so I headed off towards it. I was hurting and unsure of whether I would be quick enough. I run a few paces then had to walk. I felt a failure and started to cry with the frustration. The mind was willing but the body was knackered. I heard and then saw another car approaching and I attempted to flag it down. My attempt was half hearted and a reflection of how dejected I felt. As expected the car went pass, "Fuck it." I cried in frustration. "Thank fuck." I cried in elation as the brake lights lit up.
It was like I had found a reserve tank inside me. I dashed to the car with ease and explained the problem to the driver. Off he went to make the call and I was alone again. A truck appeared shortly after and a stout looking traveller got out. He was heading for the dump and had parked up by the gate that was locked. My blood stained clothing and distressed look meant the minimum of words were needed to explain my plight and I directed him to the scene. On arrival to my surprise and relief Colin was still alive. He was still bleeding but not with the same ferocity as when I left him. The gypsy was able to give him a piggyback to the main road. The man who had made the call for the ambulance had returned having also got the trains held up for the ambulance's arrival. Colin was now unconscious and the adults had relieved John and I of our charge. We still worried for Colin but, for the moment we were able to relax to some degree. The noise of the ambulance was a beautiful sound.
It was I who was to travel with the patient in the ambulance

while John had to break the uncertain news to Colin's parents. The hospital was some ten miles away in Southend and we travelled on a blue light all the way. Colin had been hooked up to some plasma or something like it, which suggested to me that he was going to be okay. On arrival I gave Colin's details to the reception and then phoned my parents to give them the run down. However, John already had briefed them. Colin's dad, Gerry, was on his way.

When Gerry arrived he was updated on Colin's condition. The doctor had informed him that his son had severed his tendon and artery and that he was on his way to recovery. He had lost a lot of blood but the concern for the moment was his future mobility. I was worried about the dad's arrival because I suspected that he would have blamed John and I for his son's predicament. As it was the present was more pressing.

Cause was not to be an issue. Had his injury been less serious then perhaps it would have left his mind free to consider other factors. At some stage it must have been relayed to Gerry that had Colin not got to the hospital his son would have died. When I got home there was no aggravation from either Mum or Dad. I thought the anticipated punishment would be delayed and that I was presently sitting in punishment row.

On arriving home from school the following day John and I was reminded of the deeds of yesterday. A photographer and reporter were waiting for us from the Basildon Evening Echo. We were driven to the scene of the grime - pardon the pun. Our pictures were taken. We made the front-page headlines the next day, 'PITSEA BOY HEROES IN MERCY DASH DRAMA'. We had been portrayed as 'bikeless' kids who had an accident while scavenging for parts in order for us to build our own bikes.

One reader took pity on us and phoned the Echo to make a donation of three bikes. It was an opportunity for another story and after several days in hospital Colin was able to join us in collecting them. It was a nice gesture but in reality there was only one bike that you could ride without eroding your street cred. The other two bikes ended up on Pitsea dump.

CHAPTER THREE
SCHOOLDAYS

School was now an irrelevance in the sense that it no longer dominated every moment of my life. At Westminster it was always there with either homework needing completion or it was necessary to catch up in the subjects in which I lagged. Now school was just a place that I frequented between the hours of 9am and 3.30pm. It was neither a bind nor a benefit.

The highlight of the week for many in the lower school was the Friday night school dance. The challenge was to see who could get the most dances. The big names at the time were The Jackson Five, The Osmonds, Bay City Rollers, and David Cassidy. But the one that sticks in my mind is Perry Como singing, 'Its impossible'. It was the slow number that was always the last record to be played at the school dance. Invariably if you got in on the last dance a grope was also likely. To be honest the last dance was not a big deal for me until I clapped eyes on this beautiful looking girl with a figure to match. Unfortunately, when the needle hit the Perry Como vinyl she was nowhere to be seen.

On Monday I was the first at assembly monitoring all the entrants in search of this beauty. I didn't have to wait long only pausing for a few droplets of Old Spice before making a beeline towards her. Her class was seated behind mine, which accounted in some part why she had previously gone unnoticed.

"Hello my name is Terry will you go out with me?

She looked to her mate as if to look for advice or encouragement. Her mate seemed sympathetic to my plea. "I'll think about it." She said but her eyes said, yes.

We met at break time and I arranged to meet her outside her house. I was well prepared. I had bought a pack of five Park

Drive cigarettes and transferred them into one of Mum's discarded Embassy packets. My girlfriend, Sharon, went to light a cigarette. "Have one of mine." I said, producing the Embassy packet. She took one and gesticulated for a light. I began searching my pockets for a lighter that I knew did not exist. I looked inside the pocket of my Crombie and when I had given up the pretence I looked up to see Sharon had already lit up. She offered me her cigarette with which to light mine. I regarded this as quite an intimate gesture and considered it the beginning of a beautiful friendship.

I watched her suck on her cigarette and the idea of coming back as a cigarette in my next life seemed appealing. She then took a deep breath held it for a few seconds and blew it out deliberately and slowly - cigarette flirting. Naturally I responded, I sucked on the cigarette and then blew out.

"Don't you take it down?" she asked.

"Depends."

"On what?"

I was out my depth. I was spared any protracted embarrassment due to the arrival of two mates, Dennis and Terry. Their presence deprived me of more intimate moments that night and also on the subsequent evenings. Still come Friday I would have my opportunity at the school dance.

I had now learnt to take the smoke down following many uncomfortable attempts that resulted in heavy bouts of coughing and choking. Although I mastered it I did not enjoy it. Dennis and Terry had suggested that I try Consulate. These had a menthol taste about them and the smoke seemed smoother. Unfortunately they did not sell them in packets of five so I had to fork out more money than I had intended. The consulate was quite pleasant, as were Polo Mints at a fraction of the price. As it was I did not need to invest in Polos to mask the smell of the menthol cigarettes, so there was some economy.

Sharon looked lovely on the night. She was in the company of her friend Mary but when the slow records began she danced with me. All good things come to an end and it was not quite two weeks when Sharon's friend Mary relayed the message, "Sharon doesn't want to go out with you anymore." It was a big thing for me and I was so distraught yet, outwardly I expressed

indifference.
Her next suitor was my mate Terry. Each evening it was still the two Terry's and Dennis who hung around with Sharon but it was the wrong Terry who had the girl. His dating was as forward as mine was backward and I had to witness and endure the endless groping that they indulged in. He alleged that he got a bit of tit after only two days and the apparent run down of his progress would twist my gut. I thought, it could have been me and should have been me. My anger was not directed at either of the protagonists but against myself. What I found particularly annoying was that my 'friend', Terry had still to conqueror the nursery habit of sucking his thumb. Being dumped is bad enough but then being succeeded by a thumb sucker was the height of ignominy.
I hoped, when Terry got dumped, I would be able to move in again and make up for lost opportunities but by now everybody sought Sharon. It was as if I was the trail blazer and others followed the path I had gone down. I felt as if others were getting the benefits of my efforts. Had I not made an approach to her I am sure that it would have been a considerable time before someone else did. She was very attractive and as a result many lads would disqualify themselves from being suitable. However, once I, a pre-pubescent teenager, was seen to be acceptable it made her approachable to all and sundry.

As winter approached and the accompanying dark nights so the leisure options of an evening decreased. Dad had made enquiries about boxing clubs in the vicinity and learnt of Blue House ABC (Amateur Boxing Club). The club building was a hut the size of two small boxing rings. The space not taken up by the ring was dominated by a couple of punch bags and a pear shaped ball that hung down from a frame attached to the wall. A corner was taken up with a bench for spectators. Liberally placed around the walls were huge nails that were utilised as hooks.
When I first approached the hut one cold winter night, rays of light could be seen emanating from the walls and roof. On entering the hut for the first time I recognised all of the occupants. The last time we had met I went unnoticed. However on this occasion all eyes focused upon me. Had there been a

piano playing I am sure it would have stopped. Had my entrance gone unnoticed then a withdrawal would have been made but I was caught like the proverbial rabbit in the headlights. It was smokers' corner incarnate.
By this time I had around 20 fights and was a veteran in comparison to my 'club mates' who were all still in single figures. We would train in our tee-shirts or bare skin depending on the physique and maturity of the club member. I wore a tee-shirt. The real test came when I was to get in the ring for sparring. Sparring was meant to be about practicing and learning. My first sparring partner was to be Tez. He was the eldest of three brothers at the club and the son of the principal trainer Alan Jefford. The Jeffords like the Marshes were also new to Basildon. Their father, Alan Jefford, had learnt the 'Noble art' during his service in the Army. He had been instrumental in revitalising the club along with Mick Purdy whose hippie like dress suggested that he had the opposite background to his co-trainer.
Tez was a year older and four pounds heavier than me with seven fights under his belt. I think he had lost once, whilst all those he defeated had failed to hear the final bell. It was a matter of seconds into the 'sparring' when I realised the word had to be redefined for the purposes of Blue House boxing club. I had a portent when Tez dispensed with the ceremonial glove touching. I outstretched my left hand to touch his when his right followed over the top connecting with my jaw. I hastened a quick retreat.
My Dad had always told me to move back from an attack and when I felt the ropes on my back move to the side like a matador would do to the bull. I would do this often and at times suffered from rope burns across my back but despite the painful look of them they gave no discomfort. On this occasion the pain was immense. As I hit the ropes so one of the nails protruding from the walls made it's presence felt. I had practised the retreat and the subsequent shuffle to the side to the point that it was instinctive. The move when executed on previous occasions had seen the eager attackers fall head fist into the ropes. The natural instinct of avoiding pain had overridden the nurtured instinct and I found myself returning towards Tez and his onslaught rather than the preferred option of avoidance. The impact of the

punch I received was therefore doubled.
When I sought refuge in a corner it offered little comfort. My foot disappearing quickly down a hole. I then heard one of the trainers shout some instructions, "Keep away from the hole." The first onslaught was also the last for that round only because it lasted for the duration. At the end of the round we both walked around the ring taking deep breaths and keeping our internal engines ticking over, while our heads looked to the floor. It is a routine that still persists. It has never been explained or passed down as the done thing but is prevalent in all gyms. It is as if to make eye contact would be regarded as belligerent. It is the inter-round period and a spell for calm.
The 'spar' had got the attention of all. As the calm was about to end so Tez rounded his gloves into a tight fist and the second round began. I dispensed with the 'touch glove' ritual and the 'spar' resumed. Now prepared for the onslaught and wise to the nails and the hole I was able to do justice to myself and sensed that I had measured up. As football had elevated me into a new peer group so did the boxing. It was confirmed next day at break time when I was hanging out at smokers' corner.
Membership at Blue House was not exclusive, but it did have inclusiveness about it. Those at the club also socialised together and so my evenings and weekends where shared with my fellow fighters and smokers. It was not long before I was having my first contest in the navy and sky blue colours of Blue House ABC. It was against a local lad called Mark Gibbs from the Southend Club. Mark was highly rated in the area and I turned in a good performance taking a unanimous decision on his own turf. The trainers were impressed and so were a number of others about this ex-London boy. The local Evening Echo was similarly impressed if the space dedicated to my write up the next day was anything to go by.
My dream was to win the National schools title but I failed in my first attempt reaching the semi finals. I was sure that the status of England Schoolboy champion would have enhanced my pulling power with the girls. There was always next year. I rejoined my old boxing club because the facilities were much better. It meant quite a lot of travelling but I had my younger brother John for company who also indulged in pugilism; John

was also a very good chess player.
I had some good wins during my return period at St George's and these invariably were when fighting afar. Trips as far as Wales, Coventry or the South coast were not uncommon. Dad would be full of praise for some of my performances and would give his colleagues in work an appraisal of the progress of both John and I. He was not one to see the performances of his kin through rose tinted spectacles either. However his colleagues could be forgiven for thinking such thoughts. Every time one of them came along to inspect the Marsh phenomena my performance would be abysmal. Dad was only too aware of how high he had sang my praises, "If you're going to fight like that you might as well turn it in." was a phrase he found himself saying on many an occasion.
The change of club did not enhance my title ambitions I was beaten in the preliminary round by my old foe Tommy Mooney. I was being consoled but to little effect, "Don't worry Tel you've got the Junior ABAs (Amateur Boxing Association) to look forward to." The junior ABAs was for fifteen and sixteen year-olds classed as junior A's and junior B's respectively. It came at the back end of the boxing season. After a string of victories, including a win over my old foe Tommy Mooney, I was contesting the National finals at Crystal Palace. John Traynor from Manchester was the one remaining obstacle.
I was taken in by the whole occasion. I was in awe of the Olympic boxing team who put in a show. I figured were I to be the junior ABA champion it was highly likely that I would be the future senior Champion and in turn the Olympic representative. Up until then being a national champion was an end in itself. The result of that end was, so I believed, the affections of the female of the species and the respect of my gender. But now that was the reward and not the aim. John Traynor was no longer an obstacle but the next rung of a ladder. I had a clear view of what I see as the top - the Olympic games. The subsequent contest did nothing to shake me from my ambitions. I was now a National Champion.

CHAPTER FOUR
ODDS ON

Notwithstanding my Olympic ambitions I decided that I had earned a break; 'all work and no play...' The end of May was approaching and the weather had been kind. The following weekend a party had been arranged. The host was Keith, one of the school anoraks, who was trying to endear himself to his school colleagues. He was not without problems, the most apparent being an embarrassing stammer that made him a figure of fun. Thankfully, he was spared the ridicule since it was always done out of his earshot. In a way his socialising within the new circle of acquaintances loosened him up and as he became more relaxed so the stammer lessened.
I was pretty sure that I was going to be the only Champion present. Most of the partygoers were oblivious to my ring success, but it did not worry me in the slightest. My satisfaction came from the contented smugness, if you like, from having achieved what I had. I did suffer from what might be described, as the anti- climax. It did not affect my life to any degree while, my expectation of change was great. In that regard the journey was better than the arrival yet I thought the party would be pay back time.
I had always had a inner confidence about chatting up girls which was inversely proportionate to my successes, but I was sure that the newly crowned junior ABA champion would reverse the trend of rejection. I wore my title like you would wear after-shave or eat Dentyne. As much as the latter two could be detected by the senses of those stalked they also acted like a reassurance to the stalker and it was in the context of the latter that my title was a comfort.
A group of us turned up at the party, each with our obligatory

quart bottle of cider. I always had to rely on the hairier members of the group to purchase mine. I wasted no time in search of a mate. After each rejection I thought, 'if only they knew what they had just turned down'. It was after three rejections that I got a green light from Jackie.
I anticipated the night being long. There was a queue for the phone since many seemed to be taking advantage of the free call facility. I had to wait while dial a disc was listened to by some of the partygoers. Eventually I got through, "Hello Mum, Keith's Mum said I can stay the night is that Okay?"
"If that's the case there's no need for us to wait up. We'll have any early night."
"See you in the morning."
While I was speaking to Mum on the phone Jackie was putting her tongue in my ear and her nails were exploring my back. I was experiencing all sorts of sensations, which I could not respond to yet it made it more fun.
When Keith's parents returned unexpectedly there was something of a panic. I was as quick as the next one in heading for the exit via the front passage since that was where all the shoes were. To make matters worse someone had tied the laces of different shoes together. The parents were on the other side of the front door but the catch was down so they could not enter their own house at that moment.
The son meanwhile was in the lounge having a 'fit' while everyone was charging around him looking for the alternate exit to the front door. It meant escaping into the garden and negotiating the fences of the adjacent houses until the end terrace was reached. It gave me some idea what the jockeys in the Grand National have to face not to mention the horses. I had a mishap at one fence but recovered quickly mainly due to the ranting of the tenant who judging by his garden was a keen gardener.
Having reached the road I with others ran for a number of minutes before it was considered safe. It was now about eleven o'clock and too late for me to go knocking up Mum and Dad. Jackie and I had got split up. There was some concern about Keith, left in a precarious position, but that only lasted a moment. As each went home so Lex, and I remained. He had the

same problem as I being without a bed for the night. So we walked down to the Broadway with a view to sleep in the phone boxes.
As we walked my balls began to hurt and I figured it happened when I was negotiating the garden fences. The injection of adrenaline from the shock of the parents' unexpected return and the subsequent evasion was now wearing off and so my balls hurt even more. There were four phone booths at the Broadway but only one was suitable as sleeping accommodation. The other three were more reminiscent to toilets since they carried a similar smell.
Lex's large bulk meant that room was scarce. I found myself, out of necessity, adopting the foetal position. It was both an uncomfortable night and a painful experience. I was furthest from the door so in effect I was trapped between the wall and Lex. This was considered appropriate since had I taken Lex's position I would have soon been pushed out of the door. Under normal circumstances this would have been desirable. I was free from the draught and warm but I had not figured upon the testicular torture.
It was not long before I found my position unbearable but Lex was dead to the world. Squashed between his dead weight and the wall left me trussed like a chicken. The phone and the integrated pay box were immediately above me so vertical movement was also a non-starter. To add to my problems, even if I where free from restrictions, my limbs where losing their feeling as the circulation of the blood was restricted. So I sat in the dark and suffered what was the longest six hours of my life. I very much longed for my bed. It occurred to me that there was no place like home. A week previous I had reached what I had perceived as the greatest achievement possible and now I was for the moment homeless and helpless - my bathos.
Lex awoke with the sunrise and we still had a couple of hours to kill before returning home to our respective abodes. Breakfast was a pint of milk from a deserted milk float. We then went to get a newspaper. The shop was yet to open so we incorporated the self-service facility from the pile of papers left outside. Normally I would have revelled in this, it was like a scene from the cartoon, 'Top Cat', but there were other things on my mind

and in my hands.
The only way I could lessen the pain from below was to rest the delicate items in my hand as a means of support. When they dangled freely the pain was at it's most excruciating. My walking with the legs wide apart also eased the pain. I was only too aware of the comedy of the situation, which was just as well since Lex did not think to hide his amusement.
I tried the back door and windows before I knocked on the door. I realised my return home was premature. Needless to say I soon heard someone running down the stairs. Dad answered in his pyjamas, "You're early."
"I got you a paper."
"You look like you have been up all night."
As the day progressed so did the pain. It occurred to me that this might be a stage of puberty. I had often heard the phrase, 'his balls have dropped' in the context of approaching manhood and wondered whether I was suffering from such symptoms. My parents knew that I was in pain but I had implied it was a stomach ache.
Eventually the truth came out and my balls were paraded for my parent's inspection. They had swollen to the size of tennis balls and the doctor was called. I was in the hospital within thirty minutes of being examined. My legs where bent and spread out like women in labour while the doctors examined the offending articles. "We will have to operate."
"Will he be all right?"
"We don't know Mrs Marsh, he may lose them."
"Just get on with it please." I interjected.
The anaesthetic was quickly administered and my agony eased. My problem was that I had torsion of the testicles, which had resulted in the blood supply being cut from the testicles. The fear was that gangrene had set in and such a prognosis meant the junior ABA Champion would be a eunuch. On the bright side it would mean I could drop down a weight.
Coming round from the anaesthetic was gradual and pleasant I was appreciating the pain free period. It was a while before I remembered the purpose of my presence in the ward. I quickly checked down below. I was complete but I did not know if they would ever be functional.

The start of the new boxing season saw the arrival of a new trainer, George Bowers. George had transferred from his former club bringing some boxers with him including my old adversary Tommy Mooney - we were now sparring partners

Now sixteen years old and well into my final year at school the current junior ABA Champion was going for his second title, the National Schoolboy Championship. This year I was spared the frustrations and tears of the premature exit from the championships. I found myself contesting the finals at Blackpool on Grand National day. I knew my luck was in when I had a pound on the winner, Red Rum when he recorded his second National victory in 1974.

Like Red Rum it was my second national win. Less than six weeks later I was contesting another national final, the class B junior ABAs. It was at this event that the stars of the future would be on show and I was on the short list. I won but looked bad in the process. Dad was embarrassed by the performance. A lot of his friends were there to watch Jimmy Marsh's boy and, true to form, I let him down again, "If you're going to fight like that you might as well turn it in." suggested Dad.

The Olympics was still in my sights. However, whereas some of my contemporaries had eyes on the 1976 Olympics, two years down the line, my sights were very much on the 1980 Olympics. I still had a lot of growing to do.

CHAPTER FIVE
ODDS AGAINST

I left school at the first opportunity getting a job with William Hill Bookmakers as a trainee settler at their head office. The money wasn't good. I had no disposable income. Mum would insist on the keep but allowed me to have it back over the week. It was meant to give me some financial discipline.

I was one of a dozen, 16 and 17 year olds, who where either fascinated with racing or gambling. It was a large office occupying both settlers and telephonists settling the wagers and taking instructions respectively. We trainee settlers were in effect glorified board boys, our main task being chalking up the betting odds and results of the afternoon's racing. The settlers who were a few years older than I quickly gave me the nickname Curly.

Nearly everyone who worked there liked a bet and I began to take the bets of the trainee settlers. I saw it as a way to earn a few more pennies. It started out as modest five pence bets, but, true to all gambling, it was not long before the stakes increased. I was making bundles. Everyone was betting with Curly. It was against company rules but tolerated provided it was done discreetly.

Everything was fine until I made the decision to give credit. It was a green light for some of the settlers to see Curly as a soft touch. When they won they were quick to be available for payment but when it came to paying they were not seen for dust. Losing the money to them was not the real problem. It was losing their future business that was costly. It was expedient to cancel the debt in order to get them betting again but the credit stopped.

The no credit rule solved one problem but created another. One

afternoon while working the boards one of my colleagues, Steve, wanted a bet on credit. There had been a tip going round the office regarding a horse from a certain trainer's stable. The trainer was a big punter with Hills and he had gone lumpy on one of his two-year-olds in a selling race.
Steve was unhappy that his marker was not good enough. During the afternoon he had a habit of sitting on the sill of the window fiddling with the draw cord hanging from the Venetian blinds behind him. This draw cord he would wrap around his index finger until the slack had been taken up.
The horse won and Steve was pissed off, to the extent that he wanted to take his frustrations out on Curly. The malevolent eyeballing was the first indication of trouble. He leaned against the sill playing with the draw cord staring constantly towards me. I ignored it at first but as it continued it became off putting.
"What's the problem Steve?"
"You know what the fucking problem is."
"But it could have lost."
"But it didn't."
"I can't do anything about that. I don't make the results."
"But I can."
"Can what?"
"Do something about it. You and me in the toilets."
Shit, I thought, he was bigger and clearly stronger. With all the physical disadvantages the toilet is the last place I would want a scrap. The very thought of falling over and knocking your head against the Armitage ware vitreous enamel appendages sent shivers down my spine. The tiled floor induced similar anxieties. Then there was the risk of coming into contact with the urinals – yuck.
"Is it really necessary Steve? I'll give you what you would have won."
"Its too late for that. You're gonna get what's coming."
"I'll give you a jacks."
"Nope."
"Okay a cockle."
"Nope."
"Is there anyway I can talk you out of this?"
"Nope."

"And that's your final word?"
"Yep."
I projected my forehead in to his face and got stuck into him. The combination of surprise and his inability to free his index finger from the draw cord, that had gripped the digit python like, meant he was on the defensive. The fight lasted seconds rather than minutes and after we were pulled apart Steve was in a belligerent mood. "You cunt. I'll fucking get you Curly. After work you're for it." The sequel never happened.
Unknown to us, Sam Burns, one of the directors, witnessed the skirmish. He was also involved in managing a number of boxers. He was reported as saying that he was thinking of signing us both up. I suspect he was impressed with my 'rope a dope' trick.
Now a settler, all my time was spent behind a desk. Huge piles of bets would be allocated for settlement. It was proving a distraction to my bookmaking activities so I would pay fellow settlers to do my work while I was laying bets. I also employed trainee settlers on a commission to act as runners from the adjacent office within the organisation. I knew that I had become an integral part of the organisation when one of the supervisors approached me prior to the Grand National. He wanted to place some bets for some of the blokes in the security department of the organisation.
Working behind a desk rather than on the boards meant that I would get the results second hand. It left me vulnerable to any of the board boys who could hold back the start of a race and the subsequent result. They would be able to place a bet already knowing the winner. It was not practical to take bets only until the advertised time of the race. Races invariably started late and it is a trait of betting that many punters prefer to leave their punt to the last minute. I just had to be vigilant. It was not really a case of if it happens but when it happens.
When it happened it was as subtle as an atom bomb. One of the board boys had an out of character five-pound bet on a twenty to one outsider. It was placed by one of his colleagues. Previous occasions indicated that fifty pence each way was the maximum. On this occasion it was a fiver, win only. In addition his previous investments never wavered from the first two in betting. It was a five furlongs sprint, the shortest of races, which meant that the

outcome would be known within a minute.
The alarm bells were ringing immediately. I sent someone to the adjacent office to check and they confirmed that the result was already out. I watched as the ruse was played out. When the result was announced the punter and the runner threw their hands into the air to demonstrate their good fortune and indicated they wanted paying out.
"What you going to do?" asked Bob who was seated beside me."
"Well I'm not paying 'em."
"But you know what Trucks like."
"The reason he is here is because he stuck it on the supervisor in the adjacent office." said Dave my other neighbour.
I was only too aware of the situation. Truck was a big lad and had a reputation for a short fuse. His accomplice was of little significance. They had both gone to the toilets in the expectation that I would follow with the readies.
"I'm gonna tell him I'm not paying him."
"I'd rather you than me." quipped Dave.
My aversion to fighting in the toilets still persisted but this was a situation that needed addressing immediately. They expected to be paid there and then so I had to deal with it there and then. I borrowed a penknife from Harry one of the senior settlers in his fifties. He used the knife as a pencil sharpener and everybody in the office would borrow it to chop the wood away from the pencil to expose more lead than the conventional sharpener. I donned my Harrington jacket, opened the knife and placed it in the elasticised cuff with the blade pointing towards my elbow. Dave and Bob looked on aghast. Don't worry its only meant as a deterrent. I took a deep breath and headed to the toilet.
"Done you there Curly."
"No you didn't, the result was already up. I checked in the other office. I'm not paying."
"That's what you think." said Truck as he threw his right fist towards me - I said he had a short fuse. I ducked, more out of desperation rather than design and drew the knife from the sleeve. It headed towards his stomach and disappeared from view. He backed off but I stayed close to him. Digging away at his stomach. The toilet door opened and it was cue for the battle

to cease. "What's going on? Cut it out." demanded the more senior intruder. I think the excuse to stop was welcomed by us both.
"What happened, whadde do?" asked Dave.
"I stabbed him. I told him I weren't paying and he went for me so I stabbed him.
"How come he's still there?"
"Look you can see him lifting his t-shirt looking at his stomach."
"Is it still in him?"
"No I've got it here."
"Is that blood?"
"Yeah…"
I'd sliced my thumb in the process. Word soon got around, 'don't fuck with Curly'. In this case appeasement wasn't an option.

I was getting pissed off at not getting the recognition, in boxing, which I believed was warranted. I had won three national titles and had been unbeaten for nearly four years. Fighters whom I had beaten were being picked for the England under-19 team while I was not even getting an invite to the training squad. With hindsight it was a good thing. I was still immature and matches against the Eastern Bloc countries would have entailed unnecessarily hard encounters. I thought then, it would have given me the much-needed motivation that was lacking at the time and the challenge would have brought the best out in me. However, it was not right for me at that stage of my career. I think Kenny Cushway recognised this and consequently never pushed my claim for a place in the Young England squad.
However, without such recognition or noticeable progress boxing was becoming a bind. After work I neither had the inclination or the motivation to get to the gym. First stop was the local pub where we would play bar football, pool or darts. No matter what the game, there was always a side stake. Back at the offices of William Hill my success was seen as a model to imitate. Others were beginning to copy my example and bookmaking enterprises were popping up everywhere. I still had an edge because I was good at giving early prices and my anticipation of the market was good. Curly was always the first port of call when a price about a horse was wanted.

Not only was I having luck taking bets I seemed to have the 'Midas touch' when it came to backing them. Whenever I went to the dogs I found myself coming home a winner. Southend was the local track and my good mate Richard Hallet and I would visit the stadium every Saturday. Normally when you have a bet the bookie will give you a ticket with a number that corresponds to the clerk's recording of the bets. I did not need the ticket. Instead of being allocated a number I had my own pseudonym 'Boy'. It would go something like, "Hundred pound to eight Trap six down to boy."
A hundred pound to eight indicates a twelve to one chance and it was uncanny the amount of times I successfully picked out such big price winners. Twelve to one winners in greyhound racing are something of a rarity. I could do no wrong it was all too easy. When I started to get resistance in work from the supervisors it became an irritant. "Do I need this?" I would ask myself. It got to the stage when I was asking the question too often. When I had four figures banked I decided that I no longer needed it and so Hills became history. It had been less than a year before I had a grand in the bank.

CHAPTER SIX
SO YOU WANNA BE A MARINE

The grand in the bank soon became an item of nostalgia and the days were reduced to going down the local pub, playing cards until closing time. When the pub closed it would be back to someone's house to continue the brag, pontoon or poker.
I was in the Railway Tavern with Richard when we met up with brothers Tez and Mark Jefford. They were talking about a nearby derelict house that had been brought to their attention by some builder who had some connection with the place. It became apparent that there was a good price for copper and after some deliberation it was decided that we would strip the house of its copper. The strategy was to gather all the electric cable then burn it, melting the surrounding insulation, to leave the bare copper. It was a wet autumn afternoon so the fire was made in the house. The job complete, we filled a large suitcase with our 'precious' metal and went on our way.
I felt the call of nature which meant retracing my steps to a place obscure enough to relieve my bladder. As I appeared from the camouflage a copper, of a different variety, approached me having dismounted from his bike on the pavement.
“What you up to?" he asked, his bicycle clips were still in position.
"Went for a slash."
"Anything to do with that?" he asked pointing towards the derelict house. As I turned I could see the flames and smoke protruding from the downstairs windows.
"I've just been to the toilet.”
Richard, Tez and Mark were the only other people visible. The policeman remounted his bike in pursuit of my colleagues. He already knew Mark and Tez and he began to search them and

the suitcase they were carrying. I saw him reach for his radio. I assumed it was a call for assistance. By now I had caught up with those apprehended but decided not to join them. I responded to them like you would to people you knew but continued walking, "Just a moment." I heard the Copper say in a rather polite manner. I pretended not to hear and continued to walk on in a casual manner. I knew it was only a matter of time before I literally got my collar felt. It was preceded with "Excuse me...Oi son...eh...hold up." It was followed by, "I am arresting you on suspicion of theft of metal. You have the right to remain silent. Anything you do say maybe taken down and used in evidence against you."
It was only minutes before two police cars arrived to take the four of us to the station. On arrival we were taken into the building. One of the coppers was about to instruct us where to go. "It's all right," said Mark, "I know, first right and then first right."
We followed Mark and found ourselves in the charge room. The evidence then followed us in. A policeman entered with the case full of copper and dropped it from his waist height to the floor. The case fell apart and the contents spilled out.
"Sorry about that." said the officer without a trace of sincerity.
"That's alright. It's another case you'll have to deal with." was my reply.
It met with mild amusement from both my co-accused and the police. Believing I had an audience I went on in pursuit of more laughs, "Anyway it's not ours."
"That's theft of a suitcase as well then."
We were then taken to the cellblock and placed in separate cells.
"Don't make a statement." shouted Tez from his cell.
It was advice directed towards Richard and I.
"Oi Mark," shouted Richard, "your names in this cell."
"I know, it's in every cell."
After a short inspection I was able to back up Mark's claim regarding my cell. It was about 90 minutes before we saw sight of any Coppers although the time flew by probably because of the excitement and new experience that I was going through.
We were eventually released, around eight o'clock that evening, on bail, pending further investigations. I had been expected

home for tea some two hours earlier but I was eager to join my mates at the youth club to boast about our predicament. I thought my exploits would endear me to a few of the girls at the youth club. It appeared to me that the rogues and rascals were pulling all the crumpet. I hoped that my new infamy would assist in attracting the opposite sex. However, I only walked myself home that night.
Despite the bravado of the arrest I knew inside that I was getting into a rut. My only source of income was the dole each week. I remember it being quite adequate were it not for my bad run on the gambling front. Dad saw my predicament in a similar vein, and when at the St Georges' annual presentation he had a word with Ernie Ridley the club secretary about getting a job with Tommy Newton. Tommy was the club President and a bookmaker from the East End.
I became a settler in Tommy's operation a short while later. Four months short of my eighteenth birthday meant that I could not face the punters. I was in an adjoining room settling the bets for that particular shop and assessing the overall liabilities of the four shops that he had.

I was in training for a boxing tournament, which was a keenly contested event, sponsored by the PLA. Being over seventeen I was now classed as a senior. As a senior I had managed a couple of dozen victories, but all were by guile and not strength.
On the day of the tournament the boss was an unexpected arrival. He appeared in a particularly good spirit and sent out for fish and chips all round. Having had to watch my weight for the forthcoming event I had an appetite and my discipline yielded to the cod in batter and mushy peas. Having demolished and thoroughly enjoyed the feast I thought nothing more about it until I weighed in a pound over for the event that evening. It meant either shedding the surplus weight or competing at the higher weight division and run the risk of giving as much as six pounds in weight to the opponent. The potential opponent was Dabs Eduns from the Repton boxing club. Dabs was in earshot when my trainer, Peter Morgan, put the options to me. Had Dabs not been witness to the dilemma I would have opted for shedding the sixteen ounces. As it was it would look like I was

running from Dabs and I was not going to allow that impression. I don't run from anyone.
What an idiot I was. I got bashed up good and proper. I was battered and bruised and suffered my first black eye. It was a man against a boy and the guile was left in the dressing room when I followed my heart rather than my head. Dad was unable to make the fight he was tied up in hospital. He had a history of back trouble and was under a course of traction. Both ward staff and patients were aware of the forth-coming fight through his proud boasts.
Dad was in shock and suffered deep embarrassment. Not for the first time had he built up the expectation only for me to disappoint. It was my first loss in four years. I had forgotten how much losing hurt. The situation did have a comedy to it and I added to the farce by paying him a visit. The nurses in particular were sympathetic to the bruised face that I carried and with a mix of curiosity and bewilderment asked, "Why do you do it?"
I was unable to answer. The last thing I wanted to do after work was go to the gym. I preferred playing pool in the pub and then off to the dog tracks. I would go with some of the lads from work or with my Cousin David Cupit. On the female front I was still drawing blanks. I seemed to be chasing quality women and backing mediocre horses. It caused great financial anxiety. Perhaps I should reverse my strategy.
The motivation for boxing was lacking and my dedication had waned. If I was to continue boxing I had to rediscover the dedication and motivation that I had possessed as a junior. The motivation was to come from loss to Dabs Eduns. "I told you he wouldn't make it as a senior." The 'I told you so' remark emanated from several sources. I'll show them; it was the challenge I needed. I took up the gauntlet and the dedication naturally followed.
I was entered for the National Association of Boys Clubs Championships (NABC's). Having reached the final of the London division I found myself paired with an old opponent Billy O'Grady, who I had beaten twice before. I was a strong favourite to do so again. We were contesting the second round when his right fist connected with my chin and I slumped to the canvas.
"What happened?" I asked as I my cognition roused in the

dressing room. I had no recollection from the second round onwards and concluded I must have been knocked out.
"What?" asked Pete incredulously.
"What happened? Did I get knocked out?" I enquired earnestly.
"You won." replied Peter. He then proceeded to give me a run down of the events following the knock down. I had got up and fought the rest of the contest on instinct, gaining a unanimous decision. It was the first time I had been knocked down in my career, but significantly I had got up and won, also receiving the best boxer award. I went on to win the National title.
My hormones were still dormant and puberty was still a thing to come. Now eighteen I had got the call up for the England under-19 squad. It was what I wanted and needed. I was once again back to serious training having no time for other distractions like betting. The call up entailed attending training weekends at Crystal Palace. It meant getting Saturday's off but Tommy was only too pleased to accommodate my request.
The squad training entailed a gym session on the Friday evening, which was preceded by a talk from the coach Kevin Hickey. In addition to welcoming the new faces and introducing the coaches most of the talk was about how good the Russian and Eastern European fighters were. I found this hard to accept. Their styles were very one-dimensional and seemed to lack the rhythm, spontaneity and flare of the Cuban and American boxers who were winning most gold medals at that time.
It was not long before I got my international call up for the under-19s. It was great to make a successful debut. However, the entitlement of a tracksuit with the words 'Young England' printed on the back was the real buzz. It seemed to have benefits in itself with regard to training. In particular when out running, it was as if you had something to live up to. If the going gets tough you can't be seen to be struggling or stopping as an international athlete. It was not long before I was called up again to record win number two.
The next aim was the senior ABAs. As a kid Marshy had built up quite an impressive record, National schoolboy champion, twice-National junior champion and National youth champion and unbeaten England under 19s international. The preliminary rounds of the senior ABAs were now approaching. Was I ready to

compete against the big boys? My senior record was around 36 wins with the one loss but now I was to be competing against the best of the seniors.
Like the junior championships before, this competition was made up of a series of area and regional competitions. The lightweight section of the Northeast London Division turned out to be an intriguing affair. In the red corner was Repton's Graham Moughton, the former Olympic Captain and a man of immense international experience. In the blue corner was Marshy. The two under-19 internationals I now carried was an embarrassment in such company. I was only too aware what happened the last time I touched gloves with a Repton boxer in the guise of Dabs Eduns. I had stepped up to take on the men and I was found wanting. That was a year ago. I knew, physically, I was still not quite there. There were question marks against me but at the same time there existed question marks against the former Olympic Captain, had he passed his best? Was what he had left still good enough? I saw it as a fight that neither of us could get credit for. Was I to win, I would have beaten an old man - he was 27 incidentally. Should the Repton boxer reign supreme he would have merely beaten a young pretender not man enough for the big boys.
The young pretender came good and the good fortune continued in subsequent rounds. In the quarterfinals I was against Andy Gill a Royal Marine Commando. I was not particularly impressed with Royal Marines but the Commando suffix gave me cause for concern. It conjures up images of clandestine operations, licences to kill, escape and evasion, espionage and being able to kill with one finger and above all hardness both mentally and physically. Graham Moughton enquired on whom I had drawn. I informed him it was the marine, "He'll be fit then." was his comment. He was fit but it was I who was going through to the semi final. Yet, Graham's remark stayed with me long after the fight.
The 'scalp' of the former England captain on my CV I was now looking for a victory against the tournament favourite and current England number one, George Gilbody. Unlike Mr Moughton, Mr Gilbody was not on the wane and Mr Marsh though getting stronger was not yet strong enough. I did not see

it, nor did any one associated with me, as a setback. I had finished in the final four at the senior level losing to the eventual champion on a majority verdict. Next year was going to be my year. George Gilbody went on to take the title. The next time Mr Gilbody and I were to meet was at the England training session for the senior squad.

Talk of the Olympics was no longer about if but when. But before then there was the matter of the Commonwealth Games scheduled for the summer of 1978 in Australia just over a year away.

The opportunity arose for a rematch with Gilbody in Burnley. Both my trainer Peter and Dad advised against it. They were of the view that we should wait for the ABAs. I figured that I had the measure of him and even if not I would take more from the match than he. I would have learnt more about him for when we meet in the ABAs. After the first round I felt quite pleased with my judgement. I went back to my corner, "I've got him." I told Peter, eager to get the second round underway.

"Hold still now, soon be done...three down two to go...right, now just a few in this one and that's it...one...two

"Oh Fuck."

"Sorry did that hurt...just one more, last one, nearly done *voila.* Leave it for five days then visit your Doctor and he will remove them for you. Bye."

"Cheers thanks.. What happened Dad?"

"Lost on points. He swarmed all over you in the last two."

For the second time I have left a ring with no memory of the outcome. I was just glad that it was a loss on points rather than a stoppage defeat or knockout. I began to believe that I was unstoppable. I seemed to have this inbuilt mechanism that was able to override all systems and fight on autopilot. I also realised I needed more time for training if I were to succeed.

Meanwhile I plodded along working and training and becoming increasingly frustrated with the situation. The delayed trains enhanced my frustration. Also having to stand for the thirty-minute journey tested my resolve. There was no room for me to read my Sporting Life, packed sardine like on the 8.34. So I scanned the tabloids of my fellow commuters, when I saw the inverted print ask, 'Do you think you can hack it? Have you got

the nerve?' I had to look closer. It was an advert by the navy trying to recruit Commandos. The journey complete I immediately enquired about enlisting.
After my final contest, as a civilian, Malcolm Meredith a journalist with the Boxing News approached me "I hear your joining the boot necks in January." He seemed to know more than me. It was comforting to hear though. My enlisting coincided with my full England call up. I was anticipating springing it on the Marines when I arrived - any chance of a couple of days off? What Malcolm had said gave me assurances that fulfilling my debut would not meet obstruction.
It was now November 1977 and the winter weather had already arrived. Christmas was approaching and people were getting into the Christmas mode. For me it was going to be a period of abstinence. I was busy training, running fast and often in anticipation of my International debut and the commando tests that lay ahead. There already existed this military ambience at the time due to a firemen's strike. The troops were out in force manning dated fire appliances. My daily runs would take me past the picketed Basildon fire station. The striking fireman could be seen outside the building gathered around a drum burning fiercely through the cold winter nights.

CHAPTER SEVEN
THE GREEN BERET

The training camp was at Lympstone near Exeter. I expected to be one of many but I was alone. It became apparent that I was the only new intake for that day. It was to enable me to be sworn in and signed up in time for the forthcoming boxing championships. I was to remain at Lympstone for a few days until it was time to go to H.M.S. Nelson in Portsmouth, the venue for the Navy Championships. The idea of fighting on a ship I found amusing, although I was uncertain about my ability to overcome seasickness. Meanwhile I was issued with a temporary ID card and assigned to Chosen troop.

Chosen troop was incorporated for those excused the hazards of basic training due to injury. It would be here that the injured would undergo physiotherapy in order for them to return to training. Some lads had been injured for over a year. Many considered Chosen troop as a place for malingerers and I suspected that there were a couple present in my room, which consisted of six beds and accompanying lockers.

Recruits tried to show me how little I knew by demonstrating how much they did. This they attempted through drill movements with the rifles they had under their charge. They were also trying to show themselves as being either the best at saluting or standing to attention. It did little to endear me to them, I did not see marching, saluting or standing to attention as an integral part of being a Commando. I was beginning to have serious reservations. I felt I had little in common with my roommates.

When it was time for dinner they took me down to the Galley. I had by now been introduced to a number of nautical expressions. It was all part of the marine custom. Walls were referred to as bulkheads, the floor as the deck and windows as potholes. Other expressions were not quite as obvious to me such as gash, pash, gronk, scran and many others. As we left our accommodation a couple of my roommates still in uniform began to take up a marching mode. I found their efforts amusing because they looked so much like clockwork soldiers. I guessed they were just enthusiastic, having witnessed a similar display of drilling in the accommodation. But as I looked around I found their display was the norm for all those in uniform and wearing navy berets. It soon became obvious to me that this was the recruit style of marching. I was quite glad that I was soon to be going to Portsmouth. I just could not picture myself walking in such a ridiculous fashion. I had not yet managed to calculate how I was going to avoid such antics and gain a green beret but time, it seemed, was on my side.

It became apparent that ‘scran’ was what I was eating in the Galley. As I looked around at the hundreds of fellow recruits I was impressed in the way their scran was piled high. I found myself somewhat envious of those who were filling their stomachs. They seemed to have an advantage over me. I, like them, was anticipating a gruelling week ahead in preparation for the Navy championships and my International debut, but it was necessary to forego any gastric indiscretions to make the lightweight limit.

The evening was spent listening to the residents of Chosen troop each informing me about the twenty-six week Commando course. Its fair to say that the stories were unrepresentative as everyone in Chosen Troop was a victim of the training to some degree. Some had made it as far as the final exercise only to be denied the 'green lid' through injury. The exercise was known as 'Nutcracker' and going by the accounts its title had some irony. It entailed a four-day exercise on Dartmoor. I was told tales about recruits going down with either hypothermia or hyperthermia. It seemed that there was no favourable time of year in which to take on 'Nutcracker'.

Each and everyone spoke of 'Heartbreak Lane'. This, it was explained, was the final stretch of all the speed marches. There were the six milers and the nine milers that all recruits had to pass within a specified time. It could be seen that this did

nothing to unsettle me and was informed that this was done with a weapon, which weighed nine pounds nine ounces, plus full fighting order that included magazines filled with ammunition weighing in total twenty kilograms.
There was one cause for concern and this was related to the Endurance course, part of which entailed going through a six-metre underwater tunnel. I have never been one that was totally confident in water; I spent many hours in the pool preparing for the swimming tests ahead. However, negotiating underwater tunnels was not part of the preparation.
I had not yet learnt the rudiments of rank but I knew as a rule of thumb that you could differentiate between Non-Commissioned Officers and Commissioned Officers by the way they spoke. For the few days that I was to be at Lympstone I was assigned to boxing training with three other Marines who were also competing in the Navy Championships.
Without a uniform and a proper ID it was soon time to go to Portsmouth and board HMS Nelson. We drove through some main gates and then had to do a joining routine. Some bedding was collected and I followed the path of my more experienced colleagues. I assumed that they were heading for the ship but instead went to a building where we were assigned a room. I was confused since all the talk was about going on board. It was explained to me that the barracks were referred to as ships.
"I'm having a dhouby." said one of the others. I guessed right that dhouby meant wash.
"Where's the heads?" asked another. I was to learn that was the toilet.
We shared the building with dozens of sailors who were on fire duty due to the continued firemen's strike in the so-called 'winter of discontent'. Parked outside were half a dozen green goddess's ready and willing. It was questionable if they were able. For the initial period an undisturbed night was not guaranteed.
After nine days in the services I became the Navy champion. The win took me into the Combined Services championship that qualifies the winners for the later stages of the ABAs. However, not before I made my full international debut later that week. I was fighting for England against France. My opponent was a bronze medallist in the recent European championships. I came

out of the fight a winner but if you looked at my face you could be forgiven for thinking I was the loser. I hit him three times for each punch I received but his fists carried twice the power of mine. To be fair there were a few punters at the ringside who had money on the other guy and felt hard done by and made their feelings known. Dad ended up getting in an argument with one guy, the former international cricketer and footballer, Dennis Compton. "You may know about cricket but you know fuck all about boxing." Dad informed Mr Compton. The positive side of the result was that I had competed at the top level and won. In view of the Commonwealth Games in the coming summer it was a good result and my chances of selection strengthened. I was also glad that France was not part of the Commonwealth. I didn't fancy a rematch. When I returned to HMS Nelson I was sporting a nose that was severely swollen and bruised to the point that I could see it.

Everything I learnt about Navy life was through the process of trial and error. I had been thrown in at the deep end and, in many respects, it was a complete culture shock. Normally new recruits would be taken through an induction process but the system was not designed for cases such as mine. Naval life seemed steeped in tradition, which I considered puerile. I could not understand the logic or rationality behind continuing the rituals.

Lack of funds also added to my disillusionment. My money was now depleted and having been around for over a month without pay I was getting severely pissed off. I had made numerous approaches to the pay section but my enquiries made little impression on anyone. What did not help was that my circumstances were unique. I had no uniform and a temporary ID card that was temporary both in status and durability. It was a piece of paper that had become ragged and faded due to the many times it was used. Its main purpose for me was as an aid memoir regarding my service number.

I got so pissed off I decided to visit the movements' section instead of going to the pay section. I'd discovered that you were entitled to a number of free travel warrants each year. I made an application for a single ticket from Portsmouth to Basildon. The

clerk who dealt with my request was everything that the pay clerk wasn't: helpful, considerate, good looking, slim and female. Cupid's arrow was in full flight. Earlier she had been described by one of my colleagues as ‘Ess’ - it was short for essence.
"You are entitled to a return, it doesn't have to be a single." she informed me sweetly.
"I don't need a return I'm not coming back."
"What's the problem?"
"I haven't been paid so I'm going home."
"Hold on I’ll see what I can do."
She approached a desk and spoke to the man seated behind it. I got the impression the occupant had some influence from the manner in which he was dealing with others before. He had a mixture of authority and arrogance about him that seemed to evaporate when Essence approached. There was a flirtation going on between the two of them. It was not long before I was summoned before him. He was an officer and I was asked to explain myself.
"I have asked for a warrant and I pointed out to the lady that a single was all I needed since I was not coming back."
"What?"
"I want a warrant and I am not coming back."
"What's your problem?"
"There's no problem really. I signed a contract to serve three years and I understood that I was going to be paid. I have not been paid so the Navy is in breach of contact so it is null and void. Since I am entitled to a warrant I’d like a single as a return is unnecessary."
He looked towards Essence and asked, "Is this a wind up?"
What I considered to be a fair and reasonable position to take met with incredulity. It was really a clash of cultures, civilian versus military. I was still very much a civvie. I knew very little about the military etiquette and that position was going to continue for the foreseeable future. My ‘protestations’ worked. The pay clerk got a mild bollocking and I got paid. Mickey Shone, the Navy coach, had a quiet word in my ear, "It doesn’t work like that here. Any problems see me first."
With my acquired capital I asked Essence if she would allow me to take her out that night to celebrate but Marshy drew a blank.

I figured once the bruising went down on my nose she would have second thoughts. I did not put my theory to the test in fear that busted nose or not, I would fail.

My membership to the Navy boxing squad coincided with a rise in the squads' fortunes. The squads' strength was in depth, as well as a few established internationals at least one Navy boxer from each weight division was pressing for an England place. It came as no surprise when we trounced the RAF and the Army in both the Combined Services individual and team championships. After each contest it was time for some rest and recuperation and I found myself going home frequently. I seemed to be home more often than when I was a civilian. My hair had by now grown beyond the regulation length and my curls kicked in. I did not see the point of getting it cut.
In the quarterfinals I found myself drawn against former opponent and Olympian, Graham Moughton, who had succeeded me to the London title. This contest would prove to be a good yardstick to see how far I had come since our previous close encounter. My biological clock had finally awoken and I now had brawn to supplement the grey matter. Despite now having the option I didn't discard the guile. I run out a convincing winner as I did in the semi final.
George Gilbody, who beat me the previous year, was not in the opposite corner for the final. That honour went to Eddie Gajny a former opponent. Regrettably George had pulled out in an earlier round because of illness. I was disappointed that I was not going to get the chance to avenge my losses. I was sure our next meeting would have been third time lucky no longer a boy. Recruit Marsh was now the ABA lightweight champion. It was the end of the road as far as the individual championship but I returned to Portsmouth rather than Lympstone awaiting news regarding selection for the Commonwealth games in Australia: George Gilbody got the nod. My next port of call was to be Lympstone rather than Australia. I was not disappointed Gilbody had a couple of wins over me and I was partly resigned to him getting the nod when he pulled out of the ABAs. He was England's most highly rated amateur so it was not as if I was being overlooked in favour of a stiff. Also I was keen to start my

commando training. I had been in the services for six months and military training was still at week one. More importantly I had my eye on the Moscow Olympics in 1980.

I was assigned once again to Chosen troop, where I was going to remain for a couple of weeks until a fresh batch of recruits arrived for training. For the purposes of administration I was being 'back-squaded' from 112 troop to 119 troop. In a senior troop to me was one of my brother's mates Steve Darts. Dartsy was first and foremost a school friend of brother John but Dartsy and I, through our common cause, also became good mates.

The earlier visit to Lympstone had been in January and the contrast to the then sunny June was stark. At weekends it gave the recruits the opportunity to visit Exmouth, the local seaside resort a couple of miles down the road. The recruits dressed in civvies could not have been more noticeable had they worn their uniforms. They walked around the town in packs wearing pressed denims, desert boots and tee-shirts advertising the motto of their respective troops: 'Death before dishonour', 'Sergeant Sykes horny toads' and 'When the going gets tough the tough get going' are three that remain in my memory. I had no troop for the moment so did not have a tee-shirt to show whom I belonged to. Nobody considered advertising Chosen troop on their apparel and I was not going to break with tradition, I had other ideas. The shop in Exmouth doing the tee-shirt printing, run by a former marine, was a thriving business due to the endless supply of wannabe commandos. I joined the queue and waited my turn. An hour later I had my tee-shirt 'TERRY MARSH ABA CHAMPION 1978'. Now it is rather embarrassing but then I thought I had earned the right to wear it. Winning the ABAs was a dream fulfilled and I wanted the world to know.

Unlike my earlier experience of Chosen troop this time I was to get the full works. Previously I'd go to the gym and lose myself for the day. For recruit Marsh things were now to be different. Having fallen in for inspection, part of Chosen troop would go off to receive their physiotherapy. The 'able bodied' amongst us would be assigned menial tasks like white washing rocks or pulling weeds from between paving stones - to justify our existence.

I would look on enviously at the other recruits in the more

advanced stages of their training. The more senior looked the part with their commando style cap comforters. I had seen such hats in numerous war films portraying Commandos and seeing these guys in their kit gave me an eagerness for time to move on. They were also carrying between them an assortment of weapons and looked like they could take on the world.
Another troop that caught my eye for different reasons was the King's Squad. It was the senior troop who had passed all their commando training and exercises and were preparing for their passing out parade. Wearing the navy blue surge uniform and either white pith helmets or white caps with matching white belt and gloves they did look smart, but I could not identify with it. To me it was very 'un-commando' and not what I was joining for. Ironically the King's squad that I witnessed was the survivors of 112 troop, the troop I had been assigned to on my first day at Lympstone.

The first week of the training was intriguing; the training team treated us and spoke to us like a bunch of eleven year olds – notwithstanding the expletives. We were told how we should shit, shave and shower even to the point of eradicating the 'clingons' that could occur following a visit to the toilet. We were shown how to iron, how to make a bed and fold clothing in the personal lockers. We were shown how everything was to be cleaned and warned that it should always be in such immaculate condition for inspections that were both in the mornings and afternoons. The emphasis was on hygiene to the point that it became extreme. Were a civvie to be as preoccupied with hygiene they would have been seen as obsessive.
It was to be a couple of weeks before our first military exercise. We were loaded into a couple of trucks referred to as ‘four-tonners’ and driven by Wrens dressed in army fatigues. It appeared that all the drivers of these heavy goods vehicles were generously proportioned ladies. The four-tonner description could have equally applied to the drivers.
It started out like an outing with the scouts. We were shown how to adapt our waterproof ponchos into a means of shelter. We had a demonstration of how to cook from the 24-hour ration pack, how to clean the utensils and how to keep our equipment clean

and rust free in the field. The hygiene was what separated us from the 'Army Pongos' so they were affectionately referred to - where the army goes the pong goes.
The first introduction to real soldiering then began. Having established our camp, sentry duty was the next lesson. 'Halt who goes there friend or foe?' We took our turns guarding the camp that night. That morning the training team arrived – friend or foe? It was time for inspection.
All our equipment including rifles had to be laid in the uniform manner as demonstrated the previous evening. It was another section that had been first to get their inspection underway. It gave us an idea of what lay ahead. I saw their Corporal throwing bits of equipment into the thick gorse bushes that lived on the Woodbury common. Like dogs running to retrieve a stick for their master the owners of the kit run in pursuit of the flying items. Others were seen running up a steep hill with arms held high, elbows locked, carrying their rifles.
The boy scout camping had come to an end. I was not the first in my section to be inspected. Going by the forensic examination being carried out on my colleague's kit, it was not a question of whether or not I would be found out. The question was whether it was going to be the rifle held high or scavenging through the gorse. The recruits in Chosen troop had warned me about getting 'Woodbury'. The stings from the gorse becoming infected caused it. Once the infections took root they were difficult to eradicate partly due to the demands of the training course.
'Rust' was found on my aluminium mess tins so off I went to retrieve them. I am sure that had there been an absence of mess tins the rust would have been identified on my plastic comb. My rifle however, was guilty of carrying the dreaded Ferrous Oxide. Mess tins retrieved and secured I was reaching for the sky with half a dozen others. We were a majority. "Get them fucking arms up." yelled a Corporal as if his life depended on it. Most by now had the weight of the rifle shared by their two hands and head. When we got up and back down the hill it was repeated again. I got the impression that they would not be happy until one or two started dropping. I was above such antics but a clip of the heels of the guy in front of me enabled him to bail out temporarily giving him a brief respite. The precedent made it was not long

before another fell, not of my doing, and the ‘beasting, as it was later described, ceased. "And let that be a fucking lesson to you." screamed the Corporal.

It was time to return to the barracks on foot and what appeared an even harsher regime. I was puzzled about the amount of drill that took place *vis-à-vis* soldiering and the hours spent in preparing for such drills and the subsequent inspections. Then further inspections because you were not up to scratch in the first inspection. Once caught in such a downward spiral it was difficult to extract yourself from it. You were constantly trying to catch up and it required either a super human effort or help from your colleagues. Sadly there was not much help being given. Recruits could barely keep on top of their own tasks. There was also the element of, 'there but for the grace of God go I'. While the training team is focusing on the miscreant the minor misdemeanours of the others would go unnoticed. It was not in the interests of the fortunate to assist the unfortunate.

In some respects those victimised were those with question marks against them. It was a way of testing them or getting them to leave. Those who found themselves under such scrutiny would invariably leave. Those who did not leave must have been totally stupid, totally committed or had nowhere else to go. As the sixth week approached the original squad of forty-two had been reduced to around thirty. Commando stuff was becoming more relevant in the sense that we were spending as much time firing rifles as we were marching, It was welcoming but not without a downside. Fired weapons get dirty and the explosive chemicals discharged cling and pervade every recess of the weapons that required hours of cleaning.

The time spent down the ranges was not a particularly pleasant time. There were long periods of inactivity that were fundamentally boring for the training teams. They would devise little tasks for us to undertake. I suspected these trials and tribulation were extra curricular but was not certain and not in a position to question their legitimacy.

The first time it happened to me was during lunch at the rifle range. "Marsh," shouted one of the Corporals, "do you like butter?"

If I say yes its cue to give me a massive amount to eat and if I

say no its still cue to give me some.
"Yes Corporal. Love it." rather let them think I was eating something I liked rather than something I disliked.
"There you go then, you can have that." I was thrown more than a mouthful of margarine.
"Can I put it between two slices of bread?"
"No."
"I need to give it some flavour." I began digging the soil beneath me and grabbed a handful along with the insects inhabiting it and added it to the margarine and took a substantial bite of the mixture. It was as if they found it more repulsive than I. I saw some faces grimace. It was my way of demonstrating that no matter what burden they choose to put upon me, I am able to inflict upon myself a greater burden. If someone orders you to do ten press-ups as a punishment you do twenty.
On another occasion I was ordered to run with my rifle above my head down to the hundred-metre mark on the ranges and kiss a designated post. I was warned that I would be monitored through the binoculars. I got to the hundred-metre mark and the post but continued to run towards the two hundred-metre point. Aligning myself to a post with my back to the prying binoculars I put my head to one side. The apparent tryst with the post complete it was time to negotiate the return.
"Marsh you kissed the wrong post it was the one at the hundred metre point."
"I wasn't sure which post you meant Corporal so I picked the best looking one."
"Ok, go and join the troop."
We had been shown how to strip down the weapons for cleaning and it was emphasised that the deconstruction went no further. In the interests of having a clean weapon I was more enthusiastic with the stripping. It saved valuable minutes in the cleaning process. Pat Murphy, a brummie, followed my example. He was a young man whose time was even more precious to him due to the constant punishments he was receiving. He was under the cosh. In fact what he was incurring was not a punishment but a loss of privileges. In the services everything was a privilege.
The next weapon inspection held no fears for Pat Murphy or I.

We were positioned next to each other. The working parts of the weapons were laid out on the ground before us while the carcass of the rifle balanced on the right shoulder. "What's wrong with this weapon Murphy?"
"Nothing Corporal."
"Why is your weapon different from everybody else's? You have illegally stripped it down haven't you Murphy?"
"Yes Corporal."
"You will go before the Company Commander and will be charged for the illegal stripping of your weapon. Now reassemble your weapon and take it to the armoury for correcting"
The Corporal moved on to me, "Morning Marsh." said the Corporal as he relieved me of the weapon and pointed the barrel towards the sky peering through it to check for rust and dust.
"Morning Corporal."
"You've illegally stripped your weapon down as well haven't you?"
"No Corporal."
"You see the head of that pin? It's on the wrong side that's how I know. You illegally stripped your weapon didn't you?" As each word spat from his mouth so his forehead moved closer and his eyes locked onto mine. All the recruits had their eyes faced forward and despite our proximity the stand off was effectively invisible to them all.
"No Corporal." it was said submissively not wishing to challenge the authority of the Corporal in front of his subordinates. Yet, with the eyeballing that he initiated I was not going to yield. It probably did not last as long as it seemed but I felt that I was able to intimidate the Corporal sufficiently. I've heard it said that you see what someone is thinking by looking them in the eyes. I don't know how accurate that is but what I saw in the Corporals eyes initially was confidence but when I returned the stare that confidence ebbed and was supplanted by something else. "Take your weapon to the armoury and put it right. I'll see you later."
"Yes Corporal."
He never did. My Dad once advised me, "Admit nothing." It was the right advice for that occasion.
Pat Murphy meanwhile was charged and duly punished with

further losses of privileges and more hours taken from his sleep but he hung on in. I only wish I had passed on my Dad's advice to him. There was an occasion when that advice was ignored, perhaps foolishly. It was in the latter stages of the training when we were involved in an exercise called 'Coiled Spring'. We were undergoing internal security training and staying at a camp designed for such purposes. We had by now passed on the shooting ranges and it was time to use the weapons in more realistic settings. As an a side I was surprised how much of the overall course was taken up with internal security training - was a revolution expected?
During one respite the troop was stood down. The weapons were made safe and laid on the floor with one exception which was leaning upright against a wall. We had specific instruction in the early weeks of weapon training that weapons should not be left in such positions. Should they fall the sights can be disarranged and should it be loaded a bullet possibly discharged. When one of the Corporals entered, his eyes immediately focused on the offending rifle. "Whose rifle is that?"
There was a collective silence, as if in sympathy, for the poor sole that was going to be shit on from a very big height. No one knew apart from the offender. I was just hoping it was not Pat Murphy. We all knew where our own particular weapon was but without an immediate process of matching rifles to personnel the perpetrator would go unnoticed. “Right the troop will be punished with extra duties.”
"It was me Corporal.” I said. There was at least four of the troop who must have known that I was not the offender as well as the ‘guilty’ party. I don't know whether it was the eyes, the manner in which the confession was made or simply the body language but this Corporal was not accepting it.
"Good try Marsh but it was not you."
"It was me Corporal." I insisted rather idiotically.
"It wasn't you...Well done." and we all watched him leave.
"You all owe me." I announced in a superior sort of way.

There were several commando tests to be passed. The Assault course held no terrors for me, neither did the Tarzan course, which entailed swinging and climbing on ropes. One very cold

Saturday morning we had the introduction to the Endurance course. The thought of negotiating the six-metre underwater tunnel provoked an adrenal rush. The course entailed a cross-country run. In addition to the submerged tunnel were other dry tunnels to be negotiated. These tunnels had the inconvenience of being, by design, very dark and cramped. A further hazard was broken glass that had accumulated over the years through acts of mischief from persons unknown. There was also Peter's Pool named after the recruit who was reported to have drowned in it. The depth varied depending on the time of year. On one practice run I had special memories of Peter's Pool. It had iced over and I ran across it. "Back here Marsh. You're not getting away with that. Break the ice." said the Corporal whom I had not noticed as I walked on water. Back I went and dug the heel of my DMS boot into the ice, "It won't break Corporal."
"Use your rifle butt."
My two colleagues had now caught up and helped in breaking the ice. The water erupted from below. The wading through the pool was a solitary experience but we shared a harmony when it came to our panting. It took your breath away.
I was in the first group of three being one of the better runners in the troop. This was deliberate in order to avoid bottlenecks in the cramped dark tunnels. For someone like myself it was not difficult being on the slim side. For the bigger lads it was a difficult task aggravated by the equipment being carried, which served to enlarge the body's dimensions. If you possessed a scintilla of claustrophobia it would find you out. It happened to one poor sole and as a result a jam occurred with several recruits stuck in a dark tunnel with their noses stuck up each other's arses.
I think we were all both pleased and disappointed when it came to the six metre underwater tunnel. It was certainly underwater but measured only six feet. It did not take a great deal of courage to do this. It was a matter of closing your eyes and holding your breath for a few seconds. Had it been six metres then the nerve would have been seriously tested. Every time I had seen a Commando I had a respect for them thinking that this guy had gone through a six metre underwater tunnel carrying all his equipment. It was a task that I was uncertain of being able to

complete and had often feared it would be my Achilles heel on the commando course.
While in the galley queue not long after the endurance course I overheard some recruits still in the early stages of training asking some members of our troop about what lay ahead of them. They spoke about the six-metre underwater tunnel. None of those who knew the reality challenged the fib including me.
It was not all easy stuff for recruit Marsh. A commando test that held no fears for me was the rope climbing. To continue the course each recruit would have to climb, with his equipment, a ten-metre rope. We had been shown the correct way of rope climbing in the gym and then climbed the ropes although without the equipment. The correct way was to utilise all the limbs to share the body weight as you defied gravity. I did not need to. I was able to climb the rope just by using my arms.
The instructions for the climbing test were, on reaching the top, to shout out your name. The Corporal would acknowledge your call and you could come down under control. I attacked the rope hand over hand as before and the rhythm and momentum overcame the burden of the additional equipment now being carried. I was within six inches of the top, sure that Marsh would be the first name called, but then the muscles in my arms tightened and I knew I needed the grip of both hands to stay on the rope. My legs were flagging trying desperately to grip the rope between both knees and feet but to no avail. I tried to readjust and tried again. Meanwhile I could hear "Murphy Corporal."
"Come down Murphy."
"Quinn Corporal."
"Come down Quinn."
"Linley Corporal."
"Okay Linley."
I knew the longer I stayed there the less likely it would be that I would make that reach of six inches and decided it was now or never. It was not going to be now. The one hand was not enough and I began to slither down the rope. I grasped the rope with the other hand but the downward momentum had began and the additional hand served no benefit but shared the agony of the skin being scraped from the palms of my hands. I was in free fall

for the final three metres. The landing hurt and was exacerbated by the equipment and rifle that I carried. A lingering pain also throbbed from my palms where the skin had been. Yet that pain was nothing compared to the pain I felt through failure.
It was to be another two weeks before I had an appointment with the ropes again. My hands had barely healed but I was not going to use it as an excuse or a distraction. I was not alone in having failed in the earlier attempt but I took no comfort in being one of several. Prior to the ascent I psyched myself like a weight-lifter with short sharp breaths. The signal given, I climbed it like a monkey. Hand over hand my legs being redundant just hanging. I started with great momentum and it sort of carried me up and I reached and touched the top. "Marsh Corporal."
"Okay." I heard him say.
Down I came and on reaching the ground began to feel my biceps, triceps and forearms throbbing. I was up and down before others had barely reached half way. The scabs that had formed on my palms, from the earlier rope burns, began to seep with the yellow puss that had squatted in the wounds. I wouldn't be able to do that again, I thought to myself. "Have you been up?" asked the Corporal.
"Yeah I was the first one Corporal. I called out."
He walked away and consulted his clipboard "You failed it last time?"
"Yes Corporal."
"You'll have to do it again."
I felt sick, not because I had to do it again but when I failed it would be seen as if I was trying to pull a fast one. I knew that I would not be able to do it with brute force and ignorance as I'd done previously. I'd need to use the conventional method of which I had a rough idea of but had not practised the technique until then. I grasped the rope with my hands and then gripped it vice like with my legs and recited the drill several times, "Long shift, short shift hand on top." I got there, "Marsh Corporal."
"Okay well done."
On reaching the ground the Corporal approached me, "I'm sorry for doubting you."
There was no more hiccups regarding completing the various tests to gain the green beret and all that stood between the

recruit troop and relative freedom was the final exercise, the aptly named, Nutcracker. To my amazement Pat Murphy was still around despite all the obstacles that had been put in front of him.
The exercise started with our boat rendezvousing off the coast of Plymouth with a number of rigid raiders. The small crafts sneaked us up the River Dart from where we had to disembark and make our way to the shore. It was a low tide and the water should only have reached up to our knees. However the combination of a muddy riverbed and the heavy equipment carried ensured that we sank into the quagmire. We were submerged to at least waist height. We were all top heavy with equipment and with our legs stuck in the mud the slightest loss of balance saw our hapless bodies toppling into the water. I could not contain my laughter. It was a combination of hilarity and fear. It looked a complete shambles. We were a beaten army before there was any sign of the enemy; that was the hilarity. The fear came from the fact that I was stuck and unable to extricate myself from what I was beginning to believe was quick sand. It was only a matter of time before I was a victim to what I had been laughing at earlier. The darkness hampered my judgement and I misjudged the timing of my step. I toppled over like a falling tree but less dignified because of my attempts to defy the gravity. I was totally immersed in the water.
Every cloud has a silver lining as was the case here. The greater surface area through my prone position released me from the mud. As long as I stayed on my belly or on all fours I could keep mobile and eventually make the shoreline. I had forgotten that I was with another twenty or so fellow marine. I suspect the same applied to them.
Eventually we all made it to the shore and regrouped ready to embark upon the long march on the moors. For the rest of the night we were 'yomping' (marching). On reaching our destination we were able to snatch a couple of hours sleep. The thought of changing into dry clothes and getting into a warm sleeping bag, even just for a short while, was so seductive but the thought exceeded the reality. The flirting with the River Dart had taken its toll and my Bergen (rucksack) and it's contents had taken some of the water as a souvenir.

For the next four days we were all wet, cold, hungry and tired as we struggled around Dartmoor. To help keep warm at night we would double up in the sleeping bags. Into the second day we were all suffering to some degree or another from hypothermia. Recruit Murphy had a session of doing press ups in a stream guided by one of the training team, who had hounded him from week three of training. When recruit Murphy later showed signs of hypothermia he was removed from the exercise but not to go to hospital. He remained on Dartmoor playing the part of the enemy.

As the final day of Nutcracker came we had to do a long yomp and then rendezvous with the trucks to take us back to camp. After many miles we caught sight of our destination, a bridge. The trucks awaited us on the other side. We were informed that the bridge was mined, notionally, and therefore out of use. We had to cross the river. It was a task nobody was looking forward to, although we could not get any wetter. Nevertheless, we could see the silhouette of two four tonners on the other side. That spurred us on for one last effort. The river crossing was not difficult, under normal circumstances, but it was very dark and raining heavily. Some lads had injuries such as stress fractures and tendonitis. They persevered not wishing to be taken off the exercise and denied the Green Beret. There was the equally horrific prospect of being confined to Chosen troop for an unhealthy length of time.

The river negotiated and well and truly behind us it was time to board the trucks. We were ordered to fall in.

"In three ranks." shouted the Sergeant.

There was an air of achievement relief and self-congratulations amongst us all, "We're now Commandos." I heard someone say.

"Made it." cried another.

"I didn't think it would be this hard." said someone else

"I feel sorry for Pat Murphy." was my contribution. He had been persecuted by one member of the training team and been given one hell of a time and yet had prevailed only to be impeded on the final exercise. A volley of shots interrupted my thoughts. It was the enemy or should I say Pat Murphy. The lorries drove off.

"Get moving." shouted the Sergeant.

We moved off chasing after the lorries that had driven off up the

incline. I tried helping some of those injured that I knew would not be able to run. I took one lad's kit and found that I could not manage it. I did not realise how weak I had become. So as he staggered using his rifle as a walking stick I dragged his kit that had been strapped to his back. I was told he would have to do it himself. He cried with frustration as he and one other demonstrated how their minds were willing but their bodies weak. An argument broke out between the Corporals. Some could see they were tough lads and it was only injury that prevented them from completing the course. The other side of the argument was that they had to finish on their own. One lad now unable to walk crawled up the steep incline, the rain beating down on them. I was hanging back hoping that I would be allowed to help. They were ordered into a Land Rover. Initially they refused insisting they could do it. However, orders were orders and so they were helped on board.
"You better get moving Marsh or we'll fail you too."
"OK Corporal."
Off I ran. This time we were allowed to board the trucks. The exercise was over. The next thing I remember was being awoken by the shouts of the troop Sergeant and waking amongst a mass of bodies and discarded military webbing.
The shower was the first port of call for us all. Our bodies were badly chaffed and my more delicate parts suffered more than their fair share of skin deprivation. When the shower's water hit the sensitive parts the pain was immense. The feet were deficient of a few toenails and the blisters and swelling made walking very painful. I had to resort to wearing the very baggy regulation starched white shorts to prevent chafing and white plimsolls, minus the laces, to allow the swollen feet to fit. The journey to the phone booth to phone home was very uncomfortable. I walked with my legs spread apart as wide as I could to alleviate any rubbing of the raw skin, at the same time limping because of the blistered feet. There, as always, was a queue outside the two phone booths. Eventually it was my turn and as I limped up to the booth a Corporal, dressed in civvies, made his way to the booth ignoring the queue.
"I'm next."
"You what?"

"I'm next, there's a queue. You join it like every one else."
"Do you want to make something of this?"
"Listen, I wouldn't if I were you."
"You what?"
"You're out of your class, I'm in a different league."
"Get your fucking heels together." was his response to me.
This prick was trying to pull rank and I had a choice, swallow or do something. I chose the latter. My head went into his face and my feet followed up as he went back and I climbed on top of him. It was short but nasty and brutish. A PTI Sergeant, who was nearby, saved him from my follow up. Blood was spilt by both of us. Claret emanated from his face and my sore-blistered feet.
"What caused this?"
"He pushed in the queue Sergeant." shouted out an onlooker sympathetic to me.
"What do you think you are doing? Just because you are the British boxing champion you can't go around fighting everyone for queue jumping.
I wanted to say to my opponent, "See I told you I was out of your class." Instead I worked on the Sergeant, "He tried to pull rank Sergeant."
I was dismissed and allowed to make my phone call while the other guy got a tongue lashing from the Sergeant.
It would be another two weeks before the Green Beret presentation. It was necessary to prepare and practice for the passing out parade. I was hoping to avoid it due to injury, as I was unable to get my boots on and enthusiastically reported to sickbay with my ailments.
The passing out parade was not the only event I was trying to avoid. There was also the Troop Piss Up. It was a celebration for achieving the coveted Green Beret. The training team arranged it and each of us recruits had to put in a tenner. My objection to this was not that the training team would be in attendance but they would not be contributing to the whip. I was therefore not partaking. I expressed my concerns to the troop but the training team was oblivious to this dissent.
It was payday and the troop Sergeant said that he was collecting the tenners for the Troop Piss Up. We had to line up outside his office. It was thought that I would cave in but I was adamant

that I was not parting with my tenner.
I joined the queue like everybody else. On my turn I entered the Sergeant's office and stood to attention.
"Got your money Marsh?"
"No Sergeant."
"What?"
"I'm not going Sergeant."
"Why is that?"
"I have no money Sergeant."
"What, you have been training for six months and you have not saved any money?"
"My brother got in trouble with the police and had to pay a heavy fine or go to prison. I did not want my parents to find out so I paid his fine and it has cleaned me out."
I strolled out of the office with a swagger for the benefit of my peers. They were eager to hear what happened, "I told them I'm not going and I never paid the tenner."
I had a few admirers for making a stand. However, my deception came to light when the Troop Sergeant approached a few troop members. He suggested that the troop have a whip round for me. I had to put them right.
I did not have the same success avoiding the passing out parade. I was told that I was being awarded the Commando Medal. It is a discretionary award given, if deemed merited, for a combination of Courage, Determination, Unselfishness, Competence and Cheerfulness in adversity. I think I had more of the latter than all the others combined. I was presented with it on the day of the passing out and was a particular proud moment for Mum and Dad who had travelled down to witness the occasion.
After the parade the order was given "Marines to your duties quick march." The King's Squad marched off to the tune, 'Life On the Ocean Wave', played by the Band of the Royal Marines. My duty was to be with Four-One Commando. They had an imminent trip to Brunei for jungle training but I wasn't going.

CHAPTER EIGHT
UNITED NATIONS

The combination of commando training and further maturity meant that my days as a lightweight were over. I would now be fighting in the heavier light-welter division where the maximum weight permitted was ten stone.

I was an old hand now and did not have any difficulties finding my feet with the Matelots. The Navy once again trounced the Army and RAF in the preliminary stages of the national championship but I was the only member of our squad who made it to the final.

On the eve of the final I stayed up late to watch the General Election results in the mess television room. The then Labour Government was kicked out. I was the only one in the room not cheering. I can't complain about a late night as I slept in. Come the night of my fight I was in the red corner. Was it a sign?

My opponent was Eddie Copeland from Manchester. He was an uncompromising fighter who relied on his strength to wear opponents down. The contest was widely anticipated. It was expected to be the classic fighter against boxer encounter. The crowd were not disappointed. It was a bout that the trade paper, Boxing News, suggested was the amateur fight of the year.

Eddie was out of his corner in a flash. A left hook had me grappling the ropes to prevent myself from going down. The referee intervened with a standing eight count. The onslaught, I'm told, was relentless and the referee administered a further standing eight count. I came out for the second round having weathered the early onslaught and did enough to hold my own. In the final round I proved the stronger and out-boxed him at long range to win the round clearly. It was now a matter for the judges.

It was a unanimous decision in favour of my opponent. In fact two of the three judges, numerically, scored the contest a draw but favoured Eddie for his greater aggression. Dad, John and my cousin Dennis were thrilled about my performance this year. John has always cited this fight as the defining moment in my boxing career. Tony Oxley, my new coach, said to me, "I always suspected you were a hard bastard Tel. Tonight you proved it." I was able to take something from the setback. It was not appreciated at the time, I have no memory of the fight, beyond that 'lucky' punch.

I kept a brave face and no one had any idea how much I was hurting inside. All in all it was a terrible day. It was the day Maggie Thatcher moved into Number ten and after the fight I learnt that my Paternal Grandmother had died. I'm ashamed to say it was my loss that hurt most. Still, I had a six-month stay in sunny Cyprus with Four-One Commando to look forward to, but I would have swapped that for victory if I could.

At Deal I met up with a few of the other marines from F Company who, for various reasons, had got left behind. It was simply a case of killing time, a few days in fact, before getting a flight from Brize Norton to Cyprus. It was a good induction; the 'new boy' was able to get to know some of his colleagues before being thrown in amongst the whole Commando Unit. The evenings were spent sat in the nearby pubs drinking - in my case cider. The nights were great; I'd sit and listen to the adventures of my more experienced colleagues who had done tours of Northern Ireland.

It was about Four-One's tour of West Belfast, a predominantly Catholic area. The troubles were described in Catholic and Protestant terms. West Belfast being Catholic and therefore IRA, so it was explained, was the enemy and we, being marines, would take no shit. Prior to the arrival of Four-One there existed certain 'no go areas' where the Army dare not enter, but when Four-One arrived things changed. Names of areas such as Andytown, Turf Lodge & the Devis flats were scenes of skirmishes and battles that the Green Berets had. "They only got us once," one of my 'oppos' pointed out, "Joc Andy got shot."

I also got a quick brief on Cyprus. The northern part of the Island had been invaded a number of years earlier and the

Turkish advance had occupied a big chunk of the island. It was now the task of the United Nations, to whom we were assigned, to act as the peacekeeper and patrol the cease-fire line separating the opposing Turkish and Greek armies.
We touched down at Akroteri, which was in the area known as the Western Sovereign Base Area (WESBA). It was in the Southern Greek part of the Island but was British territory. We were to be transported to ESBA, the eastern equivalent. Up until then I thought that we were joining the United Nations. It was explained that Four-one had two quite separate roles. As well as service with the UN another task was protecting the ESBA territory. F Company's first stint was to be with ESBA. We were to join the rest of the Company at a camp referred to as Hi Nic.
I had to pay a visit to the stores to get my kit and weapon and felt the part when I donned the hot weather uniform referred to as jungle fatigues. I was still short of a webbing belt, which was an essential part of the *de rigueur*, but was told, in the interim, to wear my Corp belt. The belt was a mixture of the colours blue, red and yellow hardly compatible with the camouflage jungle fatigues; I was a walking contradiction.
My troop was out patrolling and my brief was to get my kit organised and report at the next parade. Meanwhile I hit the 'galley'. The food was as good as any I had tasted. Outside the galley was a barbecue on the go with massive sides of steak. Inside was a well-stocked salad bar amongst other choices. While tucking into my scran a Land Rover pulled up and out jumped the occupants from front and rear brandishing their rifles heading straight to the front of the queue with one left behind on the radio.
I figured, rightly, it was part of my troop and was anxious to be part of it but refrained from introductions. I ate up and left with a full stomach. I had hardly travelled when a Corporal confronted me. He was the senior of the marines I had observed. He had short fair spiky hair and a similar frame to myself but a few years older. In a rather high pitched but military manner he questioned my attire. "Why are you wearing the Corp belt with that dress? It is not only irregular but looks hideous."
He was right on both counts but I felt he was digging me out in front of his subordinates. "I haven't got a webbing belt and was

told to wear this until I got one." I replied defensively.
“Right, I see, well you better get one quickly." Off he sauntered to rejoin his 'motley crew'.
I carried on not looking back but only too conscious that the Corporal was reminding me that now things were going to be different *vis-á-vis* my days with the boxing squad. I felt the reprimand was principally for the benefit of his charges and I suspect a challenge had been thrown down to him by one of them that he gladly accepted. I felt that, in a similar vein, he was throwing down a challenge to me but unlike him I didn't take it up.
I was still trying to find my feet. I should not have been surprised at the situation. I had been warned that this was the way things happened when you join a unit. Your not made welcome, nothing is done to accommodate you. It is your job to fit in. It has its own dynamics and you have to adjust to that pace before you can get aboard. As the day ended so I met a few mates from my time at Lympstone and it was good to see familiar faces. However, that was then, when we were in training together. For them it was an age ago. Since the training days they had been on exercise in the jungles of Brunei and had runs ashore in Hong Kong and Singapore. They had moved on, but I had regressed. When I last saw them I was the national champion now I'm the guy who lost in the final. The title was a comfort and now gone I would covet that comfort.
They were out that night drinking while I stayed in lying on my pit reading some adventure book by Wilbur Smith. No, I wasn’t even reading it but using it as a prop. One lad, Scouse, had a portable stereo blaring out music from Supertramp’s, ‘Breakfast in America’ while ironing his uniform. He declined the night out since he was saving up for his wedding. Going on tour was a good way to save. Super Tramp was followed by Meatloaf's, Bat out of Hell and then it was Dave Bowie with Hunky Dory: I liked his choice of music. More crucial to me was his surplus of webbing belts. Scouse was good enough to lend me one of his.
Next day I was now doing the job of real soldiering. I had been in the marines for over eighteen months and still yet to do active service. The troop Lieutenant made the comment that it was good to put a face to the name. Until then I had been the

'unknown soldier'. I had been a member of the troop for over six months but this was the first time incarnate. My first 'mission' was to be part of a four-man 'bric' patrolling the outer perimeter of Hi Nic that bordered the Turkish sector of Cyprus. We were within shouting distance of some of the Turkish encampments, separated by a skimpy piece of fencing and 50 yards of arid land. Probably because I was the new boy I got custody of the bulky radio. I held my weapon tightly ready and willing to load the chamber should the need arise.
The adrenaline was pumping and I felt alert like never before. My vision felt sharper, my vista wider, and my hearing super sensitive. We came to a halt at a spot where we were as close as we could get to a Turkish observation post (OP). I took cover, knelt on one knee eagerly scanning the ground around me. Each of my colleagues began fumbling through their equipment and I felt that I had missed out on an instruction or more worryingly I was deficient of a piece of kit. My anxiety was short lived. "Give us a smile Tel." the cameras were rolling. The Marines were posing and I was equally guilty. The photos taken it was time for the patrol to recommence and we were once again tactical until the next photo opportunity. The patrol over, the photos developed, it was time for 'swappsies'. Not having a camera I had nothing to barter with. Most had thick albums, which acted as the log of the history of F Company and their exploits. On seeing these I was able to put pictures to the narrative when the 'lamp swinging' sessions begun as we sat outside the bars on the warm nights drinking brandy sours, the local speciality. The best storyteller was Frank O'Neill, the Corporal who had pulled me up on the first day over my belt. It wasn't what he said but how he said it. It was often the case that we would find ourselves gathered round in a buckled circle and someone would request a narration from Frank. Tell us about the riot in Andy Town or when you entered the Devis flats or when Joc Andy got shot or when the Catholic Club burnt down. The tales had been heard time and time again by many of those assembled but they had an entertainment value. It was story time for the commandos and we hung on every word like a bunch of nursery children listening to the teacher reading a story. Those protagonists present would reflect in the glory of their exploits described by Frank. For those

like me still lacking in real soldiering it further increased the appetite for the real thing.
I was into my second week when I was part of a reconnaissance team. The mission was to set up a covert observation post overlooking a Turkish army camp to monitor and record the events. I was one of four and we raided the galley to prepare rations. Because of the desert like terrain plenty of water was taken and I indulged in copious amounts of egg mayonnaise sandwiches – I saw it as a picnic with attitude.
The camouflage cream was spread liberally on my face. Before setting off there was the customary photo shoot posing with bandoleers of bullets spread python like over our bodies. We were dropped off by Land Rover under the cover of darkness and continued on foot towards our pre-determined position.
The first view of our target was through night sights that showed everything in a green haze. Having scanned the camp and surrounds it was time to wonder about the stars above. It was a warm clear night and stars were plenty. My previous military excursions I remember as being cold and damp, but they were all exercises while this was the 'real thing'. Four-One Commando had been described as the sunshine commandos and I was beginning to see why.
The view ahead of me evolved as the sun began to rise and I heard a couple of cockerels doing their early morning reveille. A few guards could be seen being relieved from their night shift and the Turkish flag raised in what looked like a routine as opposed to a ceremony.
It was to be a hour or so after the early signs of life that a body of soldiers, stripped to the waste wearing fatigues and boots, formed in three ranks, began running and chanting. I felt the need to put a bullet in the chamber. I was aware that they were on one side of the border and oblivious to our presence but it did not stop the heart racing. All that I witnessed I logged. It was time to pass over to someone else and I retreated deeper into our cover and got stuck into my breakfast.
My next stint observing caused anxiety about being compromised. A young lad was tending a herd of straggly looking sheep. They crossed our position and a few curious strays felt like they wanted to pay us a visit. I don't know if it had anything

to do with the aroma emanating from the egg mayonnaise sandwiches. Had the young shepherd compromised our position it would have meant aborting the mission. I tried throwing dust at the sheep but it only seemed to encourage them. I spat at them to no avail. It looked as if we were going to be compromised when Chas the Lance Corporal in charge, in a controlled manner, exclaimed, "Fuck off." It is a sort of universal language that appears, by the sheep's reaction, to have jumped the species barrier. I duly logged the incident. 'Flock of sheep crossed our position. Cannot say how many. Every time I counted them I fell asleep'.

The initial excitement of the operation was now beginning to wear off. It was becoming routine and boring. Despite being in the shade the heat was getting to me. It now was a case of clock watching and consuming my sandwiches. That night I suffered. I'm sure the Turkish sentries could hear my psychedelic yodels despite my genuine attempts to suppress my stomach's instinct to reject the egg mayonnaise. It was a pretty horrendous experience for me for the remainder of the mission. The sound of the engine from a Land Rover was very recognisable and when I heard the whining engine in the darkness for our pickup it was as good as the sweetest music. My first real mission should have been a great memory to me. Sadly it was everything but. The only two things that I learnt from the 72 hours was never take egg mayonnaise sandwiches on missions over 12 hours and that the Intelligence guys who scanned the logs did not have a sense of humour. I got a bollocking for my sheep observations.

I soon found my feet and was settling in well. I was having a great time at Hi Nic. The weather was fine, as you would expect, the hours were good and the food delicious. The evenings were spent sitting under the stars sipping our Brandy Sours having just seen a movie at the garrison cinema while in the afternoons it was fun and games by the pool. Not to mention the occasions when part of the patrolling entailed being flown around the territory in a Scout helicopter. Furthermore, I was getting paid for it. I was also entitled to two weeks leave so I hopped on the boat to Israel for the duration. It was three months of utopia I did not want to end. Yet, as with all good things, it did. The time went so fast. We now had to exchange our green berets for the

sky blue berets of the United Nations
The accommodation was a converted box factory situated several miles west of Nicosia. Our task was to patrol a five-mile stretch of the 'green line' - the cease-fire line of the opposing armies. One of my first United Nations' tasks was as a farmer's escort. The Greek farmers whose land was adjacent to the green line would have escorts available to them. I perched myself on the farmer's tractor and off we went. On reaching his land some four miles later we dismounted and he went about irrigating his fields. We had not been briefed about the need for escorts *per se* but it was apparent that if we were there to protect them we must be protecting them from something. I concluded it was border raids from the Turks. That was all I needed to heighten the tension and get the adrenaline pumping. That lasted fifteen minutes then the boredom set in.
As I looked across the green line I could see the observation posts spread along the cease-fire line and I was able to make out the silhouettes of the Turks. Word had got round that some of the Turkish guards, who had fallen asleep, were shot by their superiors. I focused on those observation posts thinking that I may witness an execution. That lasted fifteen minutes as well. I began to question the necessity of my presence. That lasted until it was time to eat. It was the farmer's responsibility to feed me and he gave me a bottle of wine and a folded cloth that I unwrapped revealing feta cheese and bread. I had earlier indulged in some of the fruit that was being grown in the nearby orchards. The fruit eased the thirst, but it did not prevent the hunger, that was to be satisfied by the cheese and bread. Both were dry and hard and therefore the wine was drunk as a lubricant. The farmer went back to farming while his escort relaxed with a full stomach, an empty bottle, a light head and heavy eyes. I became conscious of being woken by Turkish soldiers who were shaking my leg. I thought I would pretend to remain asleep hoping they might go away. The shaking of my leg became more aggressive and I figured it best to open my eyes and surrender. I was so pleased to see the farmer, grateful that the reality was more welcoming than the dream I was having.
On returning to the Box Factory I was greeted with much laughter. I did not know why until I made contact with a mirror.

My siesta under the sun resulted in a very red face reminiscent to the top of a Swan Vesta matchstick. A few hours later blisters began to appear until my face looked like one big blister.
Despite the military indiscretions like the 'salmonella' and being drunk on duty I still felt that I wanted greater challenges. I wanted to join the Special Boat Service (SBS) I was training hard, doing runs and marches carrying heavy loads in preparation for my special forces' ambitions between duties.
I also volunteered for a pistol shooting competition that resulted in a weeks training and shooting on the ranges. I became very good with the Browning 9mm pistol. I thought it would complement my Special Forces ambitions. I also planned on buying a nine-millimetre pistol on my return to the UK.
News had come through about our next tour and everyone was upbeat about it. The tour was a four-month stint in a small border town in Ulster, or the Six Counties, depending on your political perspective. I had no political perspective and saw it as a tour of Ireland. The town was Crossmaglen, which had the nickname of 'Bandit Country'. More British Soldiers had been killed there per square mile than anywhere else in 'Ulster'. That statistic was soon to be challenged, when in that same week news came through that over a dozen Paratroopers were killed following an ambush at Warrenpoint. The timing of the tour created a big dilemma for me, it coincided with the Olympics.

CHAPTER NINE
MOSCOW OR CROSSMAGLEN

It was a cold November when I arrived back to 'Blighty' but the temperature did not deter me from wearing a vest designed to show of my bronzed tan that matched my golden hair. In addition the extra pounds I had gained gave me a definition to be proud of. I was now a welterweight.

There were at least six guys in the Navy squad with serious Olympic ambitions. It included newcomer Brian Schumacher, a young Scouser. He had reached the ABA semis the previous year and was highly regarded. I met Shoey on the first day of my arrival and you would have thought he had been there for years. Like me previously he had joined the squad straight from Civvie Street.

I must have been least likely of all the contenders to succeed having moved up a weight division. I think the general consensus was that the bigger lads would be too strong for me and I harboured similar reservations. In the earlier rounds of the championships I was meeting and beating good fighters. No one could accuse me of having an easy journey to the English semis.

I was now competing against the Country's best. There was, Eddie Byrne a former Welterweight Champion described by many as a spoiler. He was a very clever cagey southpaw. Then there was Gunter 'the Hunter' Roomes who was the London Champion. He'd left a trail of destruction behind him in the earlier rounds also out pointing Lloyd Honeyghan a future undisputed World Welterweight Champion. It was also rumoured that, as a kid, he used to beat up Frank Bruno, another future World champ, when they shared a school that had the luxury of overnight accommodation. Last but no means least was the reigning champion Joey Frost. Joe had won the

final the previous year in 12 seconds and that included the count. Not many people knew what it was like to be swapping punches with Joey Frost in the third round - he could bang.
It was all down to the draw. Was it going to be Eddie the Spoiler, Gunter the Hunter or Joey the Banger? I got the news of the draw from coach, Tony Oxley. I was getting a nap in an adjacent hotel with team mate Tommy Taylor. Tommy, a light heavy weight, was hoping to avoid the current champion Andy Straughan.
Tony, banging on the door, woke us both. When he entered his face was beaming and he was highly charged, “We have got what we wanted. Straughan and Frosty, we’re home and dry now.”
Tommy and I looked at each other confused, neither of us saying anything but both being able to recognise each other’s disappointment. “Both get your heads down I’ll give you a call at half six.” Neither of us got our heads down and we were restless for the duration.
I was first to enter the gladiatorial arena. I knew what I had to do. Joey was a puncher and it was essential that I keep him at long range with my jab, which was effectively my one and only punch. My style of boxing was different to convention and this contributed to my reliance upon the left jab.
I waited and waited for the reigning champion to appear. If he was trying to intimidate me he succeeded. The wait went beyond the normal ‘delayed entrance’. I then became more optimistic, I thought and hoped that he had tripped up and injured himself and I would be getting a bye into the next round.
Time however dispelled such notions, as he appeared ducking between the second and third rope. When it came to touching gloves I felt his cold penetrating stare; I didn’t see it I was looking at the referee while he gave the instructions.
When the bell sounded I initiated my game plan. I circled the ring and when he got within range my left jab sprang out piston like. But it was my head that went backwards from his jab. Beginners luck I thought and pain I felt. The second time it happened the pain was similar but my thoughts were about my bad luck. I was at a loss as to what to do next. He was beating me at my own game. Stick with it I thought and poked out another jab. My head went back again and then his right

connected with my chin. Time slowed, it was as if I had taken a 'time out'. I was looking for a spot were I could fall or should I say dive?
I was about to face my first stoppage defeat. I had given it a go but it was not to be. By now it was fifteen milliseconds post punch or was it one hundred, perhaps three hundred. It really didn't matter. What did matter was that the punch although accurate had not affected my nervous system at all. My legs were stable, there was no haziness in my head, I wasn't seeing two of him nor were bells ringing in my ears. "For fuck sake you're giving up before your beaten. Don't go down without a fight." said my Jimminee Cricket. He was right, "At least give it your best."
So I did and it was good enough. I don't know what I did and how I did it but it was enough. I was told it was the fight of the night and I had arrived and made my mark. I don't remember much after that punch apart from not going down. Joey had also made his mark on me having inflicted me with a chipped front tooth. It is a nice memento to carry – a battle honour. I surprised many in the way I had beaten the current champion and Olympic favourite. Many had thought I would not be up to the task and would 'fold'. They did not know how close they had been to being right.
Had that little voice not rescued me my life would have been so different. Not in a materialistic sense, more in regards to being at ease with one's self. Every night when my head hit the pillow I would have to live with that indiscretion. It made me realise how weak we all can be given the circumstances. How many other fighters have done the same but slipped over the precipice upon which I stood. Only they will know of course and very few will admit to it. It gave me an inner strength in the sense that it made me aware that people are much weaker than they would like to admit, including my future opponents.
Eddie the Spoiler got the better of Gunter the Hunter while my team mate Tommy lost on points. In the Great Britain Finals I was paired with Eddie the spoiler. I think we both saw an Olympic place as the prize for victory. In an interesting rather than spectacular contest I was judged the winner. The Moscow Olympics was there for me, if I wanted it - so I thought.

The troops of the 'nasty' Soviet Union had gone into Afghanistan, much to the chagrin of the United States of America who condemned the Soviet aggression and boycotted the forthcoming games. The British position was that it was a personal matter for the competitor. Being in the pay of the Government I had been sounded out by an Admiral, John Lee, prior to the final but it was left with me whether I would go or not. There was no arm-twisting.

I had already made my plans well in advance, namely the tour of Ireland but having now got so close to the Olympics I was fleeting from Crossmaglen to Moscow and *vice versa* - both appealed. I would think that it was not a true Olympics since the Americans were not competing and therefore debased, but then a moment later I would think that it would be easier to get the gold.

On the other hand I was looking forward to some real soldiering in Crossmaglen. The military was where I saw my future and I did not want to spend my next time in the barracks just listening to more stories about others. I wanted to be in the stories playing a major part. For the moment the decision did not have to be made. I had a long weekend to enjoy before returning to Portsmouth to hear the decision of the selectors whom had spent that same weekend choosing the Olympic boxing squad.

I was in a celebratory mood and out with John and his mates that weekend which led to an impromptu party. I lost my cherry to an older woman. She was twenty-three and a law graduate. I will say no more on her identity to save her blushes. However, some squatters hiding in a wardrobe witnessed it.

My inability to ejaculate, which I put down to my testicular torsion, meant that the lady was truly satisfied again and again and again. She was rather loud which made me feel good about myself. However, her evening came to a sorry end when as she cried, "My god what have I done to deserve this." the wardrobe began to giggle then vibrate and finally buckle as its incumbents legged it out the bedroom.

I was neither accepted nor rejected by the Olympic selectors. In their wisdom they deemed it necessary that I should exchange punches again with Joey Frost to help them decide. Even if I was to win the box off my place would not be guaranteed. The only reason I could see for their decision was they hoped Frostie could get lucky second time around. In other words Terry Marsh was not wanted. I felt I was in a no win situation, so I declined the offer, preferring to cross swords with the IRA than touch gloves with Joey the banger.

It was time to join up with Four-One Commando and begin preparation for a tour of duty in 'Bandit Country'. Within a week of my arrival we had a new Sergeant. He had seen action in Aden and Ireland on numerous occasions. He gave the typical new Sergeant's speech. We went to a training camp situated on the South Coast. The camp replicated a small town with a population of soldiers dressed in civvies role-playing. My first assignment was in an observation tower that simulated an OP in Crossmaglen, now referred to as XMG. Two 'gunmen' opened up on us from behind a garden wall and I saw the whole incident but was unable to return fire. Not getting a shot off was not something to boast about. It really hammered home to me how quickly these things happen and how difficult it is to respond effectively. I got criticism from the Sergeant

On another occasion our patrolling was filmed while the instructors monitored us from a control tower. The control tower had a bank of screens covering every conceivable angle. Eventually the inevitable happened and we were fired at. No shots were returned. I was able to identify the firing point but again not quick enough or good enough to return fire before they fled. The Marshal monitoring us made the point that it is not often that the gunman is seen. We had done well to identify the firing position and he praised the patrol in general. Nonetheless the Sergeant never saw it that way and was critical of the patrol and made such a point.

"You do that over there and we'll be bringing back body bags. I don't want to carry any baggage with me. Buck your ideas up."

"The Marshal said we done well Sergeant." was my reply.

"Don't you fucking answer me back. Right, you're going back on foot."

I gave a look of indifference.

"With your rifle above your head." he added, "Off you go."

It was time for dinner so I was going to be at the back of the queue. The run back was about a mile and it was a pleasant day

for relaxing but not running. However, I took the so-called punishment as a challenge. I must have been about a quarter of the way when a Land Rover sped pass with my colleagues in the back and the Sergeant sitting in front. I saw the brake lights come on. He leant out of the window, "I am watching."
I lowered my arms, took the prone position and began doing press ups with a smile. He looked flabbergasted. Tortoise-like, his head retreated and the Land Rover sped off. I felt that he was digging me out and it was unwarranted - I wasn't going to let him get the better of me.
By the time I got back it was time to return the rifles to the armoury. My run back meant I had no time to clean my weapon, unlike the rest of my colleagues. It was deposited with the exterior receiving a quick wipe with a handkerchief. First thing that morning a weapons' inspection was sprung on the troop. The Sergeant went through each of his charges taking the carcass of the rifle pointing the weapon into the sky and looking through the barrel. Then it was my turn. "Have you cleaned your weapon?"
"Yes Sergeant."
"No you haven't. Look at that."
The weapon was positioned in front of me, enabling me to inspect the rifling inside the barrel. Shit, I thought as I saw this piece of dirt.
"Well...what you got to say?"
"Nothing Sergeant."
"It is fucking dirt."
"I can't see any dirt Sergeant."
"Look again you fucking blind?"
I looked directly into his eyes, "I can't see any dirt Sergeant."
I expected that he would seek a second opinion from one of my fellow troopers who would then find themselves in an invidious position of dropping me in it or tempting the wrath of the Sergeant.
"Don't fucking mess with me. I'll see you later."
He moved on to inspect the next rifle. I was banged to rights but was not going to give him an excuse to dig me out. As far as I was concerned he had wrongly had a pop at me on two previous occasions. Perhaps I had faced him down or maybe put enough

doubt in his mind that he may have thought he could be mistaken about the dirt. He was at that age when the eyes begin to dim.

The troop eventually divided into two multiples of twelve men led by the troop sergeant and the troop officer respectively. Fortunately, I found myself under the charge of the troop officer. I did not have many occasions to have direct contact with the Sergeant, thankfully. We moved onto a new training camp in East Anglia designed to acquaint us with the rural side of the patrolling. Our multiple was further divided into groups of four known as 'brics'. I was assigned along with Hayes and Wally to Corporal Jock McLennan's bric. Jock, a couple of years younger than me, was a veteran of Turf Lodge whereas Hayes and Wally, like me, were still rookies.

The 'in film' at the time was 'Apocalypse Now' a movie based on the Vietnam War. The artistic way in which camouflage cream was decorated on the faces of the actors was something that was imitated by us all. There was the regulation so-called 'cam cream' but the Commandos being professional would purchase their own make up sticks in various shades of green and brown. We would wear the make up like it was war paint.

A telling scene in 'Apocalypse Now' was a helicopter attack. The commander of the choppers had speakers attached to one helicopter and Wagner's 'Ride of the Valkries' was played as the helicopters approached its target. The scene was uppermost in all our minds when it came to being flown around in the choppers as part of the training. We would fly in the aircraft with legs dangling over the edge looking for vehicles to stop. On seeing a suspect vehicle the chopper would fly ahead of the car, drop us off to perform the check and pick us up on completion. Knowing it was a case of doing more of this on the tour it was agreed that the bric would get the appropriate music and imitate art.

We were receiving regular updates of what was going on at XMG. At an assembly the Commanding Officer (CO) informed us of a recent 'contact' by the incumbent Army Company against a seven man Provisional IRA Active Service Unit (ASU). Nearly two hundred rounds were fired by the 'pongos' and they had no hits. It met with giggles from one and all, with the exception of *moi* - at least they managed to return fire. It meant the crap hats had missed on one hundred & eighty seven occasions out of one hundred & eighty seven. It wouldn't happen, it couldn't happen, to the Marines. When the CO left the Regimental Sergeant Major asked a question. "What's the first thing you do when under fire?"

I struggled to find the appropriate answer. Move sprang to mind but the collective wisdom of the audience got it right, "Win the fire-fight." was the response. It put the one hundred & eighty seven misses into perspective and gave a reality check to the commandos present.

The training was intense and comprehensive. We were even aware of the local population before our arrival. We had been supplied with pictures of all the suspects of XMG that ran into over a hundred. The actual population could not have exceeded a couple of thousand. The general view was that if there was a photo of them then they were the enemy. It had been mentioned, on more than one occasion, that our task was to assist the Royal Ulster Constabulary in the exercise of their duty. No one had given us any reason to be anything other than civil but there was an aggressive approach by most, including me, about what it was all about. "I'd like to get a kill over there." was something I heard frequently. I never allowed such words to leave my lips but it is what I aspired to. That was the mindset. It went without saying that our victims would be the 'bad' guys. We knew who the bad guys were - we had the photos. We were coiled springs wound up and ready to be let loose on the 'subjects' of XMG.

As we approached our intended destination we were able to recognise the landscape from the model that we had examined on numerous occasions. We knew the names of the streets and roads and, from the Wessex helicopter, able to point out the homes of some of the high profile members of the town.

On landing a quick exit was made and the chopper filled up with some of the former incumbent soldiers of XMG. Within ten minutes we were out on patrol to relieve a group on a Vehicle Checkpoint (VCP). We wore the war paint with pride and sported, although sheathed nonetheless intimidating, K Bar knives. These checkpoints had been part of the change over strategy. Every one of the service roads in the town had static checkpoints. Nothing could be driven in or out of the town without being checked. Before leaving the camp our weapons were loaded. We were given the okay from above that it would be okay to have a round up the chamber to allow for a quick response. From what precise level that emanated I don't know. Out of the camp I was not as wary as I would have expected. I think it was mainly due to the saturation of troops on the ground and the constant noise of helicopters landing and taking off.

On arriving at the VCP the pongos, who we relieved, could not get away quick enough and we were not fully briefed as to the situation. I had the task of having to check out the perimeter of the VCP. I felt exposed being on the perimeter of the cordon. I suspect that was Jock's thinking when he suggested I check out the immediate area. It was not a lone patrol as such I always had sight of the remainder of my 'bric' and deviated no more than 25 metres from the road-side, but at the same time I felt isolated and could feel my heart beating.

It is said that you don't hear the bullet that gets you so when I saw the flash and heard the bang I should have realised I was all right. I got up hurt but the pain had come from the hard landing. There was no bomb I had set off a trip flare that had been set up by our predecessors. I felt such a pratt.

The first two weeks consisted of stopping and searching all vehicles in and out of the town and those suspects we had photos of should our paths cross. Since most either lived or worked in the town that could amount to as many searches as there were patrols that day. At any time there were, at least, three four-man patrols working various parts of the town.

It had been known for cars to be stopped four times in the course of a journey of less than a mile: searched as they entered the town, searched as they come across a patrol on one side of the town, again by another patrol on another part of the town and once again at a VCP on leaving the town.

Our base was a fortified police station. It had somewhat expanded in order to accommodate all the troops, the helicopter pad and a series of cabins. The place was more reminiscent of a building site. There was a number of Engineers from the Army, some working hard on the main building putting in a mortar

proof roof. Others were there for the basic tasks of supplying heating, light, water and the disposal of sewage, which with over a hundred inhabitants was a necessity. It was not an uncommon sight to see a large helicopter hovering above the pad releasing an under slung load of building materials or food supplies.
There was one portable cabin that had dozens of aerial appendages and always manned by men in civilian attire. These guys did not live in the camp but would commute via the helicopters to work their respective shifts. Other non-commandos were half a dozen pongos who drove the armoured personnel carriers (Saracens). These would be utilised during the daylight patrols and was a means of transport across the town. As well as the driver, each vehicle was assigned a marine that operated the Browning - a heavy calibre machine-gun that swivelled around giving a 360-degree arc of fire. It would not be until you sat in the Saracen and the door closed behind you that you realised how hyped you were on the street.
At the end of two weeks it was time for our troop to change to rural patrols. The rural patrols had two purposes. One would be to show a presence and make it difficult for the enemy to feel that they had immunity in the sticks, while the other purpose was to draw their fire; the latter appealed most. Every time we went out it was in the hope of a contact and a fire-fight. The rural patrols were like two extremes - one patrol would be the high presence while the next one would be exclusively covert; going into a position under the cover of darkness and extracting ourselves the following night.
The most satisfying moment of the rural patrols was the rendezvous with the chopper. Like the Saracens in the town, they served as a sanctuary from the heightened tension. The sound of the swirling rotor blades ever increasing as it got closer; the launching of the smoke grenade to indicate the landing zone and the subsequent sprint to our transport was the stuff of movies.
There was intelligence that the Provos, as they were referred to, had Russian RPGs. These were hand held rocket launchers and primarily an anti-tank weapon that could be used like surface to air missiles. Despite such rumours once inside the big birds it was time to unwind following the end of the days work. On one

occasion the pilot had to take evasive action believing he was under attack but after a mega roller coaster experience it was concluded that the bang heard by the pilot emanated from a crow-scarer.
Two weeks of rural patrols were followed by two weeks of being confined to barracks - someone had to guard the fort. Guard duty was two hours on four off, alone in a 'sangar' (watchtower) with a telescope for company. There were some respites from the monotony. There was the stint in Baruki Sangar. This 'sangar' was not positioned in the base but 30 metres away designed to oversee the Town Square. It had got its name from a soldier named Baruki who was killed by a booby trap nearby. He was returning to the camp when he saw an army issue water bottle lying on the road. He picked it up thinking it had been dropped by a colleague and died in the explosion.
Unlike the other 'sangars' it was manned by two occupants so was not quite as boring, but the stints were longer. One of the tasks was to record all the vehicles passing through the square. I understood that this exercise was just one of a network of vehicle recordings throughout the Province. As well as vehicles any activity we witnessed, however insignificant, was recorded. It had been explained to us that the more intelligence gathered the better. The example of a woman hanging out her washing was used to make the point. We were told how a 'pedantic' soldier would log the items and colours of washing this woman put out each day and someone higher up was able to correlate bombings in that vicinity with specific colours of garments on the line – allegedly.
The Market Square was used regularly for cattle auctions. In the square stood a statute in memory of those who had died in the Republican cause. It was about the tenth day of the tour when the residents awoke to see the statue donning a Green Beret. There was much indignation from the local community. One lady a 'representative' of the community made a complaint and the offender was reprimanded. The general consensus amongst F Company was that it was a laugh and that they had no sense of humour. I was sure it would be one of the stories passed on to future new boys. The complainant it was assumed was a supporter of the IRA and maybe even a member. It did not occur

to any of us that both our predecessors and ourselves were probably contributory factors to that person's position.
I was able to relieve the boredom of the solitary sangars with the aid of my cassette and a tape of Madness. I also had the Wagner tape for when we did some helicopter patrols but in the meantime I would sing as loud as I could: Baggy Trousers, One Step Beyond, My Girls Mad At Me, et al.
Night time was different because it could be deemed as a residential area. Some homes were a matter of metres away from the base. The biggest problem of a night was keeping awake. Falling asleep while on duty was a very serious offence and could result in a heavy fine and or time in a military prison. Invariably, it was the troop Sergeant who was the man in charge of the operations room. From here he was able to control a camera that was situated on the highest of masts and could peruse the vast majority of the town. He could communicate with the respective sangars by an internal communications line and he would often use this to berate someone for not reporting something he had seen.
I was in 'Baruki Sangar' and witnessed a van pull up outside the newsagents in the square. A man exited the passenger side of the van at haste towards the shop. It was clear to me that he was on his way to work and stopping to get some cigarettes or a newspaper. Nonetheless I had my sights fixed on the door way and my finger on the trigger just in case. My suspicions were confirmed shortly after he reappeared and jumped in the van. It wasn't long before the tannoy bellowed.
"Are you asleep out there? What the fucks going on? I just saw someone run out of a building and jump into a van that sped off right under your fucking noses."
"We watched him go in and watched him come out Sergeant." was my response.
"Why didn't you tell me?"
"I didn't think it important Sergeant."
"I fucking decide what is important. I want to know everything."
I looked at my oppo, "That bloke is really beginning to piss me off. I hope I don't have to go out on patrol with him because I will fucking shoot the bastard. Is he mad or something? I think he must be the biggest prick in this company. I'll show him."

I then began reporting everything I saw: anyone carrying a bag or a newspaper, two people in conversation, a parent pushing a pram or a car being parked. The Sergeant took it all in his stride, to my surprise and disappointment.
"Well done. Keep it up." was his response, which only served to wind me up. I became more pedantic with my observations and he did not bite. The shift eventually finished and I'd got some food when the company signaller Geordie approached me as I was stuffing my face. Geordie, who was prematurely grey and as a result looked twice his age, was in the Ops room while I was in Baruki. "He heard all that," I was informed, "he left the 'comms' on and was pissing himself laughing." I choked on my chips.
The stint of guard duty could not go quick enough it was a relief to be out of the camp. We soon got the opportunity to play the Wagner tape in the chopper when we undertook a flying VCP. We were dropped off in an adjacent field 200 metres from the border. As we got to the road a white transit van passed. A couple of cars were stopped that we had seen approaching from the helicopter. The transit van returned several minutes later. We had been informed about a contact when three soldiers bought it in Crossmaglen. A machine gun opened up on them from the back of a truck. The van's return seemed too quick for my liking and this tale was in my mind. Jock did not stop the van; we were ready to be picked up by the chopper. I was positioned in the bushes further up the road, about twenty metres away, acting as a cut off. As it passed by one of the back doors swung open. Unlike during the training this time I was quick to respond. The rifle butt was locked into my shoulder and the barrel elevated. I pulled the trigger it failed to fire. I cocked the weapon to clear the blockage. The dud round was ejected into the shrubs.
There was no shots coming from the van that went out of sight as it negotiated a bend. I realised I acted in haste I was very lucky that the round failed to go off, but unlucky that I could not find the ejected bullet. Jock called out to me. We had to make our way back to the field to board the chopper. I returned from the patrol one round down. At the end of the tour I was expected to return all those rounds that I was issued. Failure to do so would result in a heavy fine.

I was really pissed off. The tour was also an opportunity to save some money and it looked like all my savings would be going on this fucking lost bullet that was dud anyway. Then of course there also was the risk of time in a military prison. Should I report it now? No, I'd hope we'd get a contact. If there was no contact then perhaps I should initiate one. I considered all possible ways out of the predicament, even taking a round from a colleague. It was quickly dismissed but it crossed my mind. It was an indication of how this missing bullet was doing my head in.

The town patrols were much preferred to the guard duties but it was not long before monotony was beginning to work its way into that as well. We were stopping the same people and the same cars. Those vociferous in their complaining got a harder time than the passive.

Those in their latter teens and early twenties probably had it worst of all. Yet at the same time, I suspect, they welcomed the confrontation like us in order to relieve their monotony; most were out of work. The subsequent stop and search routines were ritual like and did not appear unwelcome by those being subjected to it. However sometimes matters became more heated as the conversations flowed. The XMG youths were better rehearsed than we were, town patrols were just one of a number of tasks. We had other distractions like the dreaded guard duty and rural patrols. The young indigenous population were subjected to it every day and in most cases had grown up with it. They had heard all the arguments and knew their history and so when verbal jousting occurred the marines invariably lost and took it personally. A belated fist or boot would be brought into the argument the next time paths crossed at night when witnesses were lacking. It was not everyone doing this but a sufficient number to create a feeling of anger and resentment towards the occupiers.

It was not unknown for the victims to have a sticker placed on their foreheads. The sticker had been designed to hand out to people visiting the Marines' display teams or bands. It was not conducive to the environment in which we were operating. It read, 'I've met the Marines'.

Two factors seemed to work towards this. One was to show that

it was futile and disadvantageous to complain and the second factor was that any such altercations relieved the monotony for us squaddies on the ground. If we had a photo of them it was okay. One such father of four was particularly irate when stopped, complaining that he had been stopped minutes before. It would fall on deaf ears. The boot would be opened, the spare wheel removed along with any other accompanying articles such as toolboxes, which are then emptied in the interest of a 'thorough search'. The designated searcher would then be removing the hubcaps as the frustrated driver was reloading the boot.
Only one member of the bric would be searching while his colleagues would have one eye looking out for potential snipers or bombers. The other eye would be for the searcher and would be his audience. The real test was whether or not the 'suspect' would crack under the tormenting - because that is what it was. The back seat would come out, the bonnet lifted, the spark plugs removed - checking for bullets. Glove compartments emptied, door panels removed and carpeting uplifted. The search complete we would leave the poor man trying to put his car back together to go about his business. That is until the next patrol gets him. It was ironic how when verbal was given against us, the perpetrator of such insults would find that they had four punctures the next morning. It was all a laugh and on return to the camp it was a question of which patrol gave who the hardest time on the streets.
The best two scenarios were when one poor sole had his car keys confiscated. On asking for them back they were thrown into a nearby field of long grass for him to retrieve. The other scenario was during the evening when a driver on being stopped was requested to turn off his lights. He questioned the necessity and authority. Moments later the two headlamps were shattered with the aid of a rifle butt - the owner of the butt, recently transferred from another Commando unit, made his mark. He got a talking to but at the same time a pat on the back and he went up in everyone's estimation. My searches could never have been seen as thorough relative to what I have described but I was perhaps more to blame because I would be egging on the searchers to push it that little bit more.

When on the early morning patrol we would always lay in wait for a transit van that came in from Dundalk in the Irish Republic. Dundalk had been described as a Provo stronghold. The driver concerned claimed that he was picking up women in the town and transporting them to the south where they worked. He was alleged to be the Intelligence Officer of the 3rd Brigade of the South Armagh PIRA. The daily trips to 'XMG' were suspected as being 'recces'(intelligence gathering). It was enough for us to stop them every morning and give them a search. He was searched going into the town and when leaving and twice again when returning the workers.
The alleged Intelligence officer of the 3rd Brigade of the South Armagh PIRA was getting impatient with my searching of his van, seeing it as futile and malicious, which it probably was. In order to reach under the dashboard on the passenger side I laid low with my feet dangling out of the vehicle adjacent the near side front wheel. He drove a few inches when he stopped, realising I was still searching. The van had now stopped on my foot and I screamed at him to get the van of my foot - for effect. The new Corporal in charge of the bric believing he was driving off grabbed him and pulled him from the drivers seat ripping his shirt in the process. I had pulled my leg from under the wheel while Hayes and Wally were laughing at my discomfort.
I saw it as an opportunity to get home and welcomed the situation. The driver may have feared a charge of assault of some description. He claimed assault against us and left the scene heading, along with his female passenger, to the 'police station' to make a complaint. We followed with me limping. On my arrival I was flown out by helicopter for an x-ray and medical examination. I still had the man's driving licence and left it with someone at the base. It did not have an, 'I've met the Marines' sticker on it when it left my person but it did by the time its owner received it.
No bones were broken just a bit of bruising and no premature leave for me. I made a claim for criminal injuries but I didn't even get light duties. Which was probably a blessing; it could have been three days in sangars with the troop Sergeant on duty. The driver and his passenger brought an action against the Ministry of Defence for assault. They won and both received

damages of two thousand and one thousand pounds respectively. The Judge made the comment about the frequency of cases coming before him that involved 'I've met the Marines' stickers. I later received five hundred pounds for criminal injuries regarding the same incident. The taxpayer seemed to be the only loser.

The routines had been set - urban patrols, rural patrols and then guard duty. The highlight of the tour was a five-day stint out the camp. We dug in on a hill that overlooked the Concession Road. The road started in the Irish Republic and bisected the South Armagh peninsular. It had been reported that the Provos effected regular roadblocks on this road as a way of asserting their authority. It was to all intents and purposes an encroachment by us into enemy territory. We dug in to facilitate a base camp for the duration. We would set out from here on various patrols and lay ambushes. It was a collective regret that there was no productive end product to our hours of waiting patiently.

It was not long before it was back to the camp and the cramp conditions became more noticeable; no longer sleeping under the stars. The accommodation was a corridor seven-metres long by two and a half metres with three bunk beds, each with three tiers, against the lengths of the wall giving a total of 18 beds and occupants. I have never been on a submarine but I'd imagine it to be similar. The only natural light came from one of the two doors that led out to a small yard.

The other door led to a communal room, the focal point of which was the television. Videos were still something of a novelty and there were only two videotapes, which were recordings of previous episodes of Top of the Pops and the Kenny Everett show - all in the best possible taste. The picture had evidence of the hundreds of times the tapes must have been played.

It was at a time before 24-hour television and the tapes were the only viewing option for the insomniacs. The other popular viewing consisted of the television series, The Professionals featuring the characters Bodie & Doyle. With the exception of those on duty everyone appeared to be in the audience when The Professionals was on. The programme would be watched with a critical eye and any time something not true to our reality occurred it would get jeers and derision. The same scrutiny applied to the war films. While watching 'Where Eagles Dare' a loud bang was heard. It was clear to us all it was a bomb, but sufficiently distant not to interrupt the viewing. Had it been one of the Top of the Pops' video the response would have been immediate but the bang came at a crucial part of the film. It was not until the Sergeant Major entered the room and bellowed accordingly that the chairs were vacated and we hit the streets saturating the town with marines. The bomb had exploded less than a kilometre away.

For a period the other viewing was the Olympic games. I was able to see my former opponent Joey Frost start his second contest but did not see the conclusion as I had to go out on patrol. He won that contest and reached the quarterfinals before losing. I only got to see one round of what I saw as my proxy. I did not for one moment have any regret but the irony of it all did not escape me. I wanted him to win because it would have looked good to have an Olympic champion as a notch on my record. Yet, I also wanted him to lose and perform badly so it would expose the selectors to criticism. He did lose but performed admirably.

It was time for a briefing. We had a mission. A bomb had been detected some miles from the town. It was our task to get into position under the cover of darkness and set up a cordon to protect the bomb disposal experts due later the next day. It was a Saturday evening; we would be setting out just before midnight. Our multiple would be going out with the troop Officer. I liked him as much as I despised the troop Sergeant. He showed a faith in me by giving me an added responsibility. I was to lead the patrol out of the town. Lead scout is regarded as potentially the most precarious task yet I welcomed the position. It was something that I would never get from the 'stripey', being such a risky task.

We left the town via the Monog Road, which despite its title was a narrow lane. To the left was a bank of land, about 50 metres beyond was the graveyard that surrounded the nearby church. To the right laid a few houses and some wasteland that was sandwiched between the Monog Road and an adjacent road. The thirteen-man patrol was well spread out. From the lead scout to the last man was a distance of 100 metres. The last man had left

the town square and like his colleagues ahead was now in the shadows. As well as looking ahead I would look behind to make sure I was not getting too far in front. The troop officer, directly behind me, would do likewise and so forth down the line.
On checking behind for the umpteenth time I noticed, what at first appeared to be, a cross between UFOs and shooting stars. The subsequent movements and action moved far quicker than the words to describe it. It was heading in my direction and no sooner had I seen it, it was gone passing overhead. Those looking forward would have probably seen its departure rather than it's arrival. 'Did you see that', is what I thought. I was about to express such thoughts to the troop officer when I heard two cracks. I immediately recognised the cracks as bullets - better late than never. I threw off my Bergen and lay behind it, the safety catch of the rifle off and finger on the trigger eager to let rip. I had taken up a position facing the right of the road contrary to everyone else. They had taken cover on the left-hand side facing the high ground and the cemetery.
I was very pleased with my positioning since someone had to watch the other flank. It was known as the principle of 'all round defence'. I could hear bullets being fired at the rear of the patrol. I was aware that the front end of the patrol was not under fire. I felt for the poor bastards at the rear. I assumed they were on the receiving end. I still had nothing to shoot at and felt left out of things.
I began to unravel the flares that were taped to my webbing. They were bound with copious amounts of masking tape to prevent them being unintentionally dislodged. The trajectory paths of our machine guns could be seen shooting into the direction of the graveyard. I was aware that rounds were being fired from other parts of the town but unable to know from whom and to where.
After what seemed an eternity I released a flare. As it hits the sky so a parachute opens and delays the descent while the flare brightens the sky. It was not long before several followed my example. My second flare despatched it was time to abandon the all round defence and get some shots off. I reached for my rifle and plonked myself beside Jessie. Jessie had a Bren gun and was in his element emptying a magazine in seconds and then

replacing it with an attached inverted magazine. When he let rip it was as if the enemy had pinpointed the firing point and rounds were coming back at us. Perversely I wasn't scared, it was fucking brilliant. I still had not got any rounds off. I couldn't see anything to aim at. I didn't know whether any one else had. No one was giving any fire control orders or target indications - everyone was letting rip. No matter what else, we were winning the fire-fight.

Out of flares I thought about plan B. I also carried the M79. This was a grenade launcher and I now had the task of unpacking it. It sat nicely on the side of my Bergen secured by a series of bungees and masking tape. I dread to think what the punishment would be if I lost that or the shells that were fired from it. My conscientious packing made it nigh on impossible to make a quick extrication. I settled for breaking the weapon and squeezing the shell into the chamber still attached to the Bergen. The weapon and sights were not designed for accuracy and were very much a 'guessestimate' as to the trajectory. I had the added burden of the weight of the Bergen, which weighed in excess of 20 Kilograms. Eventually, I was able to wrestle the mass into the appropriate position and was fumbling for the trigger when another flare went up. I became aware of the bank immediately ahead with the end of the M79 close to and pointing right at it. I had already acted rashly in the sense that the weapon was not to be used at night but I considered circumstances dictated otherwise however caution had now got the better of me regarding the wisdom of pulling the trigger it was dangerous for everyone.

I went back near to Jessie his magazines would need reloading and again came under fire. It was not until another flare went up that I could see the rounds ahead ricochet against a gate and realised I was coming across friendly fire. Shortly afterwards the cease-fire command was heard. I still had not fired off a single round, much to my disappointment. Yet the trauma that hung over me trying to account for my deficit of one round I had lost earlier in the tour was now solved.

There was no return fire and it was right to conclude that they had gone but we still had to do a sweep and I was assigned point. My instructions were, should there be any contact, to hit the ground because a volley of fire would be despatched from behind me. I did not need an explanation. We had to win the fire-fight. Essentially I was the stalking horse and felt honoured to have the role. I must have been mad.

The sweep complete, we moved on with our original mission and set up the cordon. Later that day we met up with some of those unfortunates in the other half of our troop who had missed out in the action. They questioned the contact. They had done a sweep of the so-called enemy position and could not find any spent rounds. We accused them of sour grapes because we had been involved and they hadn't. Still when we get to the debriefing facts will win.

We heard that a four-man patrol on the other side of the town also had a contact. In addition the two marines in Baruki sangar not wanting to miss out let rip into No 43 the Square. There had been suspicious activity around this vacant building positioned adjacent to an alley. An order went round that should Baruki come under attack, let rip into this vacant building opposite. The order had something of a shelf life that had by now expired but the two Marines must have forgotten. The resulting volley of fire from Baruki created further ricochets, some of which struck other sangars drawing their fire as well. It was estimated that around two thousand rounds were fired that night with no casualties.

At the debriefing it was further concluded that the first two rounds were those fired against the patrol on the other side of town. The bullets had overshot their intended target. Those were the two initial rounds that I had witnessed flying overhead. Following this, the rear of our patrol was fired upon. This was drawn from the accounts of those at the rear. It was concluded that our patrol had interrupted a 13 man active service unit (ASU). How the figure of 13 was derived I don't know. This ASU was in the process of preparing for a co-ordinated attack on the camp. The view of the indigenous population was that we were shooting at each other. I was later to discover that the indigenous population were right.

As the tour progressed so the more futile things appeared to me. The strategy worked in that everyone returned home safely. However the bitterness and hatred of the local population towards the British increased further. That was no longer our problem it was now the problem of those Pongos taking over. I suspect that our presence did nothing to undermine the IRA war effort and am sure our presence aided them in the terms of recruiting. Many of those we had disputes with must have signed up to some degree – I would have.

CHAPTER TEN
AMERICAN EXPRESS

I was now quite flush with money following the lengthy isolation in Crossmaglen. I had even made some cash selling Lonsdale tracksuits and tee-shirts while at XMG. With my new found entrepreneurial sideline and the associated income projection I was able to apply for an American Express card; it had a degree of exclusivity then. I also treated myself to a .44 Magnum revolver and a Browning semi-automatic pistol. The Magnum according to Clint Eastwood, in the film Dirty Harry, was the most powerful handgun in the world. In theory with my .44 Magnum in one hand and my American Express card in the other I could have anything I wanted.

Now weighing twelve stone seven pounds I wondered whether I would have to move up another weight but once I got in the gym the pounds came off comfortably. My progress through the Combined Services and the subsequent ABA championships met with no problems. On one of our post-fight periods of rest I travelled with team mate Cliff Storey to Stoke his hometown.

I met a 19-year girl called Jacqui. I gave it the big'un with my American Express card. The card facilitated the booking of a hotel room. I could not believe my luck. I thought she was really attractive and had a good figure. I would have considered her a perfect catch were it not for her aligning herself with me.

When it came to chatting girls up breaking the ice was not a problem. It would go down hill when they discovered I was a commando and British boxing champion.

"Yeah, and I'm the Queen of Sheba." was the general response.

When the line was used on Jacqui the response was different or more to the point indifferent. I questioned her indifference. "Somebody's got to be duck." was her response cosseted in a

strong Potteries accent, which I found as equally engaging as her response.
On my return to Portsmouth she came along. It did not occur to me that she may have had a home to go to. It was not a consideration. Accommodation was rented and things were going nicely until the next month's rent was due and the American Express bill dropped on the doorstep. Then we had a visit from the police. They were investigating the whereabouts of Jacqui; she had been reported as a missing person. On establishing she was alive and well it was the end of the matter for them. However, for me it was becoming a bind and I suggested that she returned home, now I knew she had one.
I never had enough money to buy her a train ticket but I had a moment of inspiration. There was a special promotion by British Rail fronted by Jimmy Saville - 'Let the train take the strain'. By purchasing a rail card you were entitled to a free return journey to anywhere in the country. The money was borrowed, a couple of photo's taken and Jacqui was on the next train from Portsmouth to Stoke.
It was a big weight off my mind and I moved back into the barracks no longer burdened with paying visits to the supermarket or worrying about cooking meals or having to travel to and from the barracks every day. I kept in touch with Jacqui by phone and on one occasion she even phoned me, "Did you get the letter?"
"No not yet, perhaps it is delayed in the post."
"No I gave it to the man on the gate."
"When was this?"
"About 20 minutes ago."
"How did you get down here?"
"I used the return ticket."
I went to the main gate to meet her and we stayed at a hotel that night - thanks again to American Express. After a few days we both were put up by my team mate Shoey who had naval accommodation with his recent wife Dawn. That was the arrangement for a few months. A disagreement between Jacqui and Dawn led to Jacqui, now in the early stages of pregnancy, returning to Stoke and me back to the barracks. The pregnancy never lasted the full term. It was a close call. I knew that I was

neither capable of nor wanted to look after children. But I knew even more so that Jacqui wasn't equipped. She may have had maternal instincts but not maternal skills. We kept in touch.

As the championships progressed so I found myself the only naval boxer contesting the finals. I was to meet in the final a young up and coming fighter who had excelled as a junior boxer by the name of Chris Pyatt. I gained my third ABA title. Chris fought a good fight and I was sure he would go onto better things (he went on to win a world title light-middleweight title). For me it was time to hang up my gloves. I felt that winning the title again helped prove a point regarding the 'Olympic snub'. My ambitions now lay in the military. However, for the moment it was time for a holiday in the Philippines.

It was to be a working holiday; I had been selected to attend a Multi-Nations Tournament for England along with my mate Shoey and another boxer Cameron Lithgow. I hoped to lose the first fight. I had no intention of throwing the fight, but my preparation left a lot to be desired and did not expect to win with that mindset. I was looking forward to enjoying the remainder of the fortnight on the sandy, palm tree covered beaches. On arriving at the Philippine's capital Manila we were escorted to a luxurious hotel where 'chaperones' were assigned to us. The hotel earned the tag of luxurious relative to the surroundings. The boxing tournament was known as the President Marcos Multi-nations tournament. It received blanket coverage on one of the Philippines' television channels. It was good timing on the part of the President because it was the final fortnight of the general election campaign.

It was a well-represented tournament with teams from the top boxing nations including Cuba, the United States and the then Soviet Union. It was the first time that the boxers from these countries had competed against each other since the American boycott of the Moscow Olympics. I drew an Indonesian in the first round of the tournament and it was difficult to lose against him. Later on I had my equipment, credit cards and wallet stolen and so there was not going to be much for me to do outside of the tournament.

I concentrated on my next contest against a Korean. The Korean was very strong and powerful, seriously bashing up his previous

opponent. He was too dangerous to take lightly. So, during the fight he got my undivided attention and again I was a comfortable winner. Next I was against a Filipino to decide who was going into the final. The other semi was between a Russia and Kenyan. By this time Shoey and Cameron had fallen by the way side. My semi-final opponent was not able to capitalise on the home advantage and I found myself facing the Kenyan in the final. I won the fight and the President Marcos 'gold' medal. The down side was standing on the podium listening to the National Anthem 'God Save the Queen'.
Back home my success had made a few paragraphs in the sports' section of some of the national papers. One, The Mail, had a quote from an ABA official conceding that it may have been an error in not selecting me for the Moscow Olympics.

Due to defence cuts 41 Commando was being disbanded and its former marines were to be disseminated to the other Commando establishments. I was assigned to Royal Marines Poole. The base was for amphibious training and the SBS, the Special Forces arm of the Marines. The camp was pleasantly situated adjacent to a holiday camp and opposite numerous tributaries of Poole Harbour. I was accommodated alongside a group of marines who were on a Landing Craft Course. I was assigned duties in the gym, spending the day walking around in a tracksuit. It was summer and the weather lovely. At alternate weekends I would hitch hike to Stoke to see Jacqui and the weekends in between would entail enjoying the pubs and cider in Poole.
Whilst in the gym I would witness those guys in the SBS working out and I was in awe of them. There were numerous tests that I had heard about for those aspiring to join the SBS. I trained for and mastered them all and I was keen to do it sooner rather than later.
I was sleeping heavily one early Sunday morning, as a result of copious amounts of cider, consumed in the adjacent holiday camp, when awoken by one of the guards. As the torch shone in my face I thought I was dreaming. "There's a phone call for you at the main gate."
"Is that Mr Marsh?"
"Yeah."

“This is Lime Street Police station Liverpool. We have a Jacqueline Bethell here. She has been robbed and assaulted. Will you pay her fare?”
“Yeah.”
“You’ll have to go to the local police station and deposit the money and inform them to contact us.”
I didn’t have any cash or any idea where the local police station was. It was not as if the camp was situated in the city centre. Money wasn’t a problem I had a chequebook although there was no cash in the account. Some of my roommates on the landing craft course had recently purchased a car and I asked if I could borrow it. They were all asleep but one of them in a daze pointed to the keys. That was good enough.
I made a couple of kangaroo starts before finally mastering the relationship between the accelerator and the clutch and off I went. It was about two o’clock in the morning and the roads were clear. I made good progress and headed to the town centre. It was then a matter of stopping and asking for directions. Eventually I found the police station. I parked up in their car park and ambled in, with a manner a few notches over and above my usual disposition. I figured that an air of confidence had to be radiated in view of my illegal car journey.
“I've been contacted by Lime Street nick. I have to deposit some money regarding paying someone’s train fare.”
“Sorry, can’t accept cheques. Has to be cash.”
I hope and prayed that I would not do a kangaroo start in the car when I pulled away. Luck was with me. I was still very nervous about the whole affair and only too aware of the ramifications if caught. The windows had to be wound down full to stop the windscreen steaming up. As I was motoring along I even indulged in listening to the radio. Clear of the police station and a clear road ahead of me lead me into a false sense of security. I was not aware of the roundabout until I had driven across it demolishing a flowerbed in the process. On reaching the sanctuary of the camp it was back to awaken my unsuspecting roommates.
“Lend us a score.”
I’m sure had it been in the cold light of day I would have drawn a negative but timing is everything and I was back on the road

heading for the police station. As I negotiated the roundabout that displayed a carnage of flowers a cold shiver travelled along my spine. It was eerie but only marginal compared to the shiver and cold sweat I got when I saw the blue light flashing behind me.
"Shit." Only then did it occur that I had more than my share of cider a few hours earlier. Drink driving, no licence and no insurance. They would lock me up and throw away the key. Perhaps it was a dream after all, I could only hope. I was out of the car before the coppers.
"I'm looking for the Police Station..."
"Is this your car?"
"I was contacted by Lime Street Police station..."
"Is this your car?"
"No I borrowed it. I have to... "
"Can I see your Licence?"
"I have to deposit some money with the Police Station in Poole. Can you take me there?"
"What's the problem?
"I was contacted by Lime Street Police Station in Liverpool. They told me I had to deposit some money with them to allow my Fiancée to get a train ticket. She'd been raped."
It did the trick.
"Follow us. We'll lead you back to the station."
My two concerns were whether I would manage to pull away in the car competently and on arrival whether it would be discovered that I had already been to the police station, and my earlier protestation was a sham.
Things turned out favourably and I was at Poole train station later that day to meet Jacqui. She only had the clothes she was wearing and the task was to kit her out with new apparel and the sexiest underwear available in Poole - thanks once again to American Express. I still had use of the car and that night we slept in the car parked on a deserted beach.
I was still figuring out what to do about accommodation until something more permanent was found. I sneaked her into the barracks. My roommates positioned their lockers so that they acted as room dividers and the lady had some privacy. The one-week in the barracks was a bizarre time. Food would be brought

back from the galley at the various meal times. During inspections a chair was placed in the locker for Jacqui to sit on with a book, a torch and some food for company while the locker doors were closed and padlocked.

We eventually got accommodation, sharing a house, with a couple of lads that I worked with at the gym. Our new accommodation was quite spacious and pleasant. The one bugbear was the distance from the camp - five miles. I found myself running into the camp most mornings. It was all contributing to the time when I would take the SBS course.

As much as there was certainty about what I wanted to do, there still existed doubt in my mind about the strategy. It was not enough for me to be in the SBS. I wanted to be able to make a greater input. That, I felt, could only be done as an Officer. I had a no academic qualifications so a Commission was not presently a consideration. It occurred to me that if I was to take a couple of years out I could get suitably educated to apply for a Commission. That was the preferred option but getting there was problematic. My circumstances and bank balance conspired against me.

CHAPTER ELEVEN
FIGHTING FOR AN EDUCATION

I'd just finished a work out when I received a message that I had a phone call from someone by the name of Frank Warren who left his number. I did not have a clue who he was but was curious as to the purpose of his call.

"I've seen you fight and I think you can go a long way. I would like to manage you. I'm down your way this weekend. Could we meet up?"

I took Jacqui along to the meeting and met three blokes. They introduced themselves as Frank Warren, Frank Maloney & Kieron Murphy. Ginger haired Murphy was the more portly of the three. He held a Managers licence with the British Boxing Board of Control (BBBofC). Warren looked the fresher faced of the three and appeared quite shy in comparison to Murphy who was doing most of the talking and selling. Warren had a habit of moving his neck as if it possessed an itch that he was not allowed to scratch. His eyes looked like they had permanent conjunctivitis and he possessed a pigeon toed gait. The third man was Frank Maloney a rather diminutive figure. He was introduced as the trainer. Maloney was in the process of acquiring a pub, where a gym was to be situated for the likes of other top amateurs, in addition to me, whom they were eager to recruit.

I was able to realise that there was an opportunity here for me to go to college and earn money from boxing at the same time. However, not before I made a few enquiries about Frank Warren. I was spuriously informed that he had 'gangster connections'. He was a nephew of Bob Warren, who had been involved in some turf wars with some other gang in London's Soho, but Frank was still wearing short trousers when all this was going on. In addition, how could a person possessing a pigeon toed gait and a wobbly head with permanent conjunctivitis ever be mistaken for a gangster?

Frank Warren had been involved in what some people described as 'unlicensed fighting' but it was as equally legitimate as those boxing matches seen on television at the time even if the standard of the 'unlicensed fights' were rather average.

A contract was signed whereupon Kieron Murphy was to be my manager. At this stage, unlike Kieron, Frank did not possess a manager's licence with the BBBofC although it was he that signed the cheque for a thousand pounds. It was to represent payment for my first three fights. I now had it all planned out. I'd be able to go to college and get the necessary qualification for a Commission. The fighting would enable me to pay my way. Things began to move fast. I applied to the local college in Basildon where I was to study 'O' Levels in Maths, English, Physics, Electronics and Chemistry. I made a request, which was subsequently granted, for a premature release from the Marines to attend the college. Mum and Dad had only recently moved from Pitsea to a house near to the college, which was highly convenient. Now I had some money behind me I used it to set Jacqui up in a flat in Poole. It coincided with her getting work at the local Tesco supermarket on the checkout.

I had been at college around a month before my first fight, which was under the banner of Pirate Promotions. It was a tongue in cheek title emanating from the so-called 'unlicensed' period. It was a Murphy, Warren Promotion. I sold enough tickets to justify my purse money and that of my opponent and there was a bit to spare for the promoters - a marginal profit. I won a six round fight on points. My opponent was Andrew De Costa. In the Boxing News ratings I noted that there were around 105 boxers rated in my weight category, Andrew was rated 102. My victory probably put me just in the top 100.

Kieron Murphy was not impressed. He was reported as saying, "He can't crack eggs." He was right. My amateur record was there for all to see. I had in excess of 170 fights and had not knocked any of my opponents out. I don't think I had even knocked anyone down. A few opponents had visited the canvass having slipped but none had taken a count. The coach load of supporters diminished to a minibus for my second contest. I wasn't unduly bothered. It was a payday and a means to an end regarding my studying. I had more fingers than fans they included Nicky Bolger who became a friend and my elder Cousin Dennis Hill.

Dennis, a Millwall supporter, had followed me all through my amateur career and would tell anyone who would listen how good I was. He had a similar optimism about his football team. Brother John was still in the Army serving his final months so he never witnessed the earlier contests - lucky for him.

I could not sell enough tickets to cover my own purse let alone that of my opponents. I worked it out that my opponent was probably getting more money than me since I was the house fighter and the favourite to win. It sounds at face value perverse, but that is how it works at that level of boxing. The promoter wants the house fighter to win and therefore restricted in the supply of opponents. This puts the opponent at an advantage when it comes to negotiating the purse. Another factor which has an inherent sense of justice, unique to boxing, is that it should be only right that the loser gets more than the winner since defeat implies greater pain and suffering. From the point of view of the house fighter it was another victory notched on his belt, further recognition and a step forward towards the title.

Things were going according to plan until Jacqui turned her job in at Tesco and could no longer afford the flat that she had rented in Poole. By now Frank Maloney had secured a pub in East London and converted the first floor of the premises to a gym. He gave Jacqui a job as a live in barmaid. He was of the opinion that she was a liability and tried to fix her up with other suitors but to no avail. I would have welcomed such an outcome, as I felt obliged not to leave her homeless and destitute. The novelty of courting was wearing thin and becoming a bind. The only good thing about it was the sex. It was no longer everlasting but I thought it was a good trade off. But it was not long before she had fallen out with Frank Maloney and his wife; finding herself homeless again.

I got digs for Jacqui in Pitsea and, with the bit of cash I had, started laying bets on the horses in a local pub. One of the punters as a perk of his job would acquire all sorts of spirits and would sell anything at three pounds a bottle. I would buy all his stock. He would often lose the money back to me thanks to the slow horses and dogs that he backed. The bookmaking became a regular ritual and very profitable, far outweighing any money made from boxing. Jacqui got a job behind a bar which meant late nights for her and undisturbed nights for me to concentrate on my studies.

Meanwhile I had knocked up my second points win. By now Frank had acquired a manager's licence and I signed a standard BBB of C managers' contract with him. Kieron was no longer on the scene. He didn't even say goodbye. By now Frank Warren had acquired a good team of young boxers mainly from Liverpool. I had known most of them from my time with the England amateur squad such as Keith Wallace, Jimmy Duncan, Jimmy Price and Stevie Johnson. It was just as well that Frank had other fighters to call upon. If he had put all his eggs in the Marshy basket then he would have had a lot to worry about.

My third contest was against a guy named Kid Murray. I looked up the record books and erroneously found that he was effectively a bloated featherweight with more defeats than victories to his name. I had looked up the wrong Murray. I anticipated my first inside the distance triumph but it was not to be. I was always winning the fight but he proved stronger and more resilient than anticipated. The biggest scare came in the third round when I was beginning to see two of him. I don't recall receiving any telling blows but I was clearly suffering from double vision. Following the win I was vomiting. It looked like blood due to a blackcurrant drink I had after the fight. Off to hospital I went and kept in overnight with suspected concussion. I was discharged the following afternoon, but not before getting a visit from Frank Warren and Ernie Fossey. Ernie, the matchmaker, was becoming increasingly noticeable within the Warren organisation.

It was to be another two weeks after being discharged from hospital before I was to fight again. I did not have the aggravation of having to sell tickets this time. It was a dinner show and the promoter, Johnny Levene had already sold the tickets to the members of a sporting club that he administered.

I was fighting a guy called Gary Brookes. My support was

restricted to friend Nicky and Cousin Dennis. The initial seconds of the contest assured me that it was going to be an easy night and then suddenly I was on the floor with Mr Brookes looking over me. I looked over to my corner to see the jaws of the two Franks hanging. Despite the dire circumstances it was a comical sight that I witnessed. I was up before ten and went on to win the fight. But the performance did not bode well for the future.
Christmas of 1981 had now passed and I was now officially an ex-Marine although still a Reservist. Up until then I was at college at the discretion of the Marines. I had been allowed a premature release in order to facilitate my studying. Yet that ended in the New Year. Prior to then I was still on the books if not the payroll. Sufficient time had passed since my early release, for the rumours of suspicions, in some quarters within Navy boxing, that my premature release was purely a means of getting out of the mob in order to turn professional. That was never the case. Being a pro was a means to an end rather than an end in itself. My future was to be an Officer.
My immediate future was to have another fight, since funds again were tight, but it was to be fifty days into the New Year before the next contest. It was against a guy called Arthur Davis whom I knew nothing about; or so I thought. When I saw him in the opposite corner I recognised him as someone I had seen training at the Thomas Beckett gym, in the Old Kent Road, and knew him to be at least ten pounds heavier than myself. He would train like a Trojan. I thought at first one of us had got the fight order wrong and had appeared for a contest earlier than scheduled. Inwardly I was not happy I felt I'd had been compromised. Fitness in itself does not concern me and neither does size/weight disadvantage. Yet the two combined is difficult to overcome. Pulling out, even at such a late stage, is what I would have advised others to do but it would have effectively meant walking away from the fight. I could not do that. Our eyes had met. It would have been seen as weakness on my part. I remember a similar scenario occurring against Dabs Eduns in my amateur days that I alluded to. I should have walked away from that one but pride dictated otherwise. I got bashed up.
As the battle commenced so it became apparent that Arthur did not carry as much skill as he did commitment and endeavour

and another victory was notched up again on points. The money came in handy as well, although it would be no consolation had I lost.
Top of the bill that night was British and European Champion Clinton McKenzie defending his light-welterweight title against Steve Early who had recently signed with Frank Warren. I watched the fight, having got changed from my own encounter, and was impressed how McKenzie stalked his man for the first three rounds and took him apart in the fourth. He looked awesome and light-years away from anyone I was facing.
Meanwhile I was endeavouring to get accommodation from the local council. I drew a blank. I could not get a place unless I was married. Jacqui and her landlord had differences so she was homeless again. We got married in order to qualify for accommodation. I skipped a physics lesson to take my matrimonial vowels.
There was no honeymoon period I was fighting five days later against Gerry McGrath. It was a clash of two unbeaten fighters at Hornsey Town Hall. With the exception of my handful of followers, who were more like part of the team, all present seemed to be cheering for McGrath. It understandably was a partisan crowd for the local man although a Frank Warren promotion. I was very aware of the crowd's preference for Gerry and tried to tease them by playing the matador against their man who liked to charge forward. This was scheduled for eight, I had two extra rounds in order to gain a stoppage but it wasn't to be. It just meant an extra two rounds in which to wind up my opponent's supporters. I was criticised by John Pritchett, the Official in charge, who accused me of trying to incite a riot.
It was only a couple of weeks before we were allocated a spacious two bed roomed flat in Pitsea on the same estate that I had spent my teenage years. Money was now a bit tight, having taken a hit on the horses. I sold my guns to help the cash flow. The new flat was modestly furnished but well stocked with a variety of drinks - far too many to count.
April arrived and so did news that, after a three-hour battle, Royal Marines guarding the Falklands Islands' capital Port Stanley had surrendered to Argentinian forces. I was glued to the television thinking how I had missed out. I had put in for

that posting when 41 Commando had been disbanded and would have loved to have been involved. There were a number of ex Four-One and in particular F company veterans in the thick of it. A task force was launched a few days later that coincided with my next fight. I was in the ring waiting for the bell to ring. I don't want to be here. I shouldn't be here. Why did they not invade four months earlier? I did not give much thought to Lloyd Christie, my opponent.

I received a cut above the eye in the fifth round. I had identified cuts and stoppages as being different sides of the same coin. For the remainder of the fight I was ultra negative, protecting the wound. It worked in the sense that I did not get stopped and did not lose, but I never won either - the referee made it a draw. It was just as well that I had no ambitions in boxing. Fortunately for Frank others in the stable seemed to be making better progress and impressions. The star attraction was former England amateur flyweight Keith Wallace. Frank was keen for him to challenge the then top flyweight Charlie Magri. It was a fight everyone wanted to see.

The only fight I was interested in was the one in the South Atlantic. I was so envious of those Commandos I saw on the news. I had worked with some of them. I had drunk with dozens of them. I knew loads of them. I envied them all the experience that awaited each of them finding out what they were made of in a way that is difficult to replicate in civvie street. Perhaps boxing is the best simulation, but it was not enough.

I was beginning to suspect that Frank Warren was seeing me as a lost cause and it would not be long before we were parting company. Frank Maloney had now left as had Kieron earlier. Kieron seemed to have other business distractions, the most grave being a petrol bomb that had been thrown into his pub. Both of them were expendable and more experienced people were around to replace them in Ernie Fossey and Vic Andretti. Vic was a former British Champion and a good fighter. He had also managed a fighter called Colin Powers who had won both British and European titles. I had the displeasure of sparring Colin. Being hit by his jab was like being hit with a mallet and it made me question whether I was in the right game or not.

Ernie was in his fifties and had been in the boxing business a long time in varying capacities. It included a spell as a fighter but he was not in the same class as Mr Andretti. He had been involved, to varying degrees, in promoting, managing and matchmaking. Now he was firmly in the Warren set up. Ernie had lots of contacts and experience. Experience was a department that Frank Warren was weak on in comparison to his other qualities. I certainly must have been a drain on his pocket I was not selling enough tickets to cover my own costs let alone finance the wages of the opponent and a margin for the promoter.

The exams complete, it was time for my next contest. The pressure of ticket selling was not a problem for my next fight. I was on the bill of other promoters Greg and Alex Steene. It was at the Lyceum ballroom in the West End.

To kill time between the weigh-in and the fight I had gone to the cinema to watch Rocky, with friend and supporter Nicky and Brother John, at nearby Leicester Square. The Rocky phenomena must have had an effect upon me as I recorded my first inside the distance win. No knockout just the intervention of the referee. I still couldn't crack eggs.

My 'O' levels passed it was time to take 'A' Levels in the three sciences. I had a mark time fight against a lad called Robert Armstrong. It predictably went the distance and allowed me to start the new academic year a few quid in front.

Once again I found myself fighting away from home when I had the dubious task of fighting Chris Sanigar of Bristol. Chris I had known from my amateur days when there was a fierce rivalry between him and Navy team-mate Wayne Green. It was a big test for me and some may have questioned the wisdom of taking such a fight. Vic Andretti was now my trainer, having recently secured his trainers licence following a brief spell out of the game.

On attending the weigh-in Chris, on seeing me, shouted out, "You fucking turned up then." I didn't respond but Vic did not remain reticent, "He's going to do you, you cunt." I was slightly concerned that Vic would take it a stage further and risk losing the licence that had only just been returned. I was preparing for the fight when John, who arrived later with Dennis and Nicky, made the point that not many fighters have all their supporters

with them in the changing rooms.
I was only too aware of Chris's style. His was very durable and aggressive and wore down many of his opponents. I considered it prudent to pace myself and refused to be drawn into a slugging match. As Chris rolled forward I would hit him with quick punches never more than three then move away. He stayed there long enough for me to connect with more but I was having none of that. In and out that was the strategy and it continued for the first three rounds. I felt good, I felt sharp and I felt strong. Towards the back end of the fourth Chris lumbered forward again and I caught him with a crisp right upper cut and he stayed there hands held high bent forward with his elbows tucked in. I backed off, had a look and risked another two shots and stood back. There was time to go back with another flurry and Chris remained steady stone-like. It appeared to me that he was out on his feet. I quickly opened up as best I could. I thought there was a good chance of a stoppage but the bell either saved Chris or spared me from my delusions.
I was eager to start as I finished in the next round but Vic advised me to bide my time. The opportunity to finish him would come again. I had to wait a couple of rounds though. I slipped on some water while keeping my distance from the 'Bristol thunderer'. When I touched the canvas there was plenty of daylight between Chris and myself but the gap was short lived as Chris pounced while I was climbing to my feet. It did not hurt but it did not stop me from feigning that I was in no condition to carry on. It left the referee with no option but to disqualify the house fighter much to the anger of him and his supporters.
On announcing the decision I made a quick recovery and grabbed the microphone from the MC, "Ladies and Gentlemen I'm sorry that the fight has ended this way but I will give Chris a return any time anywhere..."
"How about now?" shouted Mr Sanigar as he ripped his gloves from his hands. We made a sharp exit to the dressing room as the crowd became more agitated. John made the comment, "Your boxing was world class, but you're acting pathetic."
I did not see the corollary of the agitation until the next evening on News at Ten, where I, along with millions of others, witnessed me being hit while on the canvas and an irate woman

is seen subsequently attacking the Master of Ceremonies. For those not there it would seem that I was on the canvas because I had been put there by a punch as opposed to a slip. It is a source of much regret when I am asked why the opponent was disqualified. I have to say, "For hitting me while I was on the floor."

Frank had got me a fight in France in the mining town of St Armand. Again Frank and myself were each spared the respective burdens of making a loss and selling tickets. The anomaly in all this was that I was in effect the opponent for the house fighter and it was not the job of the promoter to bring in an opponent who is going to beat their man. Why should this promoter go to all the trouble of flying Terry Marsh into St Armand? It is not as if I could sell loads of tickets. It was the same case when I went to Bristol to fight Chris Sanigar. Chris had nothing to gain from the fight unless of course he and the promoter were confident of victory. It must have been my previous poor displays that had lured their matchmakers to see me as fodder for their respective protégés - good amateur, crap pro who can't crack eggs.

My French opponent was Didier Kowalski and on meeting him at the weigh-in I could not help notice the scar tissue that inhabited his face. Early in the evening I met up with my team, all three of them, John, Dennis and Nicky. They had brought Jacqui along who, following some wines on the ferry, was tired and emotional. It was suggested that she sleep it off in my room but on entering she became more emotional than tired and I easily succumbed to her advances. I did not give the oncoming fight a moment's thought and later feared that I may regret my indiscretions. I entered the ring accompanied by two scantly clad tasty French ladies. The team had ringside seats and Jacqui still tired and emotional shouted out, "I love you Terry. I love you."

I was quite embarrassed and shifted my gaze only to see John and Nicky exchanging French francs with the locals. It was a pressure I could have done without.

Kowalski pushed forward and I pumped out my jab and knocked his head back frequently. It was not long before the scar tissue began to open up on the Frenchman's face and his blood flowed freely. I anticipated the intervention of the referee but to no avail. The fight lasted the full 8 rounds and I was declared the winner. It was by such a margin that Vic and I did not even consider that a hometown decision in favour of the bloodied warrior was feasible.

The tasty looking French ladies, who during the fight displayed the round cards, escorted me out the ring. Jacqui was sensitive to this and demonstrated her frustration by throwing a punch at me. I had just boxed eight rounds with a former French champion and he did not lay a glove on me. Jacqui succeeded where he had failed: it was also hard enough to blacken my eye.

Despite the recent successes I could not see much light at the end of the tunnel. I had become somewhat resigned to the fact that I would not be returning to the Marines. I figured being married might hamper my application. If marriage, itself, were not a problem the disposition of the spouse would be a consideration. I now perceived that as a major problem. I began to notice the bottles of drink were diminishing and I was not consuming any. When I came home from college early one afternoon I understood why. Jacqui was crashed out on the floor face down with an empty spirits bottle lightly grasped in her hand. I poured the whole supply down the toilet.

I'd had eleven fights since turning pro in September 1981. It was now March 1983 and I had grossed around £4000. It wasn't enough to support my studying. The bookmaking sideline could not be exploited enough. There did not seem to be much cash around in Basildon. This may have been a factor in the lack of ticket sales but my style of boxing and lack of punching power probably played a greater role.

I applied for a job as a fireman. I thought that could be the answer. I understood that firemen had a lot of time off and figured fire fighting and studying would complement each other. I knew competition for a place would be fierce since there was a lot of unemployment. A year earlier it was announced that unemployment had passed the three million mark for the first time since the 1930's.

I sailed through the examinations, tests, and the subsequent interviews. The start of my new career was still a few months away. In the interim I was still punching for pay. My last two performances were pretty competent and now I was fighting at

Cheltenham during the National Hunt Festival meeting. Frank had mentioned the idea of promoting a show, during the Festival meeting, the previous year. I thought it was a good idea. I was still without an opponent as I travelled to Cheltenham. Not withstanding yours truly Frank was beginning to make progress in his attempts to break into big time boxing.
Joe Bugner, a former heavyweight champion, had aligned himself with Frank and he was the type of big name needed to get the television involved. As it was then only BBC covered boxing and it appeared, to those in the game, that the Beeb were very selective as to whom they would work with. ITV were keen to get involved in boxing but big names were needed. Bugner was a way in for Frank. Joe Bugner was doing an exhibition at the Cheltenham show.
It did not look like I was going to get an opponent but Ernie managed to secure one at very late notice. He did not come cheap. Ernie informed me £900 was the price for his appearance in the opposite corner compared to my £300. The turnout for the show was abysmal. There were more officials than paying customers and Frank must have done a lot of money. I told him to forget about paying my purse but when we met up again a couple of weeks later he insisted that I take the money.
Next I found myself challenging for the Southern Area title against Vernon 'The Entertainer' Vanreil. I had met Vernon at a gym in the Old Kent Road and we sparred together. I remember, as we touched gloves, Vernon saying, "Lets take it easy we're not getting paid for this." I wrongly interpreted this as weakness and felt good about my prospects.
The fight was with rival Promoters who had won the purse bids for the fight. I was going to be getting about £1500 which was a big jump for me. Being the rival promoters I never felt the need to push the ticket side of things. However, a coach load turned up after considerable effort on John's part. My preparation was interrupted by a cold. Frank was keen for me to pull out of the fight. I'm sure he would have been equally keen were he the promoter. Had I not sold many tickets then perhaps I would have taken his advice.
Having weighed in at midday Frank suggested I book a day room in a hotel and have an afternoon nap. I'd already decided to go

home to the new house we were recently allocated. I thought it would be a surprise for Jacqui and it certainly was. She was pissed and appeared annoyed at being discovered intoxicated. She chose what she thought was her best form of defence and that was attack. She went for me verbally and then physically, which aggravated her even more since I would stand there while she would lash out. I was able to duck or parry anything she threw at me. Inside I felt like a volcano ready to erupt but I would laugh because that, I felt, was the opposite of what she wanted. She stormed up the stairs slamming doors behind her. The cheaply built house meant that the whole building shook and shuddered. "You fucking twat. You and your whole fucking family." she screamed.

Best to leave her to get on with it, I thought, and made my way to the front door. I saw her, out the corner of my eye, standing at the top of the stairs but did not acknowledge her. Reaching for the catch on the door I thought I caught a glimpse of her jumping from the top of the stairs. I looked up to see one of my dumbbells, used for training, heading towards me. I dived out of the way. It put a sizeable hole in the plaster that a moment earlier I had stood in front of. I made a sharp exit.

Vernon 'The Entertainer' Vanreil was a good ticket seller and the atmosphere was charged as we entered the ring at York Hall. Vernon entered the ring with a sequinned hat and cane with an equally pretentious dressing gown to match. I was gob-smacked in the sense that my only knowledge of him was the sparring session months earlier at the Old Kent Road. The image I had seen then was an image a million miles from what I saw now. He certainly was an Entertainer.

I was conscious of my cold and the interruption it caused to my training and feared that I would be found out in the later rounds of what was to be my first ten round fight. Uncharacteristically, I was out the corner quickly keen to stamp my authority. I had not planned it that way and in view of my fitness doubts it was a reckless tactic. I reckon I was deluded by our previous meeting. That was knocked out of me in round three. The expression 'I felt it in my boots' was a phrase I was familiar with but not intimate. That changed in the third round. It was as if 'The Entertainer' was allowing me a few moments of glory before he started work.

Fuck this for a game of soldiers, I thought to myself. I don't want to take another punch like that. I didn't think I would be capable of receiving another and remaining on my feet. My brain must have spun inside and copious amounts of brain cells damaged. Vernon could certainly crack eggs. Having had a taste I was hoping and determined not to take any more and survived the ten rounds. To my surprise I did not flag towards the end. Not a bad way to finish a career undefeated Southern Area champion.

CHAPTER TWELVE
SO NEAR

Following the twelve-week Fire-fighting course I was assigned to Tilbury Fire station but I was not in a celebratory mood. Within months of my new occupation Jacqui informed me that she was pregnant. I thought how could she do such a thing to me, as if it was a unilateral action. She had been on the pill and I considered that I did not have to worry about such calamities. She decided to come off the daily dosage and Bobs your Uncle or more to the point Tels the father.
Children were never in my plans and just as I seemed to be making career plans and moving into what was a fairly predictable and stable future I've got the burden of a kid or as I saw it another kid. I was already married to one. I had to do all the thinking for the both of us.
At the training centre we had been warned about so-called initiations. Every new recruit had a 'welcoming' of some description. Having been assigned my appliance and checked my breathing apparatus equipment I did not have to wait too long for a taste of being the new boy. One of my early tasks was to get into the grease pit to inspect the underside of the appliance that was now sited above. After several minutes I was drenched as water flowed towards me. Before the assailants could be identified they were gone. I shook the surplus water from me and made my way to the Sub Officers office.
"What do you want? Why are you wet?"
"There must be a leak in the radiator." was my reply.
"Okay get dried off."
Off I went, "Have you forgotten something?" I was asked.
"No."
"The puddle, mop it up."

It was not the most hospitable of places. At around eleven o'clock it was time for tea with cheese and onion sandwiches. It was the one positive thing about the day. There was much talk around the mess table and laughter, which I did not find funny. 'In jokes', I thought to myself.
When I was brought into the conversation so the questions began. "What's your fiddle?"
"Haven't got one."
"Everyone's got a fiddle. You can't get by on what we're paid. You married?"
"Yeah."
"Got any kids?"
"One on the way,"
"What d'ya use to do?"
"Student."
"All the time?"
"No I was in the Marines."
"Wooooooh."
I'd only been at the station a week or so when it was time to come out of retirement from boxing; I needed a fiddle. My new colleagues were right about the money not being enough. Furthermore things had developed. During my period of inactivity I had climbed up the ratings and was now the number two contender for the British title. I was nominated to fight a final eliminator for that title
The eliminator went to purse offers. This meant that the controlling body invites Promoters to place bids for the right to stage the contest. My Southern Area title fight against Vernon Vanreil was another of my fights that had gone to purse offers. Frank Warren lost that bid, assuming of course that he made one. In view of my lack of pulling power at the box office it would have been folly to go in at too high a price.
I may be giving the wrong impression that Frank was not putting on any Promotions, far from it. It was just that I wasn't featured on them. Frank was now clearly number two to rival promoter Mickey Duff. Despite his innovative attempts to wrestle the hegemony from Duff and his partners they remained dominant. All the other fighters from Frank's stable, which had grown tremendously, had hitherto fallen when the big question

was asked. Soon the big question was going to be asked of me subject to a successful eliminator and warm up fight in Southend that Frank had arranged with the local promoter, Johnny Levine. I also had to get permission from my new employers, the fire service, to have an additional occupation. It was hardly a money-spinner though. I'd been boxing 'professionally' for over three years and still had no tax liability.

The warm up fight was with Lee McKenzie, a cousin of the champion Clinton. I was top of the bill yet I still could not pull the crowds even though it was, effectively, my own back yard. The missing fans could not be blamed since they were clearly blessed with an accurate foresight. It was a points victory for me, bland boring boxing. People wanted knockouts, knockdowns or punch-ups and they were getting none with me. I even contemplated going down just to put some excitement into the fight but dismissed the flirtation. Still it was a win and after over 6 months of inactivity good to get it out of the way. Christmas was just over a month away and the additional money would, not for the first time, come in handy.

I was also now legally a driver, having passed my test with the fire service. I bought a new mini metro. It was good coming out the gym and just jumping into a car rather than have the tiring walk to the underground. All my energy had been left in the gym and there was the added problem of carrying a massive sports bag containing my bulky sparring gear. It seemed to me that this bag was with me wherever I went and I longed for the day that I would be able to go somewhere without lugging it around.

Frank lost the purse bid for the eliminator. It meant travelling to Bradford. Tony Sinnott from Liverpool was the opponent. Although the Lancastrian was fighting in Yorkshire he was considered the house fighter, which was a role I was only too glad not to have. To add to the confusion Sinnott was also the all Ireland champion of the, higher, welterweight division.

The venue for the fight was in the banqueting hall of a hotel. Vic and I stayed there on the eve of the contest. It was the first night in six weeks that I experienced an uninterrupted sleep being relieved from the cries of Kelly my recently born daughter. The hotel was as good as my sleep and the hotel food looked delicious, but due to weight making I had to refrain from the culinary

facilities and mini-bar. Abstinence included breakfast much to my frustration. Still I slept late and once the midday weigh-in was over I would make up for the deprivations.
At the weigh-in Tony said something disparaging to me to which I did not respond, but Vic did and it looked like I was going to have to stand between the two. I had heard that he struggled to make the weight - as if I never. As he mounted the scales Vic looked close to see that the scales balanced: they didn't. He was over and had to lose the excess pound within the hour. I came inside and was keen to get some grub inside me but at the same time we wanted to witness Tony making the ten stone limit. Fighting away from home we trusted no one. Eventually he returned looking rather flustered but the work out was sufficient enough to shed the excess. I was in a fight tonight.
Ten rounds lay ahead. He was something of a puncher and quite strong. I was concerned about it going to points and being the victim of a hometown decision. The weight making would have blunted some off his strength and I suspected it would find him out as the fight went into the latter stages. I adopted the tactic of sitting tight with the purpose of coming on strong in the latter rounds and getting a knockout - well, a stoppage anyway. It was the best I could hope for in view of my previous fights. It did not go according to plan. As the final bell sounded for the end of the tenth round we both walked towards the referee, but I knew it was going to be my hand that was raised.
Vic travelled back with Frank Warren who had travelled up from London that day. I was left with my supporter's club of John, Dennis and Nicky. On visiting the toilet that evening I passed blood. It made me feel like a real fighter. As a kid I had been a great admirer of Britain's greatest ever fighter, Ken Buchanan and remember reading how after a title fight with the legendary Roberto Duran he was passing blood. Buchanan was a warrior and now so was I.
My fiddle was now becoming a point of interest at the fire station. There would be this informal overlap period when one watch was coming on duty and the other going off. Invariably all would congregate in the watch room and banter would be exchanged. "So your telling me that you are fighting for the British Title?"

I think many found it hard to take in and thought it was some kind of wind up. The fight was scheduled for September but I had an outstanding commitment, a sponsored canoe race, which was an annual occasion for the Tilbury firemen, from Bristol to Windsor We were to stay at a Bristol Fire station with numerous others on the eve of the race. That is of course if we found our way back to the station after the night out. Our team split up, half wanted to remain at the fire station bar enjoying both the company of fellow firemen and cheaper ale while the other half wanted to see the city and enjoy the ambience. I opted for the latter group.

The fight was only six weeks away but not uppermost in my mind. I was a fireman who happened to do a bit of boxing enjoying a weekend away. I probably had a couple of ciders more than I should have. I returned to the station with my fellow firemen slightly worse for wear. To give some indication of my deterioration I broke in to song singing, 'If my friends could see me now'.

"And his fighting for the British title next month?" asked an incredulous Bristolian fireman.

Vic Andretti would not have been pleased. Vic and I got on well together and apart from my Bristol indiscretion the preparation went well. There were no niggling injuries to worry about although weight, as always, was a problem. Domestically it was as rocky as the preparation was smooth. The cries of the hungry baby, screaming for her milk, I had an empathy with. I had little sympathy for the mother with regard to her new maternal responsibilities. I did not think there was anything I could do to help, as my time was taken up with working and training.

I had attended a number of press conferences before but not as the main attraction. On this occasion I was sharing the top table with Frank Warren the promoter and Clinton McKenzie the Champion at the Bloomsbury Crest Hotel where Frank had an office. Clinton had a solid record. We had in fact met on one occasion before, at the Thomas Beckett Gym. We did spar a couple of, maybe a few, rounds. Both Frank and Ernie Fossey made reference to this, stating that he was unable to lay a glove on me. It was true, but meant nothing to me since I remember how he destroyed Steve Early after three innocuous rounds.

Clinton could not remember the occasion, which really goes to show what little impact I had made on him. However, it was a good line to feed the journalists. A press release had been circulated and journalists invited to ask questions, but not many questions were asked. After a significant pause Frank called an end to the conference and it was time for the two protagonists to leave the building for photos.

I was both surprised and embarrassed when I saw a Fire Appliance in the hotel car park with two lads from White Watch accompanying it. Under instructions from the photographers a ladder was placed against the appliance, firemen's axes where taken from the cab and the champ and I posed to order. There was the Laughing Policeman, the Singing Postman and now the nation, through the tabloids, was witnessing the Fighting Fireman.

Come the day of reckoning I surprisingly came in a couple of pounds over at the check weigh-in. Vic Andretti gave me a brisk workout in a small gym he had situated over his restaurant, The Ringside, a short walk from the venue in Shoreditch. The promotion on paper had a lot of promise. There was of course my fight, which was a true title fight; the challenger had gone through the tried and tested path of an area title and an eliminator. This made me a legitimate challenger. Invariably the champion gets to pick and choose his opponents but this was a mandatory defence for the champion.

It was reported that Mickey Duff, McKenzie's manager advised Clinton against the defence seeing it as a distraction from bigger fish. The bigger fish being the recapturing of the European Title he had lost through a low blow when looking the better fighter. He also had world championship ambitions having a world rating of number four. His next fight could easily be a title challenge.

I still saw the fight predominantly as a payday. I trained hard for the fight but my motivation was not to win the fight but ensure I did myself justice when the shit really hit the fan and big questions were being asked. When I say I trained hard I mean that I took no short cuts. 'Short cuts' are always options open to you and dangle before you like a temptress. The alarm

Top: Taking on my kid brother John while Dad looks on.
Bottom: My trophy collection aged 16.

The emaciated and dehydrated champion

Top: The lady (Jacqui) and the champ.
Bottom: Frank Bruno, Dennis Andries, Jim McDonnell, Charlie Magri and yours truly holding Lloyd Honeyghan: At the time we all held European titles.

March 4th. Our wedding Anniversary, Kelly's third birthday and the day of my World title challenge.

Top: A six round fighter?
Bottom: Back to work following a title win.

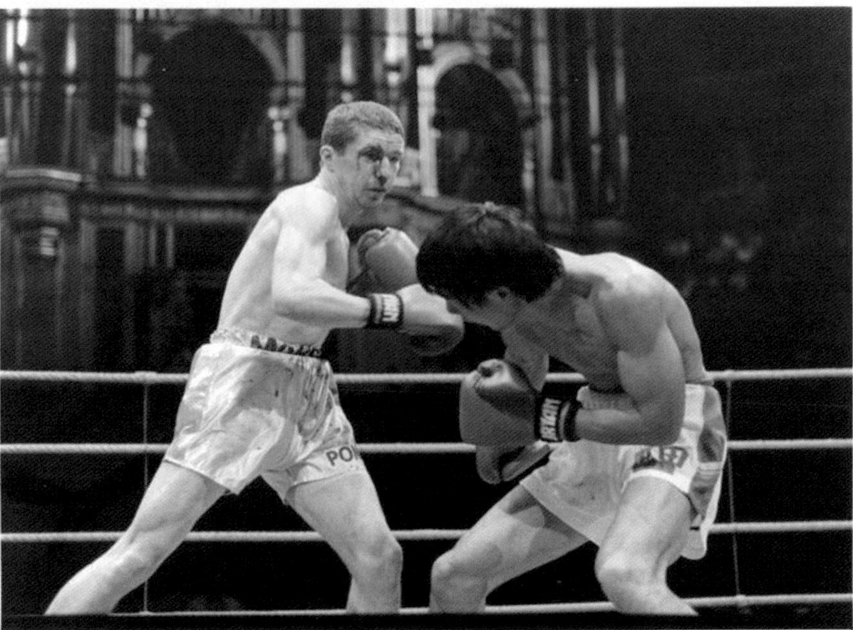

Top: A presentation with Jacqui and Jimmy in attendance.
Bottom: My last fight within the ropes. Despite the cut I remained undefeated.

At one of the betting shops with Dad and John.

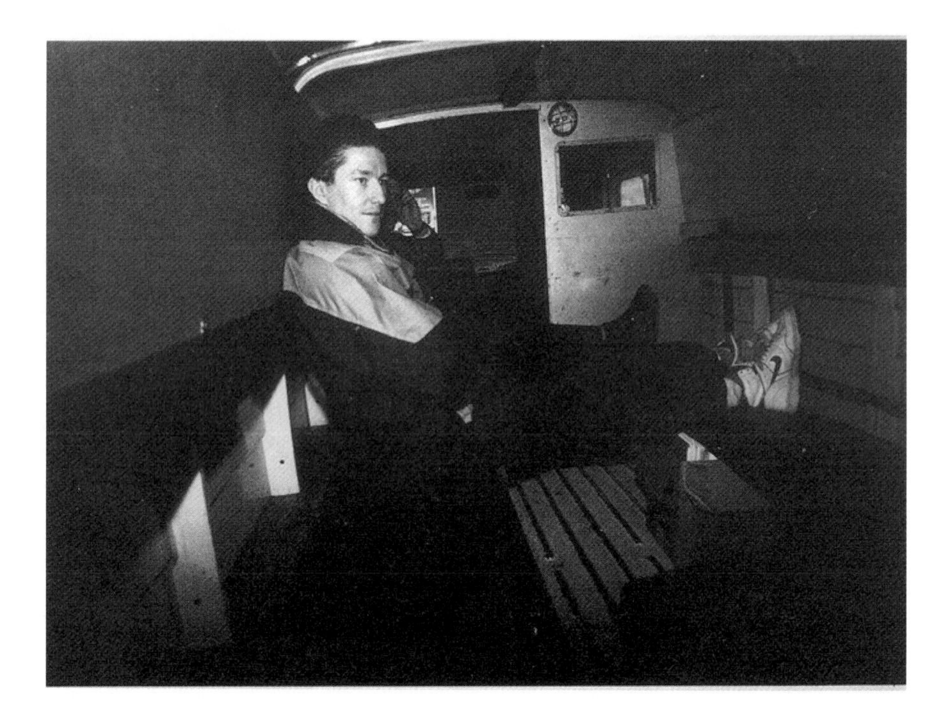

Top left: A reception at the Savoy hotel with Jacqui, Jim, and Mum present. Top right: My acting debut. A scene from the film Tank Malling.
Bottom: Being taken to Barking Magistrates court charged with attempted murder.

goes off at six in the morning you get up and ache from the training the afternoon before and you're also carrying an injury. Everything tells you not to run. You're tired and stiff. You have just left a warm bed with warm flesh beside you. It's raining and dark outside. So you jump back into bed having convinced yourself that it was the right thing to do. For any other sport it is probably the right decision but for boxing it isn't.

In most other sports if you get injured you can leave the arena without disgrace. If it occurs to boxers the general view is, 'they bottled it'. Boxing is perhaps the one sport where you have to continue training with injuries to condition your mind to go through that pain barrier. The general rules for sport is train with your head and compete with your heart. In boxing I took the approach of training with my heart and competing with my head. Training with my heart was about not taking short cuts. I'd learnt how to fight with injuries and when fatigued.

In the gym sessions in the afternoon I would do most of my sparring with Johnny Andrews. Johnny was a weight above me. He was challenging Rocky Kelly for the Southern Area title on the same bill. This contest also had all the ingredients for an explosive fight. Rocky Kelly did not know how to take a backward step while John was uncompromising and technically the better boxer. In one sparring session I got an imprint of his teeth on my shoulder as we were negotiating for superior positions in a clinch. Over the duration I felt that I barely held my own, still he had the weight advantage so on balance I was happy with the preparation. I was very interested in how John fared, as it would be a good indicator of my own condition.

Another fighter on the bill was young Errol Christie he had recently turned professional and had attracted much acclaim because of both his youth and success. There was no superlative that had not been prefixed to this young man's name and great things were expected of him.

When the news filtered through to my dressing room that Johnny Andrews was giving Rocky a battering and Rocky had taken a count it cheered me up no end. It was a good indication that our preparation had been right. It was encouraging for the task that lay ahead. It did not last. John seemed to come apart in the middle rounds and Rocky stopped my gym partner. It was

not looking good.
As I entered the arena I was amazed at the packed hall. It was a sell out. Since I was top of the bill it must have been partly due to me. Although in all honesty the fights sold themselves. I had not made a personal effort to sell tickets since this fight was being broadcast on the Independent Television Network (ITN). Frank had a number of televised promotions before but none involving me. Who would want to watch me? A boxer who can't crack eggs. I figured my purse was coming from the television. The bid, won by Frank, was around fourteen grand of which, as the challenger, I would be getting forty percent.
I entered the ring to a fanfare from bandsmen from the Royal Marines school of Music. The atmosphere got to me. "You can't lose this Tel." I said to myself aloud. As I witnessed the champion enter the ring and discard his gown I saw his muscled body that was the antithesis of mine having boiled down to ten stone. I had a number of inches over him but at that moment I would have willingly swapped my obvious inches and bones for his muscles. I felt that I now knew what it would be like in those final seconds before a soldier leaves the trench. Twelve rounds lay ahead of me probably less if Johnny Andrews, my sparring partner, was the yardstick. "Don't go down without a fight Tel." I said to myself only too aware it fell short of my earlier soliloquy.
The early rounds were as expected. Clinton stalked me and I kept my distance trying to keep him on the end of my jab. He did not rush in but played a patient game. My work rate was far greater than his and I figured that this was part of his strategy. It was a ploy to wear me down and take over in the later stages of the fight. Clinton had done this successfully in the past. I knew I did not have enough fuel in the tank to keep running for the full twelve rounds and so I would occasionally come off my toes and draw the fire of my opponent and take the sting out of his punches. Taking the sting out of the punches meant allowing the opponent to hit you, but where you dictate. If you can do that you are able to anticipate and block the incoming assault. It further has the effect of being more exhausting on the puncher rather than the receiver.
Clinton put me under immense pressure but was never able to take full control. The pressure increased as the fight went into

the later rounds and he desperately tried to land a telling blow. He had allowed himself to get too far behind on points to make up the deficit other than via a stoppage. As the final round approached I knew it was in the bag and felt comfortable about the three minutes that lay ahead. I wanted to make the final round, one where I stood and fought rather than run down the clock protecting my lead. In addition Clinton had sustained a cut eye and I optimistically thought there was a chance of a stoppage. My supporters did not share the same confidence. It was clear to them that I was the more tired and if anyone was going down it would be me.

As the round progressed so we stood toe-to-toe exchanging blows. Clinton was the heavier puncher but I wanted to show I was not afraid to mix it. It was a conscious decision by me but if the truth was known I did not have enough in my legs to do anything else. As the punches were exchanged so the crowd rose to their feet in appreciation. I responded by finding a bit extra I was not aware I had. It felt as if Clinton did likewise. As the bell sounded I turned to the referee offered him my arm which he raised declaring me the new Champion.

It was not a time for celebration but more a case of recuperation. I had given it my all and there was nothing left to give. When I eventually got to the dressing room I sprawled myself out on the padded table knowing I was the champion and for the immediate future no more questions were going to be asked of my body. My mind wasn't given the same reprieve. Numerous reporters, asking questions, surrounded me. My sentience was sufficient enough to notice how the national press had pushed themselves to the front of the press pack. The likes of Terry Poskitt & Len Whaley of the Basildon Evening Echo and the East London Advertiser respectively, who over the years had given me a fair crack, were left struggling like the runts of the litter. I was not beaten, battered nor bruised but as I was sprawled out I must have looked anything but a winner.

Then I heard a voice, “Stand back please.” As the pack parted Ambrose Mendy appeared with a cup of tea for me. It was like manna from heaven. “Ambrose, I'll never forget this moment for as long as I live. ”

Ambrose Mendy was a man I had been very aware of; he was a

friend of Frank Warren. He worked in Frank's office but gave me the impression that he was more than an employee. Frank had been best man at his wedding.
The questions came from all angles and I barely had the energy to respond. I thought to myself, 'just give me five minutes'. Then I heard a voice shout, "Christie has been knocked out." Young Christie's loss was my gain; the press pack departed leaving me to lie in peace with Dad and John close by. For the first time John had trouble getting into the dressing room. The Commissioner responded "Every ones his brother tonight."
"And I was his brother last night and the night before that as well," was John's hasty riposte.
As I got my strength back so I jumped on the scales nearby and weighed in at 9stone 9lbs - I could make the lightweight division. It transpired that the ventilation in the packed hall had failed to work. As the evening progressed so did the room temperature. During my fight it was reported that spectators were removing items of clothing to keep cool.
Understandably I missed the broadcast of the fight on TV that night but watched the recording the next day. Not to put too fine a point on it I was fucking brilliant. In parts it was reminiscent to Ken Buchanan and some of my moves were equally as effective. The two commentators were Reg Gutteridge and Jim Watt. Jim Watt himself was an ex-fighter and was there to give an insight into the technical side of the fight. He was unfortunate enough to be around at the same time as Buchanan and was very much in the shadow of the maestro having lost to Buchanan a couple of times. However, his opportunity came when Buchanan retired. He fought for the vacant British title then the vacant European title followed by the vacant World title. It was ironic that he never beat a champion. Jim was good at commentating though.
I was later whisked off to the Thames Television studios by chauffeured car for an interview on the post six o'clock news programme. After fifteen years of boxing winning national titles at every level I became an overnight success. After the interview I was invited into what was referred to as the green room. There was a party atmosphere. During the talking and bantering it was revealed that the celebration was for 'our victory'. It was

explained to me that Thames Sport, in particular, now had a champion and was in the driving seat when it came to arranging dates for fights. Challengers seldom dictate the terms and conditions. Frank now had a champion whom he could bring to the table when it came to negotiating with TV. It had been attempted with others but they had fallen by the wayside.

I had been a professional now for slightly over three years and my contract with Frank Warren had reached expiry. I picked up my cheque for £5880 and a new contract was signed for a further three years for Frank to act as my Manager. Frank, as I was aware was also a Promoter and there was an inherent conflict of interests between both roles. As my manager Frank was entitled to 25% of my purse as laid down by the standard British Boxing Board of Control contract. To be fair that was never the case previously and that was the understanding when we first met. As my manager his job was to extract as much as possible from the promoter. While a promoter's job was to make a profit on the show and the payment of the fighters was the biggest cost. Keep that down and making a profit becomes much easier. So it is a fine balancing act the manager *cum* promoter has to perform. He gets up to 25% of what the fighter gets but 100% of what the promoter gets. As a fighter, being aligned to such arrangements can have its advantages. Sometimes a promoter can take a loss in order to get you exposure that reaps dividends further down the line. He can invest both time and money in you knowing that some other promoter will not reap the benefits of such investment. Now a champion I did not need to align myself with a Promoter. I had arrived but I was happy to sign a managerial contract with Frank. What I needed was a good manager.

I was now vying for the European title being in the top two. Also I was in the top half of the world top ten. I remember watching the film 'On The Water Front' in which Marlon Brando gives the line "I could have been a contender Charlie I could have been somebody." I was now a contender - I was somebody.

The response, by the media, to my victory was beyond all expectation. The fireman angle certainly gave me an edge in the publicity world. I started to get invitations to all sorts of functions. I would at every opportunity take Jacqui along but they always seemed to end in disaster. My wife would get pissed or simply disappear and sometimes both. On one occasion she was gone for over two hours. I began to think she might have been murdered. I started to think of the consequences of such a tragedy. As long as it was not I doing the crime, I think I could have recovered from her misfortune. Either Bridie, a neighbour and friend of Jacqui or my Mum would look after Kelly. When it came to Mum looking after our daughter she was always returned to us in a much tidier and cleaner state than when she was dropped off.

Frank talked about the next fight being a world title fight. Understandably, it was not dependent on him. Were that the case, I'm sure it would have happened but as the challenger we were always going to be dancing to another person's tune. Frank would cover himself at the end of the, ifs and buts. He would knock his knuckles against the nearby desk saying, "Touch wood."

In my status as British Champion I was in a much stronger position I could dictate terms, as could my manager on my behalf. However, defences were not what it was all about. This was only a base camp towards higher ambitions. In that context a defence is a negative step. You can only go backwards regarding positioning. The bank balance of course is enhanced but I found my bank balance being enhanced anyway. Now I was the champion I'd be getting exposure on television. I also no longer had to worry about selling tickets, which was a huge relief. The television paid for me.

As the British champion my first fight was completed in two rounds, through the referee's intervention rather than a knockout. The commentating team of Reg Gutteridge and Jim Watt made the observation that the new champion was punching harder. It was more a case of the opposition was lacking in preparation and vastly inferior. But they couldn't say that, their employers were banking on me.

I always had an advantage since I knew the actual date, many weeks before the fight, whereas I only became aware of my opponent in the later stages of my preparation. I assume they did not have as much notice nor preparation as I. Ernie Fossey was doing a good job matchmaking. Ernie had also taken over Vic's position as my trainer. There was no formal parting, one-

minute Vic was there then he was gone. He had allowed others, unknown to me, to give him the message that I did not want him as my trainer. Similarly, I had allowed others to let me believe that he was no longer interested in the game.
Under such an impression I was happy working with Ernie. We had a good rapport and I think he respected me because I wasn't a ‘messer’. All too often in the gym you would see fighters who really look the part and played the part well but when it comes to sparring they always have an excuse or injury.
The title Frank was angling for was against the WBA champion Gene 'mad dog' Hatcher. It seemed close to happening. The manager of the Champion had come over from the United States to watch my second post-title fight against Peter Eubank. Eubank held a verdict over the highly touted Barry McGuigan. I won in the seventh with Eubank complaining of an eye injury. It was an unsatisfactory ending but it would have done nothing to dissuade Mad Dog Hatcher's manager from allowing his fighter to share a ring with me.
There was talk of fighting in Las Vegas and I had already visualised the fight poster, 'Mad Dogs and Englishmen'. It wasn't to be, Argentinian Ubaldo Sacco tamed the Mad Dog. The Falkland’s war was still in the minds of many and the thought of a former Marine Commando fighting an Argentinean would have made the promotion of the fight an easy task.
However, securing a World title fight was only going to be achieved through negotiation, as I was not the number one contender for any of the three titles (WBA, WBC & IBF). I could of course fight my way to the top as I had done with the British title, assuming I was good enough, but that could take time. You find yourself achieving the number one contender spot when your better days are behind you. So I focussed on the European title.
The European distraction came in the guise of the then champion Patricio Oliva. It was the man rather than the title I wanted. Oliva had won the Gold in the Moscow Olympics. Not only did he take a gold medal home with him but was also awarded the boxer of the tournament: the best of the best. Wouldn’t it be great if I could take this guy? The Olympics had been some five years past but it would be my way of

embarrassing those who chose to omit me.
Oliva had eight successful European defences to his name. He had taken on most around with the exception of me. It was my turn next. I knew I was the official contender but unaware of the timetable of events when it came to purse bids for the fight and the timing of the fight. Being a boxer, fireman and parent not to mention a tormented spouse did not leave much time to pay attention to such details. That's why I employed a manager.
However, when it came to the purse bids for the fight the outcome was noted by the Press Association. I saw the headline on the boxing page of teletext, 'Money Man Marsh'. Italian promoters had won the purse bid for the forthcoming Oliva - Marsh fight with a bid of seventy grand. This meant as challenger I'd be getting forty per cent, £28,000. What a windfall? I've heard the saying, 'If it looks too good to be true, it probably is' - this was. Oliva vacated his European title since it was becoming a distraction for him and his sights were set on the World Title. It looked as though I'd be fighting for a vacant European title against at that moment an unknown opponent. The notional twenty-eight grand became a benchmark figure.
In the interim another win was notched up this time inside six rounds against a white American fighter Randy Mitchum. On discovering he was white it was hard to get the adrenaline going for the fight. I've never come across a white American who could fight. My next fight was another television fight the venue being in Manchester. I was topping the bill against Lee McKenzie a former opponent. It was a meaningless fight since I had now got a date for the European title, which was six weeks later against the former challenger to Oliva, Alessandro Scapecchi. The Manchester fight from my perspective was nothing more than a payday. Apart from the money there did not seem any upside. Was it worth it? It was a date Frank Warren had been committed to with the Television for some time. I didn't mind helping out. It was not as if I was doing it for nothing. If I really did have European and World title ambitions the likes of Lee McKenzie, although a capable fighter, should not hold any terrors for me.
That in fact was the case for the first two rounds. Then as my left jab pumped out with a purpose it struck his forehead and it

was a case of this is going to hurt me more than it hurts you. I felt the crack of bone in one of my knuckles and immediately realised I was in trouble. It was broken. Even the adrenaline being pumped around my body failed to kill the pain. The only consolation was that my opponent was unaware of my problem. My style of fighting was wholly dependent on my left hand: I was a lame duck. I was there to be taken but Lee failed to take advantage of my apparent passiveness. I was able to kid my way through the remaining eight rounds. Not surprisingly the Manchester spectators were not that happy with it. Throughout the fight there were periods of slow hand clapping. I was worried that the display of disapproval would spur Lee into being bolder in his approach. Fortunately for me and unfortunately for the audience that was not the case. My run of three inside the distance victories had come to an end as this excuse for a fight went the distance I was both an embarrassed and relieved victor - I still took the money; ten grand.

I made regular trips to Harley Street receiving treatment for the broken knuckle but what the knuckle needed to heal was something I did not have - time. I feared that if I pulled out because of the injury another opponent would be brought in to make up the numbers. As and when I was ready I could then challenge the winner as the 'preferential challenger'. However, should the champion not fancy the fight, I'm sure tried and trusted tactics could be used to stymie me.

I trained well and with a greater intensity than ever before. When I sparred or worked the punch bag I spent much of the sessions shaping up as a southpaw allowing me to use my right hand as my jab. Understandably, I did not punch with my left hand at all. My sparring partners were unaware of my handicap otherwise I would not have been able to carry out the deceit effectively.

I found I was beginning to enjoy the challenge that lay ahead. It took a lot of pressure off me, I was in a no lose situation. Should I lose I could take comfort that I was greatly handicapped and it would not be seen as a disaster. Too often in boxing, more so than in any other sport, there is no easy routes back from losing. It takes so long to position yourself in the ratings then one loss undoes or undermines many months or years of progress. It's

like a game of snakes & ladders without the ladders.
The fight was scheduled to be in Monaco on a Saturday afternoon. It was to be screened live on the ITN sport's programme World of Sport. It became apparent that the whole programme was going to be presented and broadcast from Monaco. I had trained so seriously for this fight, notwithstanding the broken bone, that coming in under the ten stone limit was not the problem it had been previously. Although my selection of food still had to be modest. The hotel room had a tempting mini bar but the cost was obscene and a cost benefit analysis quickly dissolved any previous temptation.
This really was a playground for the rich. I had taken a stroll around the Principality and I could not help notice the absence of litter and how clean everything was. I wondered whether it was because things were so expensive that no one bought anything. The litter absence was more than compensated though by the presence of dogs. In the early morning or late evening when I took my walks I seemed to be the only pedestrian not walking a dog. I've heard it said, that stepping in dogs' shit is meant to be lucky. On the morning of the fight I received two portions of luck. Luckily I had a surfeit of training shoes thanks to benevolent sports companies. They had unilaterally decided I was a suitable recipient of their products and accordingly parcels would be sent to me. So the contaminated trainers were placed in the bin outside the hotel as I entered the foyer in my stocking feet.
The bandages had been placed on my hands and inspected by the European Boxing Union officials as well as the opponent's representative. They would check that the regulations regarding amounts of bandage and tape were adhered to and that it was not done to excess. Because of my injury the bandaging and tape was applied to the limit. The inspection passed the official signed the bandages to prevent subsequent alterations without detection. My preparation for the fight had one additional requirement *vis-á-vis* previous fights. I had a local anaesthetic injected into my left-hand seconds before leaving the dressing room. I was advised that it would only last for a maximum of 15 minutes.
The pre-fight ceremonies were drawn out eroding valuable

painkilling time. The respective national anthems were played - Italian, British, and Monaco's. None of which inspired me. Finally and fortunately, since we were in France, the 'Song of Marseilles' was played in full blast. It fired me up. It would compensate for the now diminishing effects of the anaesthetic. The first round went fairly smoothly. The hand hurt but the pain was tolerable and if it were an indication of the rest of the fight I would have been happy to settle for it.
Round two was interrupted when Scapeechi's glove split. The referee returned him to his corner to have the defective glove replaced. When the fight recommenced there was a clash of heads. A warm liquid flowed freely down my cheek. It was not tears and it was not sweat that I was feeling. I could see the heavily blood stained body of my opponent but it was my blood.
It was going to be a cruel way to lose a fight. Ernie managed to stem the bleeding from my eye during the interval using a combination of an adrenaline solution, petroleum jelly and direct pressure but was it going to be enough? Had the cut come in the later stages of the fight and I had a lead to sit on then the approach would be different to what I decided to do. There were nine rounds ahead of me. The fight being only three rounds old meant there wasn't much of a lead, if any. I could protect the cut by taking a safety-first approach but such an approach would lead to a points verdict but probably not in my favour. I don't think I was the house fighter. I just resigned myself to going home without the title.
In the meantime until the result is official I'll just go down all guns blazing. Carrying such an injury I was perhaps reckless getting stuck into my opponent and exposing the cut to further damage. However, I just saw this as bringing forward the inevitable, but having the saving grace of being stopped while on top.
I fought every round as if it was the last and knew that come rounds nine or ten I would have little left in the tank. I ran the risk that should the fight get that far I'd be beaten on a possible knockout. I had felt the Italian's right hand in the second round, which managed to penetrate my central nervous system. If a similar punch landed on my chin when in a fatigued condition I may not be able to get up in time.

Round six continued where rounds four and five left off. The blood flow, stemmed by Ernie in the break, began to flow again during the combat. Towards the end of the sixth I anticipated the feared right hand and came inside the expected arc of the blow. I threw a couple of feeble punches in the process and my opponent sank to one knee. I was sent to the neutral corner while my opponent looked distressed looking to his corner. The count reached ten and I was the new European Champion.
It felt so good. It was a special moment. It wasn't because I was now the champion although that was a good enough reason to be elated. It wasn't the win in itself; I'd had better. During the fight I was grinning and laughing outwardly not wanting to show my opponent any sign of weakness or reason for encouragement but I felt tormented. Then within ten seconds I was experiencing the other end of the emotional spectrum. To go from one extreme to the other in such a short space of time puts you in the clouds. During the fight, if I had the time, I would never have dreamed of pulling it off. All I was hoping for was a defeat with dignity, but instead it was zero to hero. I was my own hero as well as everybody else's. Its not what you do it's the way that you do it – I got a result. In the post-fight interview I was asked how I felt by the presenter Jim Rosenthal. "There is only one word to describe the way I feel now and that is voluptuous."
It was a mimic of my sparring partner Sylvester Mittee who had used the line after winning his Commonwealth title several months earlier. Sylvester's remark was not picked up then but now it was something to run with - It's the way you tell 'em.

CHAPTER THIRTEEN
TOUCH WOOD

On my return home I was asked to appear on the Terry Wogan show. I was picked up from work having quickly changed into a dinner suit and the accompanying black tie for a later engagement. The several stitches in my eye made a nice contrast to my attire. I was kept occupied with food and drinks in the green room and patronised by the employees of the programme from all levels. I was being told how clever I was, how good I was and how brave I was. It certainly gave my confidence a boost, which was a good thing as it was a live broadcast in front of an audience of over ten million viewers.
This programme went out three nights each week. Wogan was a master at work. He was smooth and slick and I was in awe how the words just flowed from his mouth when I watched the programme at home. On my introduction I joined the set. I got a big cheer and an enthusiastic applause from the audience. I was both pleased and impressed with the reception until I saw a guy on the studio floor orchestrating the adulation. I tended to walk towards the audience but was prompted towards the host and the vacant chair. The audience was positioned off centre of the studio floor that faced a number of television cameras one of which blocked the view of many of the audience. In between the cameras were big white cards with prompts written on them, for Mr Wogan I presumed.
I found myself sharing a platform with Henry Cooper. Mister Cooper was a former British & European heavyweight champion who had the distinction of putting Muhammad Ali on his arse. Unfortunately for him Ali got up and bashed him up. Henry was something of an institution and the *de facto* ambassador of British boxing and here I was sharing a platform. Henry and I now had some common ground, a susceptibility to cuts. However,

it seemed that the cuts got the better of him.
At the other event later that evening I met an old friend of my Dads, Connie Donovan. He gave me a lift home in his Bentley. As the car pulled up on the council estate where I lived I was somewhat embarrassed. European champions should be able to afford not to be living on a council estate.
I could now afford to move on but I was conscious of not over stretching. I remember watching a programme, several years earlier, on a then current British World Champion boxer. The programme portrayed him with his young family in their luxury house with the obligatory swimming pool. He seemed to have all the trappings of success. A few years later he lost it all. I did not want to move up the property ladder until I could be sure that it was an irrevocable move. I knew where I wanted to live I would make a detour on my runs to inspect the area and the for sale signs. Price wise it was still out of my reach but that was my goal.
In the interim I bought a townhouse in the same road as my parents and Jimmy. There was still a degree of doubt on the move but house prices were moving and I did not want to be left behind. I kept control of the council house as a fall back. The council was not too happy about it and insisted I give up the tenancy.
My boxing future still had much uncertainty. The injured hand would require some rest so I would not be able to cash in immediately on my new title. But the title purse was a nice windfall and put the bank balance in the black. It fell considerably short of the £28,000 benchmark – it wasn't half as much. But Frank, I believed at that time, did the best he could for me as my manager. It was in his interest. For this fight, so I understood, he was not involved in the promotion so the conflicts of interest between manager and promoter did not exist. I speak with hindsight when I say he should have let the fight go to purse offers.
The uncertainty I felt about my boxing future was eased because of my job. The boxing money I had rightly described as a windfall. It was not money I relied on and the vast bulk of it could be ring fenced from the demands of bills, the mortgage and the general cost of living. The fire fighting money took care of

that, just, but with the comfort of the other money in the bank it was no longer a struggle.
The fight over I was back to my old routine of making up for the previous culinary denial. I had now got into the habit of foregoing sugar in my tea. The lack of sweetness was supplemented by a bar of chocolate invariably a Mars bar from the watch nutty locker. I would have several cups of tea during the course of a shift and the corresponding number of bars of chocolate.
Jacqui's twenty-fourth birthday was approaching. It had become customary for my friend Richard and his wife Pat to go out with Jacqui and I as a foursome on the wives' respective birthdays. It was a pleasant evening at a Chinese restaurant. We were waiting for the next course and the conversation was flowing. I had everyone's attention when I felt a strange feeling in my throat. It's difficult to describe but was similar to being choked in the emotional sense. This was distracting rather than worrying. Then I began to feel light headed. I thought I would shake it off and continued talking. My fellow diners heard my mumble and then witnessed my head slump face down onto the table. I came round a short while after and aware I'd passed out. Jacqui understandably was upset, Richard also showed concern,
"You OK?" he was asking.
"What happened?" I was asking.
We were both more concerned about getting an answer to our own question than giving an answer that our questions were repeated.
"You just passed out."
"How long?"
"It weren't long."
"Did anything else happen?"
"No. You alright?"
"Yeah, don't worry. I'll go to the Doctors."
"Make sure you do Tel."
The evening continued. I made a special effort to reassure everyone that I was OK, which was the case. I intended to go to the Doctors at the first opportunity. Other commitments meant it was going to be later that week, but as the end of the week arrived I felt fine and reckoned it must have been a one off.

I was back in the ring near the end of January defending my European title against Frenchman Tusikoleta 'Tek' Nkalankete. The first two rounds went well. I remember thinking the matchmaker and promoter have done a good job getting me this opponent. This is going to be an easy night. I took both the fighter and the two rounds for granted. Tek must have been on a scouting mission. He had looked at me, sized me up and was now ready for me. I talk with hindsight, at the time I saw his delayed challenge as an act of defiance I was content to let him bang away at my ribs for a couple of rounds before fading away. He never did fade away and was there to the end. He was a good fighter.

Another defence in the Isle of Man came shortly afterwards. This fight had a similar format to the fight in Monaco being a Saturday afternoon. Also on the bill, arguably topping the bill was the British Heavyweight title fight between Horace Notice and Trevor Curry. The Heavyweight fight was pretty entertaining, which was just as well as my fight was abysmal. My Italian opponent was competent but not at all dangerous. I was given to understand that he had not had the easiest of journeys to the Isle of Man. That should have given me a further edge but I was unable to finish him off. It went to points after 12 boring rounds. The highlight of the fight, for me, was in between rounds when the rounds card girl, who had the title of Miss Isle of Man, would parade the ring. It was from around the fourth round on that I began asking her, "What you doing tonight?"

After the fight we met up and she agreed to show me the sights that evening.

Word soon got out that I was going out with Miss Isle of Man. "You lucky bastard." was one response, "In your dreams." was another. For those who doubted me I simply replied, "Be in the foyer at 8 O'clock tonight." Several of my fellow boxers could not resist checking out the authenticity of my claim. When she arrived I felt ten foot tall. We approached her car, I took the passenger side looking into her eyes as she opened her door and entered so did I. Our eyes met as half of our bodies where still outside of the vehicle. "This is my boyfriend.." I never did catch his name I was too shocked. The three of us visited a few clubs and a restaurant.

When I was dropped off I sneaked back into the hotel and to my room. At breakfast the next morning I was asked, "Well?"
"Well what?"
"You know. Last night."
"Oh yeah, we went for a drink had a bite to eat nothing more."
"Well, did ya?"
"It was purely plutonic."
"That means you did."

Patricio Oliva the former Olympic Gold Medallist had taken the WBA World title from Argentinian, Ubaldo Sacco and my sights were set on the Italian once again. It seemed as though things were moving in the right direction. There was a meeting in Frank's office with the Italian's Promoters. I was invited along and was privy to all the negotiations. I was offered a purse of ten thousand US dollars, which I considered derisive. As it was I would have been happy to fight him for nothing. The sticking point concerned options.
Options were something the Promoter appeared insistent upon. Initially I thought the meeting was a meeting between his people and my people but I was to realise that Oliva did not come into the equation. What this was about was securing the Promoter's interest. If I was to beat Oliva then the Italian Promoter is left in the lurch, unless he has a piece of the action with the new champion. They wanted options on my next three fights with pre-determined purses that were quoted in dollars with a gradual increase starting at $50,000. At the then exchange rate it was only fractionally larger than the £28,000 from the notional European purse bid. I was beginning to see the game in a completely different light. The people promoting Oliva would be winning no matter what the result. Would Oliva be getting a piece of me should I win? If that was the case it would be more acceptable but I suspect there would be no redundancy for the beaten champion.
Following it through, were I to win, then the only fighters who would be allowed to challenge me would be those fighters prepared to allow options to the promoter, at the pre-determined purses. It is a good way for a promoter to get a fight on the cheap. I just wanted the title and would have signed anything

and I was happy to put my signature to the contract. The matter of options did not bother me because were I to win I would have vacated the title rather than allow the options to be implemented. I figured that I would have broken the chain liberating the next two challenges for the vacant title from the burden of options.
I was lucky that Frank had allowed me to partake in the meeting. Ironically, I would have sacked him had he negotiated what I had signed up to. As it was I made the decision and signed the contract. It was the first time I had signed a contract for any fight. Up until then Frank, I presume, had done all the signing on my behalf. I left Frank's office so up for the challenge that lay ahead some time in September.
Before then I had a fight scheduled in May against Ricky Kaiser another white American. I was giving quite a lot of weight away, about ten pounds. I don't think it was by design. It was a case of finding an opponent who was available. I recognised and noted the dilemma that Frank was facing as both the manager and promoter. But it was not an issue for me. This was all necessary preparation for Oliva. Kaiser was just an opponent he wasn't brilliant but that night I was. I felt so good and sharp. I only wish it was Oliva in the opposite corner. It was as if my opponent was a sloth. I anticipated everything he was doing. I was so tuned and responded rapidly. It was technically a knockout, he being counted out in the seventh round. It was not due to a blow on the chin but a punch to the stomach that winded him. He was on the floor gasping for air in round seven while I wasn't even breathing heavy.
It felt good training during the summer months. It was something of a novelty. It seemed that most of my training was on cold winter mornings. Training in the heat was less restricting as you did not need the layers of training apparel to keep warm. Training in just shorts and tee-shirt was rejuvenating. I trained harder and faster. My times on my runs were coming down big time. I was doing so much more than a year ago when I was training at my maximum. I've always had doubts and insecurities about every fight, with the exception of white Americans, which was safe guard against complacency. The greater my doubts the less the complacency. This one was

different. There was no doubt and there was no complacency. During my runs I would play out the post fight interviews as the winner. On previous occasions I would be rehearsing speeches for defeat.

I received a phone call from Neil Allen who was a journalist from the London Evening Standard. He had heard that the fight was off. Frank was on his holidays at the time and it was several days before it was confirmed that Oliva was going to be defending his title against some other lucky bastard. I was still being accommodated on the under card but no money was mentioned and I wasn't going put the gloves on for $10,000. I believe I scared them off. I looked too good against Kaiser.

I was still training in the hope that this was a ploy by the Italian promoters to fuck me around and interrupt my training. If they can alter a contract once they can do it again. What did become apparent was that the contract, I signed, accounted for nothing.

I have heard it said that at the time of peak condition an athlete is finely tuned and more susceptible to infections. I don't know if it based on any scientific research but what happened to me gives weight to the assumption. I developed a virus and could not shake it off. I was due to make a mandatory European defence but was genuinely not fit to train let alone fight and the European Boxing Union stripped me of the title. I was a bit pissed off but it was the right decision by the EBU. The example should be the policy adopted universally. It keeps the interest in the title alive and gives everybody a chance. It also gives the edge to the controlling bodies over the promoters.

In many ways mandatory defences can be to the advantage of the champion. The fact that it is a mandatory defence puts the negotiations for the fight in the open. Any promoter interested in the fight can submit a sealed bid before the specified deadline. The biggest bid gets to promote the fight and both the champion and challenger get more money.

Ernie Fossey, who had been in the game many years, advised me to always let fights go to purse offers – 'any one who doesn't is a mug', he would say. I was beginning to realise why. It would have been interesting to see what purse bid would have been generated for the European mandatory. Had it been in the £70,000 region, I would be entitled to a 60%, I may have had a moment of madness and took the fight. The reality was, as I had demonstrated on a number of occasions, you can fight with an injury but you need a good engine. Your heart and lungs need to be working efficiently and mine weren't. The virus had knocked me back many months.

All that good work and training had been undone. I was without any title, no longer the British Champion having relinquished the title and no longer the European Champion having been stripped. I was concerned that I would not be able to replicate the fitness level and the general feeling of well being I had previously experienced.

Christmas was now approaching and I had made a recovery. It was time to get fit so that I could get back in the gym. My approach to my early stages of training, I think, was something of a novel approach. Most fighters go to the gym to get fit whereas I would not go to the gym until I was fit. A fight was pencilled in for January and was being touted as a warm up for the IBF title fight – touch wood.

Gary Hinton had lost the title to Joe Louis Manley in what was one of the American fights of the year and these two Americans looked the business. Hinton had taken the former champion Aaron Pryor to a split decision. Pryor had been touted as the best pound for pound fighter around. When Hinton fought him there had been some slippage of the World's best but Pryor was still a force. Hinton had to be respected and even more so Hinton's victor Joe Louis Manley.

More immediately there was the task of beating another American fighter Dave Taylor. This guy had etched into his front tooth the '$' sign in gold. Dollars were what I was chasing. The fight was in Croydon and I was crap. My timing was out, I was out of distance and bloody embarrassing. Fortunately for me, we clashed heads in the second round and my opponent received a cut eye. It was nowhere near as bad as the cut I had received in my European challenge but the referee stopped the fight. If the next fight was going to be for a world title I deserved to be 100 to 1 against.

In my defence I had not tuned myself for the fight. I had trained up to the eve of the fight seeing it as a sparring session for which I was being highly paid. The only thing about the evening that had a scintilla of world title status was the journey home with Dad. We were chauffeured home with Connie Donovan in his Bentley. We watched the broadcasting of the fight on the television in the car. It did not look any better. When we got out the Bentley Dad said, "If you're going to fight like that you might as well turn it in."

The IBF World champion Joe Louis Manley had a good pedigree. He had been in the American 1980 Olympic squad but did not get the chance to fight for medals as the USA boycotted the Moscow Olympics. This guy appeared class. I did not watch his title victory against Hinton although I must confess to seeing a short clip when being interviewed on a sports programme and asked for my opinion. I remember saying I could see something to work on. What else could I say? 'It looks like I'm in for a beating', was what I was thinking. I did not like watching fights of prospective opponents it is always easy to see their shortcomings. The real reason though was that it took away the edge I needed. Prior to fights I would form an image in my mind's eye of the complete fighter and prepare for combat against that image. That way you're ready for anything. My sole loss in the four ABA finals, I contested, I put down to preparing for a particular opponent. The game plan I had didn't work and I stuck with it for longer than I should have. Fifty odd punches too long.

The championship fight was to be held in Basildon. There was not a venue big enough so Frank hired a circus tent. Frank Warren was promoting this and the tent was a demonstration of how innovative he can be. Training was going well in the gym. I would do nine rounds of sparring with three different opponents. Mo Hussein, a Commonwealth champion, was one of my main sparring partners. He also was on the Basildon bill. As Mo and I sparred I was amazed at how tough and brave he was. I was sharp and seldom failed to miss but he would keep coming. When he did get close I'd let him bang away at my ribs. It was a sort of *quid pro quo, i*t gave him encouragement and I would get a couple of more rounds out of him the next day. Without that trade off I don't think sparring with me would have been be the right thing for Mo. I would work the trick with lots of sparring partners. Give 'em some success and they're up for more rounds.

If you marked up the points won and lost in sparring over my whole career, it would probably be a points defeat. But sparring was about learning and practising. Too many fighters see it as winning and as a consequence fight exclusively to their strengths.

Mo banged away as I let him have one of his moments. It may have been that I allowed him too long a time punching away or that I did not ride the punches. Either way it was the final straw for one of my ribs and it gave way. There is nothing you can do with a rib fracture. It heals in its own time. Not for the first time, 'time' was not on my side. It was difficult finding a comfortable position in bed and it would take me an hour to nod off. Further sparring was out the question and was concluded earlier than otherwise, as was my running because of tenderness in my ankle. Ernie had said to take it easy and against my instincts I took his advice. In all candour, my obedience stemmed from sharing the burden that lay ahead. Up until then I had done everything my way. It was not that I was a *Prima Donna* it was just the reality. No one was with me when I went for a run in the mornings nor after those runs when I would do circuit training. Therefore, in the gym later that day, only I could really know what further efforts were needed of me.

I was my own trainer. I would not go away to training camps since I had a full time job and I would not abstain from my conjugal rights. That is not to say Ernie was surplus to requirements. He encouraged me and really was a kidder but that was what I needed. If he were not there he would have had to be invented. So now I was taking Ernie's advice to ease up – there was no alternative

I finished my visits to the gym well over a week before the fight. The weight was not a problem. During the preparation Connie Donovan introduced me to an associate of his, Ray Watson. Ray had an interest in sport in particular concerning physiology. He was impressed with my resting heart rate, which at the time was thirty-four beats per minute. He gave me some advice on the weight making side and recommended some supplements that included Amino Acids. They had a slimming company called Natural Vitality.

The fight was scheduled for March 4th. Coincidentally it was

Kelly's third Birthday and our Wedding Anniversary. It was good copy. The press conference witnessed my first meeting with the world champion. “Are you confident?” I was asked.
"March the fourth was a significant day. I'd checked my biorhythms for that date and I have checked Joe’s. Mine are at their peak while Joe’s are at a low point.”
I had read an article in a magazine about biorhythms a month or so earlier but did not know how to interpret them. Whether it affected my opponent only he will know. It impressed former England squad colleague Jim McDonnell who was keen to understand about the Biorhythms’ phenomena. He used the ploy against Barry McGuigan.
"Will you give up your fireman’s job? What are your plans after this?”
"No, I will have one defence then retire undefeated."
The majority of those present, understandably, did not believe in my words. To have a defence you first have to win the title. That was odds against. My understanding of boxing was that it was not until you became champion that you can really cash in. However, I looked back at the road of past World champions and it was littered with disaster and defeats. No one gets out of this game without getting damaged and discarded to some extent. Not many finish as winners. The last fighter to retire undefeated was Rocky Marciano – a white American and that was well over a generation ago. Why not retire on winning the title? I wanted a payday and to show that the win was not a fluke.
What I had, that was very special to me, was the title of undefeated. It is hard to keep that tag as a champion as every defence is an ever increasing pay-day. For a champion to retire undefeated means he is effectively walking away from his biggest possible purse. It is the equivalent of a redundancy payment. Assuming of course you are not tied into options then you could not afford to retire. It was reported in the press that I was receiving £70,000 for the fight. When I was asked by a journalist to confirm this I replied "As much as that?" I did not know what I was getting. Frank had said he'd look after me.
I perhaps could be *blasé* about retirement because of my other occupation. I wasn’t fighting to put bread on the table; this was pin money. It did not have to be dipped into. It was not my

living. I had something to fall back on. Retired undefeated champion of the World had a nice ring to it. I really did not want to lose this fight. Not only because of missing out on the title, but I knew that defeat would condemn me to fighting on. One loss on your record is no better than six losses as far as I'm concerned. Next there would be losses at the European level then at the British level finally hanging up the gloves with a respectable 42-1-7 record but a loser nonetheless. Many fighters seemed to spend half their career working their way up the billing and the second half working their way down. I wanted to show that I was in charge and get out of the game at the top.

I was under no illusion about the task that lay ahead of me. I knew the smart money was on Manley. There existed three title holders because of the competing boxing associations but Manley was reported as the lineage champion. John was now working, managing a betting shop. His head office contacted him. "We have a top promoter who wants six grand on Manley at five to six what do you think?" John was asked. "Take it" was John's reply. Despite my training interruptions John was sure of my condition.

This was to be only the second time I was to meet a decent American fighter. The first was as an amateur when the Navy competed against the US Marine Corp in North Carolina. I beat the highly touted Capers D'Antagnac. Many had D'antagnac down as a future world champ until he was killed in a plane crash.

Selling tickets was not a problem. John had banked twenty-five grand from ticket proceeds. There were many people from Basildon and surrounding areas buying into this fight. Most had never been to a professional fight before. I only hoped that they would not be disappointed. Sadly there was disappointment for an equal number who could not get tickets. Going by the demand for tickets, had the tent been twice as big it would have been filled.

The day of the fight began with Kelly opening up her birthday cards. Later in the day, after the weigh-in, a car was presented to me from Foster cars the local Toyota Dealer. I ate at home and slept later that afternoon. When I awoke it was early evening and I went for a walk alone round my neighbourhood. A few of

the locals were amazed to see me wondering around expecting I would be locked away somewhere. As I walked I seemed to get a rush with each step, it felt that I was being pumped with energy for the task ahead. It was not quite divine intervention but it felt like unknown forces were at work. It wasn't scary and I wasn't curious, I just felt good that I felt so good with the fight only hours away.
My mate Shoey was also on the bill against a local lad. Shoey had left the Navy and was also under the management of Frank. As an amateur, unlike me, Brian had made the Olympics and also had the distinction of being the Captain of 1984 team. He was Liverpool based and his professional career was not going smoothly. There was a tension between him and Frank. I felt bad about the situation he was now in, having introduced Shoey to Frank and persuading my mate to take him on as his manager. It was not a harmonious business arrangement. Still as Mickey Duff once said, "It does not say anything in the contract about us having to like each other." Maybe, but it helps. The manager can leave the fighter but the fighter can’t leave the manager. Shoey was put on a weekly wage, which looked, at face vale, a good deal, but it never lasted. After one televised fight Shoey was critical of Frank in the post-fight interview. It was downhill after that. Shoey claimed he once phoned Frank and threatened to travel down from Liverpool and shoot him. "Don't forget to bring your gun." was Frank's alleged reply. Shoey struggled but got the win.

CHAPTER FOURTEEN
TOP OF THE WORLD

It was a cold night. The journey from the nearby hotel, that facilitated the changing rooms, to the tent entailed a stop off at a caravan. It served as a sanctuary from the elements while waiting for the cue to enter the arena. I had wrapped up well still wearing my tracksuit bottoms as I entered the ring. The reception was fantastic and as I looked out of the ring I saw so many familiar faces from the Basildon area, surely they hadn't come to see me get bashed up.

Then the champion entered. He did not have the same respect for the elements as I. Entering the arena like it were seventy degrees. 'Big mistake', I thought. The early rounds were going to be mine. He could not have warmed up sufficiently. The densely packed crowd helped create some degree of heat but not enough.

The preliminaries out the way it was a case of coming out fighting. I had an idea on what I had to do. I had based a strategy on an article I read about the new champion in a boxing magazine; Joe had served in the US Army representing them as a runner in the 400 metres. This suggested to me that he had a good balance of speed and power, but it left questions about his stamina. If I were to have ambitions as a runner it would be over the much longer distances. I lacked that explosive power required for speed. It probably also explains why I have not knocked anybody out. I needed to test his stamina.

The article quoted the champion as overcoming initial problems thanks to his new management. It was as if they were responsible for his new success. By definition it means his previous management team caused his initial failings. I have always seen it as it being the fighter who makes the decisions in the ring. No other outside influences should affect that. The buck stops with the fighter. By all means have reasons why you lose but not excuses. My take on this was that Joe would not face his boxing shortcomings; It was other people's fault. In reality the only person you can blame for your failings is yourself or your opponent. Joe had weaknesses that he was either ignoring or not noticing. It is not a problem to have weaknesses, provided you both recognise and understand them. I was only too aware of my weaknesses - I couldn't crack eggs.

The article also reported Joe as being a great fan of former heavyweight champion Joe Frazier. "When things were getting tough during the Hinton fight I kept repeating the name Joe Frazier." Joe informed the author of the article.

I went out for the first round nervous and apprehensive. I needed to take a look at this guy but not allow him to get settled. I thought it better and safer to have a look at him from close range rather than at a distance. You can't get into too much trouble close up. I nicked a few points with punches as I came in close managing also to negate his counter. It was a scrappy affair but it was suiting me more than him. This was not meant to be the strategy but it seemed to be working. Come the third the same approach was taken but for different reasons. It was no longer based on caution and sizing him up but more about recklessness and bashing him up. At the bell for the conclusion of each round so my hand went up to claim the round. In the corner water was given to me, as were instructions. Both Ernie and Jimmy Tibbs were giving advice but I was on a another planet. The referee Randy Neuman would visit both corners in between rounds, "Everything okay?"

"Top of the world." I would shout out to him.

In the space of a minute I had gone from being on another planet to top of the world. The rest of the fight was a blur. I recall being warned by the ref for going in with my head. "I was coming inside his punch." was my reply. I remember falling to the canvas when I lunged towards the champion with a wild swing. It was one of only a few he avoided. The momentum carried me to the floor but the smile remained on my face. As I climbed to my feet my legs felt like lead and I was concerned that they may not last the trip, but my smile got bigger. Then I found Joe and

myself banging away at each other in his corner. I could hear his corner men screaming instructions to their man and complaining to the referee about my tactics. I looked towards them as I pinned their fighter against the ropes with my head and shoulder, "You can't help him now I've done him." I shouted at them. Their jaws dropped.
The referee came in to break us up but I was on him again. When we were again pulled apart, I was back on him. I don’t think I was hurting him with my punches, but I was wearing him down. As we broke apart I saw Joe take a couple of deep breaths during the respite and roll his gloves. He looked determined and focussed. It was like he was trying to regroup and compose himself for a counter offensive. I charged in head and fists. "Fucking Joe Frazier ain't gonna help you now pal."
He was no longer composed. He was no longer focussed. He was, to all intent and purposes, no longer the champion. My moment came at the end of the ninth. A series of hooks connected to his jaw and his head twisted on his neck, back and forth, as one came from the left then the right. I have never connected in such a manner before and I don't know where the punches came from. It was not a conscious move but they were delivered viciously and they landed perfectly. No one could get up from that, I thought or perhaps hoped. He was saved by the bell. As he rose to his feet, so it sounded.
It was time to stop the mauling and start the boxing. Picking the punches from long range to finish him off. It became one sided and there emerged some guilt about what was happening. I backed off momentarily and thought about how this was going to destroy his life and affect his family and children. He was going back to America without a title; an ex-champion.
In all my fights I have seen myself as the prey fighting off the predator. And it has been my instincts of self-preservation and survival that has got me through. This fight was no different. Even my aggression could be justified as the best form of defence. I was always able to justify my boxing in these terms. But now I was the one doing the stalking and I felt uneasy about it. I had in front of me a beaten man who could be seriously hurt. As the prey I should walk away. It was no longer a fair fight. A moral dilemma I faced. Spare him or go for the kill? "Fuck it, its

him or me."
He toppled the referee stepped in. Or was it the other way around? It appeared to happen simultaneously. I'd pulled it off; a world champion. To quote the boxing Commentator Reg Gutteridge "... and it couldn't happen to a nicer fella." [sic]
I gave the credit to Ernie. It was only fair. He would have got the blame had I lost. It would have been down to my lack of training in the latter stages. But it would not have been the cause of my defeat but I believe it was in part the reason for victory. I had been on the weight about a fortnight before the fight. It meant, injuries notwithstanding, the scales did not dictate the training. My body could acclimatise at ten stone. All too often a fighter only makes the weight for the few seconds that he is on the scales. The weigh-in is too close to the fight to be able to replenish those essential minerals and salts that have been squeezed out in the days before.
The media interest again was taken to another level. I made the national news and for me the indication of truly making an impact was that even the newspaper cartoonists where making sketches alluding to me. I conducted numerous television interviews starting with the breakfast programmes and worked through the day. The frequent question asked was "Are you going to give up your job?"
My view was why should I? I enjoyed it and now I had a nice few quid in the bank I could afford the job. The money was crap but the hours good. At home Jacqui also had the media to contend with being followed by photographers as she took Kelly to school.
The next day it was back to work and back to reality or so I thought. As I drove up to the station I saw hordes of photographers, cameramen and reporters. I felt a bit embarrassed by it all. The adulation was great but in another sense I felt empty. The desire I had to reach my goal would torture me but I liked living with it. I only realised that now it had gone. I've heard it said of fighters softening when they become champions their willpower weakening. If I was anything to go by it was not about lack of willpower, but lack of direction. What do I do now? Where do I go from here? Having the title felt better, I guess, than having missed out on the title. The rest of your life you are asking, 'What if?' or wondering, 'If only'.

However, in some masochistic way wanting it was a better feeling than having it. I felt more alive wanting than having.
Later that week Connie Donovan, carrying a Gratton's Catalogue, visited the house with Sally Ann Voak, a newspaper journalist, from the Sun. She was asking me about the diet I had been assigned by Connie's colleague. Meanwhile Jacqui was given the Gratton's catalogue to choose whatever she wanted. She still looked at the prices. It was the catalogue version of 'super market sweep'. No limit was put on it. Inside the Sun newspaper the next day was the heading, 'Terry's a mino fighter' readers were able to get a months supply of these Natural Vitality tablets for £9.99 plus postage and packing. Connie introduced me to a number of the people from the Sun including the editor Kelvin McKenzie. Being a 'lefty' I did not like the paper's politics but could see nothing wrong with Kelvin Mackenzie now having met him.
I was in demand. I found myself appearing on many television programmes including the Terry Wogan show, again. Although interviewed this time by, stand in, Bruce Forsyth. I couldn't get a word in. I was also getting regular spots on the ITV sports programmes. I seemed to be constantly in one studio or another. I was also asked to attend many charity presentations. It was difficult to say no. I seldom did which left much misunderstanding. Because I did not say no, it did not follow I meant yes. On several occasions my silence was taken as consent only to find the organiser blaming me for my non-showing when no such promise had been made. It was quite a pressure because I still had a full time job to fit in. It was often the case I'd find myself being picked up at the fire station by a chauffeured car.
Any programme that had the so-called 'celebrity' guest appearance I seemed to be on. I enjoyed them all and felt I entertained and made a real contribution. The researchers seemed to confirm this by telling me how good I was. This was not just one researcher it was most of them. Was it true or was it part of their job? I hope the former I suspect the latter.
I felt like I was doing everything for everyone else. I was going here and there as a favour to everyone. It was not those close or friends. They avoided me thinking that I was too busy. Many others, however, inundated me with requests. Everything else

being equal I would have found it easy to say no, but things weren't equal. I was the world champion and went out of my way to show I had not changed. If the truth was known it was not people putting on me, but I putting on myself.
On one such occasion I was at my niece Fallon's birthday party. I would normally not have gone but now I had to make the effort. My cousin Connie had travelled from Romford. It required a protracted bus ride or changing on the train with her young kids so I offered her a lift home. I really did not have the time but I wanted to show I hadn't changed still having time for everyone. Mum came along for the ride. I had just got out of the town when I came over funny. I recognised the signs and symptoms that I had experienced 18 months or so earlier when I had passed out in the Chinese. I wound the windows down, turned the air vent on full blast and slowed the vehicle. I began actively making conversation thinking this would keep me alert. The feeling subsided and I was able to drop off Connie and the kids and return home safely.
I made an appointment with my GP and explained what happened. He thought I was probably over doing it and suggested I slow down a bit. He described it as 'flaking out'. I took his advice. Paradoxically I would be able to slow down because a fight had been arranged. It was easy to say no in a pre-fight period. Everyone understands when you say you are in training.
When Frank and I got down to talking about my next and last fight he pointed out that we were committed to options on the next three defences. "That's not a problem I'm only having one defence." was my reply.
He explained that the first defence would be for fifty thousand dollars. Frank always spoke in dollars. "That is not a problem either, I'll retire now."
It appeared to me that the agreement Frank Warren my manager reached on my behalf was similar to the contract I had signed with the Italians. I suppose he thought if I was happy to sign that contract then I would have no qualms about being committed to a similar contract for another world title fight. To be fair I got more than ten thousand dollars. I netted about twenty-three grand but I was disappointed. I signed for the

cheque using the name M Mouse.

CHAPTER FIFTEEN
ONE MORE FIGHT

July first was the date for my defence it was to be at to the Royal Albert Hall. The official contender was a fighter named Frankie Warren and a mandatory defence against him was due in a few months. I thought about hanging about for this because of the large purse it would generate when the rights to stage the fight went to purse offers. Only having one defence I wanted as much cash as I could get.
Frank was very much aware of this but he had plans for a voluntary defence. He put proposals to me regarding the purse for the voluntary defence. This was new ground; hitherto I had taken what was given. I was now negotiating with my manager or was it the promoter? I was in a strong position. It was as if Frank wanted the fight more than I. "What I'm offering is the equivalent of a gross £147,666." he exclaimed.
"I'll take the headline figure £147,666 and live with the deductions." was my reply. Frank had asked me if Connie Donovan's Company, Natural Vitality, would be interested in sponsoring the fight. I broached Connie on this and a meet between him and Frank was arranged. The deal was done and Natural Vitality got their money's worth. As with boxer's purses the sponsorship headline figure fell short of the reality but it exceeded my previous purse.
I think my purse was good money but a sign of the times. This was 1987 and the year of the Lawson boom. House prices were rocketing but I was still reluctant to move upwards until the money was in the bank. It was probably costing me thousands being left behind on the property ladder by remaining in the present house. But I wanted to be sure that I could afford a bigger house both in the short and long term. An election was

approaching but it did not mean a lot to me in the sense that the result was another inevitable Thatcher victory. All I could do was vote.

I was too busy to notice much outside the world of Terry Marsh. In fact was there a world outside of Terry Marsh? Wherever I went I was the focus of attention. Whatever I said seemed to be either quoted in a newspaper or broadcast on a radio station, be it a national or local. Cars were always there to pick me up or drop me off. Invitations to events and dinners were plentiful. I was even invited to Westminster by the Basildon Constituency Conservative MP David Amess. David lived in the same neighbourhood as me in one of the bigger houses that I was aiming for. I made it clear that my attendance was not an endorsement. We had dinner at the House of Common's restaurant. I went into the Commons and sat where the Prime minister sat, I was informed by my Constituency MP that such practice was frowned upon. We then went onto the terrace overlooking the Thames, I felt like I had arrived.

I was also a guest of the sponsors of the Ever Ready Derby at Epsom. Frank and I along with his friend and business partner John Botros were taken by helicopter to the meeting to beat the traffic. I had to leave earlier than everybody else, by helicopter, as I was on nights at the fire station.

Frank was involved in many things other than boxing. He was a director of Rex Williams a PLC. He also had a project at Docklands concerning the building of an arena. He was keen for me to attend the site for a photo opportunity but I always had to decline because of fire-fighting duties. Still he was able to get Barry McGuigan down there. McGuigan had parted company with his former Manager cum Promoter Barney Eastwood and there were some recriminations. It is funny how fighters and managers appear to fall out. It would appear that Frank's sympathies were with the boxer.

Barry had recently lost his world title fight in Las Vegas to Steve Cruz, the last minute replacement was the ideal opponent. It was reported that the heat had got to him; it was the same for both fighters. I thought it was bad tactics, but in defence of McGuigan he only knew how to fight one way. He could not adapt. He would have made great soldier but a lousy General.

My opponent was to be a Japanese fighter Akio Kameda. He had suffered a six round stoppage against former champion Aaron Pryor but not before putting Pryor on the floor. At the first press conference I had primed a couple of journalists to ask particular questions. One of which was, "How much is Terry getting for this fight?"
Frank brushed the question aside. I interjected "Tell 'em Frank I'm not afraid of the tax man. I'm getting £147,666 is that right Frank?"
Frank nodded sheepishly. Ernie later alleged that Mister Warren was not a happy bunny.
I was due a medical before the fight and as usual booked an appointment with my GP. But on successive occasions I was called to a press conference – tickets were not going well. I had to cancel the medical appointments. Eventually a medical was arranged with a doctor in Harley Street. Numerous questions were asked one of which was have you ever had any blackouts or fits. I answered no. It was no different to any other medical. I also signed the bottom of the medical giving the boxing authorities permission to contact my GP – they never. Several days before the fight I mentioned to Frank that I had not seen the contract for the fight. It was pretty radical stuff, as I had not seen a contract for any fight that I had been involved in. Frank needed a reminder before the contract was forthcoming. I noted the signature read Ernie Fossey. The signature I did not recognise as Ernie's. I sought Ernie's confirmation of the signature but he equivocated. I'm sure there was an innocent explanation for what appeared to me as strange. After all, these two men, who played such a big part in my boxing career, were both frank and earnest.
The final press conference had a surprise guest in Hector 'Macho' Camacho. He was a big name in boxing and a big draw. He was flamboyant, flash and could box a bit. The American based Puerto Rican was the former undefeated WBC lightweight champion. Camacho was moving up to light-welter and looking for a title. A fight between him and myself was being touted. Of course, subject to retaining my title and getting my mandatory defence out of the way. Although, I reckoned that the mandatory challenger could be bought off - everyone has a price. I had heard

of fighters being paid to step aside.
It was a fight that I would have prolonged my career for. It was the opponent I was looking for, a name. He wanted to fight me only because I had a title. I wanted to fight him because of who he was. It turned out to be a distraction as I was now thinking about this potentially big money fight. I don't know what was the bigger motivation, the money or the fighter. It was probably the fighter but the consequence of a fight with such a name would lead to a massive purse. It was the conviction that drove me to want to fight a name but the purse was welcomed and expedient. When conviction and expediency run together it can be a powerful mix.
Another fighter that would have had the desired effect was fellow countryman Lloyd Honeyghan. Lloyd had won his fight against the undisputed welterweight champion Don Curry and was highly regarded. Lloyd was a more complete fighter than me and had competed and won against the best. He was regarded as bigger, stronger and better than me, which he was, but I felt that I could nullify him and master him tactically. Still these two desired opponents were conditional on remaining the champion.
The week prior to the fight Kelly had to attend hospital to have her tonsils removed. Jacqui and I were informed by the Doctor, on bringing her home that she had to stay indoors for a couple of days. The first day, Saturday, entailed me flying up to Bradford for a fete that involved Gratton the Catalogue Company. I had been introduced to the company and it's then boss David Jones by Connie Donavan.
On my return I came home to an empty house. In view of what the Doctor had instructed, concerning Kelly, I was a little put out. It was a couple of hours before Jacqui arrived with Kelly. Kelly was clothed in just a vest and knickers while Jacqui was either pissed, stoned or both. My concern was for Kelly. I had to go to the gym the next morning to monitor my weight. The fight was days away. Not being sure about Jacqui's state I contacted Mum on the cordless phone and asked if Kelly could stay with her that night not letting on about the reasons.
I neglected to disconnect the phone and Mum could hear Jacqui going into one. Listening to Jacqui's ranting introduced Mum to a different side of her daughter-in-law. She had a very spiteful

tongue. I had tried to hide this side of her from my family. She later stormed out the house with Kelly still not fully dressed. Upon realising her departure I rushed out in pursuit but as I looked left and right there was no sign of either of them.
There was a genuine worry about Kelly. There was concern about her being out, although mid summer, underdressed so shortly after coming out of the hospital and against Doctors orders. Also her Mum was intoxicated. I decided I had to get the police involved and went down to the station to report Kelly missing. After a few hours Jacqui phoned. She spoke to one of the coppers who was now at the house. They established that Kelly was okay. She returned home the next day. I discovered she stayed at a house about 4 miles away in Pitsea. This was not the best preparation for a World title defence. Although it helped take my mind away from the food I had to refrain from. Food was always an annoying temptation the days prior to a fight.
Frank acknowledged that I wanted this to be my last fight while he wanted me to continue fighting. However, he said, he'd respect my decision if that is what I want. Come my time things did not get off to a very good start. Before the proceedings the National Anthem was played. I wish I had been consulted I would have vetoed it. I was not going to be standing to attention. I jogged on the spot while the anthem was played. "God save our gracious Queen. Long live our noble Queen. God save our queen. Send her victorious, Happy and glorious long to reign over us God save our Queen." What a load of crap. As the anthems were doing their bit I looked around the venue and noticed many empty seats. Despite being a world champion I still could not pack them in. I reckon Frank, if he could put the clock back, would have chosen a re-run of the circus tent in Basildon for the defence. However, another factor affecting the gate was probably it being broadcast live on ITV.
It went well for the first couple of rounds then the heads clashed. I think it hurt him more than it hurt me but I was the one who got the cut eye. It was bad. I knew that the injury could not last the remaining 12 rounds as did everybody else in the hall and the millions watching from their lounges. I just had to fight every round as if it were the last. I'd been there before of course but the last time I was a challenger. I now had more to lose, the

title as well as my unbeaten record. Defeat would also have meant that it would definitely not be my last fight. As I had said before with no unbeaten record to protect there was no reason to stop fighting and earning. It looked as if there was to be no happy ending. I tried hard to repeat the punch that had found Joe Manley's chin but failed miserably.
I was under the impression that should an accidental injury occur, that requires the intervention of the referee, prior to the end of the sixth round, the points, up to the intervention, would be totalled up and the decision awarded to the fighter ahead at that time. I still don't know if it was a misapprehension on my part but it had resulted in the belief that it was the deadline.
I could afford to be reckless with the injury until the seventh round providing I was ahead on points. I tried so hard to nail him probably too hard. Come the sixth I thought I'd try something different against the man who had put Aaron Pryor on the floor. I stood close to him raised my elbows exposing my stomach and ribs and invited him to take a shot. He took two. I smiled but inside was hurting. I made the invitation to him again he accepted with another two punches. I felt a rib give, but I continued to smile. It was meant to be a trade off - he breaks my bones while I break his heart. It did not work we both survived to hear the bell at the end of the sixth. I returned to my corner reconciled to an eventual defeat. Ernie worked frantically on the cut to stem the flow of blood but, I knew, it would only last momentarily once I came out fighting.
I was too preoccupied with my own plight to pay attention to what was going on in the opposite corner. My challenger had faltered as he approached his stool and was in a fatigued condition. The ringside doctor Adrian Whiteson stated he could not continue. Sitting on your stool is no way to win a fight. I was deprived of that moment of conquest. But at that stage I was happy to take victory in any shape or form. It was an inconclusive ending and did not go down too well with the television viewers. The end of round six was time for a commercial break and when it was time to go back live to the Albert Hall the fight was over. The ending was messy and untidy and not a good time to announce retirement. Another reason was Hector Camacho. He had been at the ringside and was now in

the ring grabbing my belt and feigning a tug of war.
My position now was that I was effectively retired. Only the right fight could get me back. I still kept in trim but this was through habit and liking the feeling of being fit. The difference now was that when the training or running started to hurt I could stop. I was also playing football regularly with the TV Entertainers XI and the games were the highlight of my week. I've got to add I was a crap player.
It was about a couple of weeks before I collected the purse money. I went to Frank's office and received a cheque with the accompanying invoice. The format was the same as before in the sense that there was the purse then the deductions. Frank would take his managerial percentage. The contract we had signed entitled him to 25% of the purse but the maximum was seldom charged. On this occasion it was expected. Other deductions were for the trainer Ernie, whom I presumed Frank passed the money onto. Then there was the expense incurred, like medicals and sparring partners. The difference with this payment, compared with previous invoices, was that the VAT had not been added to my purse. It included the VAT, as was the case previously on both the managerial deduction and training deduction but for the first, time since it became relevant, the VAT was not added to the purse.
On pointing this out Frank suggested that I send him a VAT invoice. I believed that I handed one in the next day to his secretary but it was later said that it was not received. I can only conclude that I had foolishly given it to someone who was masquerading as Frank's Secretary; a consequence of taking too many punches to the head – perhaps it was a good time to retire. It was not really an issue for me in the sense that I would only have to send it onto the HM Customs and Excise. What I did not know was that the HM Customs still expected me to pay the VAT whether or not I received it. It amounted to £22,000.05 and payment was not forthcoming. Knowing that still would not have bothered me, I would only pass it on when I received it. I live by my own rules
On one of my days off Jacqui and I went for a stroll down the town centre with Kelly. We stopped and had a brunch in a department store. We were chatting away when I began to feel a

bit light headed. It was similar to the occasion in the car. I managed to overcome that and I thought I would do the same this time. My indifferent bladder brought me back to consciousness. I could not get out of the store quick enough. It was a combination of embarrassment and wet denims.

I now realised I had a problem and went to the doctors at the first opportunity. He suggested that I should see a colleague of his who was a neurosurgeon. I had a full diary and it was difficult to make a mutually convenient time. As the days went by so did my urgency and it withered.

Life went on. The invitations continued to arrive. They were easier to accommodate because I did not have the distraction of training and the need for early nights. Back at work I was due to go on a HGV3 driving course. On completion and passing I would be behind the wheel of the appliances. An HGV licence was a requirement and so at the last minute I rushed to get one. A medical was required so I made an appointment with the GP. He informed me that, because of my history of passing out I would have to see a specialist before he could pass me fit to drive. Because of my urgency to get the licence, as the course was days away, I saw the Neurologist the next day. Mum came along, not out of concern, it got her out the house and she enjoyed going out for the ride.

I met the specialist and told him the history and he made the diagnosis of epilepsy form attacks. Tests were arranged but the diagnosis was not dependent on the test. The tests would either support the diagnosis or be inconclusive. I was told that I should not drive and was given a prescription for tablets that I should take every day. My only concern was with regard to the fire fighting. The boxing side of things was not an issue. It was clear that the touted Camacho fight never progressed beyond rhetoric. Had Camacho been my next opponent then boxing would have been an issue. I would have taken the fight.

The fire fighting involved bigger dilemmas. Working in a team meant being a potential liability to colleagues. The situation I could find myself in may be difficult to extricate oneself from. How could I now retire, which was always the likelihood, in the manner that I would have liked? Now retirement would be because I had to, not because I chose to. I needed time to think it through. Despite being told not to drive I drove home from the hospital. Mum had got chatting to a young mother from Romford and I offered her a lift. Following her consultation she had been told that she only had a year left of her life. She was a mother with young children. Her presence helped put matters into perspective.

The diagnosis itself was not a problem. It was the restrictions and limitations that others would now impose upon me. Driving was not an issue for me. I did not regard myself as a danger either to myself and more importantly anybody else. There were early warning signals, which I could now recognise and therefore take preventative measures.

It was not a sad period in my life. Neither did I see it as a crisis. I just did not know how to play the next move. I booked in sick from work and pondered the options. I now had a hundred grand in the bank but knew that without another regular source of income it would diminish either in the short or medium term. It was not as if I could go into another career. I thought there might be opportunities in the media, but it was a transient environment. There was also talk about being a co-commentator for boxing matches with Thames television. Yet, it was all ifs and buts.

If the truth was known I, probably like everybody else in a similar position, got seduced into television. We are there as guests on the programmes and help sell the show. You begin to believe you make the show what it is. The presenter is invariably obsequious which gives you a feeling of superiority and it does not take much imagination to fancy your chances of doing their job.

I went to Frank's offices a week or so later. I asked the secretary about the VAT money due, "Oh Terry I'm really busy at the moment." I had a chat with Ernie in his office that was situated in the basement of the building. I told him about the epilepsy diagnosis and he was understandably surprised. He had been advising me to turn it in anyway. For Ernie the diagnosis was not an issue regarding retirement. Ernie had never shared a corner with me knowing that I 'suffered' from epilepsy. He had been in my corner when I had busted ribs and hands and colds, but so what? This is professional boxing. Frank and I were both

due to attend a meeting at Thames Television's offices that was a short walk from his office.
Frank later went on record to solemnly state to the best of his knowledge and belief, that we did not meet that day in his office, having met up at the Thames' offices, and I did not mention to him on that, or any other occasion that I had seen a doctor who had diagnosed epilepsy.
The meeting was about the forthcoming weekly boxing show 'Seconds out' featuring Frank Warren promotions. It involved some other independent networks that included Anglia and HTV and one or two others. I was to be the co-commentator and a press conference was arranged for the following week. I found it an interesting meeting, it indicated to me how far Frank had travelled from the day we met some six years earlier when he had ambitions of being a 'licensed' boxing promoter and manager - he had arrived. He was effectively the television producer. He produced the shows that were then broadcast. What impressed me in particular was how he was pitching for Harry Mullan to be involved as the statistician. Frank believed he was the best man for the job and he only wanted the best. Harry was also the editor of the 'Boxing News' magazine. He was a good man to have on your side. Mullan was not a man who could make things happen but in his editorial role he could cause obstruction and difficulties. He still could now that he was the statistician but it is more difficult if you are on the payroll. This is not a reflection on Frank but a test for Mullan should the time come when there are potential conflicts of interests.
I noticed also there was as strong bond between Frank and Trevor East who was the Executive Producer. I had met Trevor on several occasions but had seen him as just another face from the television side of things. I had once shared a car with him when he spoke highly of Frank. Now seeing him across a table in his Executive capacity was, for me, a further indication of how far Frank had come. Alongside this was Frank's arena that was being built in Docklands and his involvement in a PLC. It certainly seemed that it was all coming together for him.
For me it was coming apart. There was no good way out. It was more a case of choosing the least bad scenario. Time was ticking away and I could not stay sick off work forever, eventually

questions would be asked. Questions were asked but not about what I expected, or from whom I expected. The knock on the door was a Sun reporter, Ruki Saiid, and her accompanying photographer, "Is it right your wife has left you?"
If only it was true was my thought, "No Comment." was my reply.
They seemed pretty sure of their story. I refused to confirm or deny their questions, which seemed to encourage them to believe their information was true. The more convinced they were of the accuracy of their information the more persistent they became.
"We're going to print but thought you would like to put your side of the story."
I thought print and be dammed. I'll sue them. I was teasing them. After all, it was not long after Geoffrey Archer had received £500,000 from the Daily Star for an alleged libel. Despite the truth of the Daily Star's story they were unable to prove it and so they lost. That case like many before was about proof not truth.
The journalists would not leave until they had seen Mrs Marsh. Jacqui was not coming out so we were 'door stepped'. After an hour or so the two Sun people would appear again and that was the pattern of the day. The no show of Jacqui was the confirmation they needed to back up their story. "We're going to print the story anyway."
Perhaps, I should have let them go ahead with it but instead yielded, "Okay if you want a story I've got one but you'll have to pay for it."
Had it been any other paper I would have told them the story there and then but the Sun would have to pay. Fifty grand was the figure I had in mind. I wasn't giving any information until we reached some understanding. A representative would be paying me a visit when money would be discussed. Shortly before the meeting I had read or heard a story about Joan Collins asking for a payment for many thousands to appear on a German television programme and the programme makers refused to pay. I figured, in view of Miss Collins place in the celebrity pecking order, my demand for fifty grand was excessive. It was not quite comparing like with like but it downsized my valuation of the story. When Nick Ferrari the Sun

representative called at my house a letter was produced which guaranteed the confidentiality of the story subject to agreement of a price that I lowered to twenty-five grand. It was accepted and a deal was done.
A number of days later at the Thames Television buildings at Tottenham Court Road a press conference had been arranged by ITV. Frank was there and various photos were taken of him and I. I mentioned that I had been door stepped by the Sun but did not elaborate. I was asked numerous questions about my new 'career' but I was not able to give much information not having seen or signed a contract. I did not know how much I was getting if anything. Although the money was not really an issue it was all about getting a foot in the door.
The Sun journalist whom was assigned the task of interviewing me was Neil Wallis. He explained that nobody should know about the story, as it would spoil the exclusive. The story was planned for the following Monday and Jacqui, Kelly and I were to stay at a secret location. I was already committed to dinner at Ernie's on the Saturday. Having messed around Pat, Ernie's wife, several times with cancellations I was determined it was not going to happen again. I was having lunch with Ernie and Pat no matter what. I also had a football match on the Sunday afternoon, which was also non-negotiable. The week prior I had to do some filming which would be used for the promotion of the exclusive. It only took a few minutes or so. 'Why I will never box again', or some bland lines like that. My paymasters wanted fight footage of me, which I did not have, either rights to or claims to. I explained that was the property of the Promoter Frank Warren. I left that with them.
Later in the week I got a phone call from Frank's secretary. I was hoping that she had phoned to say that she remembered receiving the VAT invoice. She said Frank wanted to see me at Ernie's. Frank's eagerness to see me was out of character. I concluded that the Sun had alerted him with the enquiries about my fight footage. After all I had only mentioned to him the previous week that I was being door stepped by them. Neil Wallis was keen that I should not meet him but I thought otherwise. It was only fair to tell him about the agreement with the newspaper. I once again put off the lunch with Ernie and Pat

to the Sunday and also the meet with Frank. Pat was really being messed about but I did not see it that way. I thought turning up inconveniently was better than not turning up at all. Jacqui, Kelly and I arrived early. The earlier I arrived the earlier we could leave so I could play the football match before being whisked away to the 'secret location'

After a delicious lunch Frank arrived holding an executive style brief case. He opened it and produced what I recognised as the standard British Boxing Board of Control Promoter Contract. I looked at it and focussed on the parts that are later inserted. I read the opponent *'Frankie Warren USA'*, the date *'TBA'* and the purse *'$250,000'*. Frank was wearing his promotional hat. It was the eve of the deadline for purse bids. He did not want this fight to go to purse offers. I felt that was a breach of the Boxer/Manager contract, in the sense that it was the duty of the manager to get the best possible deal. That was only possible by considering all offers. I felt let down. It was an academic exercise but Frank had his own interest before mine. That is perfectly human and understandable for a promoter but not for my manager. I was only too pleased to sign the contract knowing it to be dubious anyway. I had already signed one contract for a world title and that proved not to be worth the paper it was written on. Just to put a few touches to it I haggled about the exchange rate. My signature on the paper off he went. He seemed in a hurry. No need for purse offers now, he's got the fighter signed up.

I did not tell him about the Sun Exclusive but knew he would find out that evening if he was watching Independent television. I made the second half of the game. Neil Wallis was there for the final whistle. He drove Jacqui, Kelly and I to the secret location - a hotel in Bournemouth.

When I read 'my' story I got as far as the fifth paragraph and found it difficult to come to terms with what I was reading. I began to scan the script focussing on what I saw as bad parts - most of it. There were quotes in there that I did not recognise. The syntax was wrong. Anyone who knew me could recognise it and did. I felt like I should get up and walk out but they had the story and I did not have the money. I liked Neil Wallis but I don't think he did me any favours but probably that was what I

was getting paid for. It presented me as a person who was devastated, in despair and desperate.
The secret location served the intended purposes of keeping the subject of the story away from other newspapers thus diminishing their rival's chance of spoiling the so-called exclusive. It also had the unintended consequence of sheltering me from the press backlash. The main focus of attention was Frank Warren. He was quoted as saying in one paper, "I've got a contract here I don't understand it." He felt betrayed and let down. I knew the feeling.
In the tussle for publicity it was an interesting conflict. The Sun versus the rest or was it Marsh versus Warren? The Marsh story was about me and there was no mention of Frank Warren. The Frank Warren story was about what he thought about Terry Marsh. The words attributed to him caused me a lot of damage. I could not relate to much of what was allegedly said. Perhaps, like me he also had been misquoted. Things were beginning to go against me. Terry Marsh the image had been badly damaged thanks to accounts that I did not recognise and other misrepresentations by the Sun. At least the latter paid for the privilege.
A big talking point generally was how I was able to go undetected despite all the 'stringent' medical examinations by the boxing authorities. I did not go undetected as such. I had seen my doctor after two encounters and he, aware of my history, described it as flaking out.
There was also the discussion that it was boxing related. It gave reason for the anti-boxing brigade to be trooped out. I then found myself accused of letting the sport down by Harry Mullan the Editor of Boxing News. I could not believe what I was either reading or hearing. So what? It can only harm me. There was such a stink of hypocrisy from the boxing world. Eager to know how I could have escaped the checks and balances. In boxing the only checks and balances the authorities are concerned with have the prefix 'bank'. The medical checks were basic while the concern about boxers' health I found highly amusing.
I have seen boxers come out of retirement and fight with barely a week of training. The week's training was not designed to get them fit. They would get no benefit from it for a fight seven days

hence. The aim was to get down to the specified weight. The Board would do nothing. They pretended they were unaware or turned a blind eye.
While at the hotel John Botros, a friend of Frank Warren, contacted me by phone on behalf of Frank. Where he got the number from and why Frank could not have made the call I don't know. A meeting was arranged with Frank and me at a hotel in London. We could not agree on how the events unfolded. I gave him the benefit of the doubt and did not respond publicly with my version. Neil Wallis came along and later joined us. He asked Frank some pointed questions as a result of matters that I had alleged. Frank was on the back foot and Neil was going to run with the story. I retracted my account having been won over by Frank. Neil was pissed off with me but I still had £22,000.05 VAT money to get from Mr Warren. It was already two months overdue.
I also met up with my brother John at the hotel. He informed me that the television cameras were waiting outside. I wanted to avoid them, as that was part of the agreement with the Sun. When they saw me leave they followed and I ran off. They managed to get it on film. I looked like a fugitive with something to hide. It did not look good when it was broadcast on the television that night. What a brilliant way to end a career. What really riled me more than anything else was that it was portrayed that I retired because I was suffering from epilepsy - totally untrue. I retired because I wanted to.

CHAPTER SIXTEEN
SANTA SACKED

I later met up again with Connie Donovan who told me to put an invoice into the Sun for forty grand. They paid promptly and included the additional VAT. I was still waiting for the VAT payment from Frank Warren and fired off a solicitor's letter. His solicitor came back saying that they had not received an invoice and that it was being withheld in lieu of monies due to him from money I had made from Natural Vitality and the Sun. Of which they claimed an entitlement of twenty-five percent. My view was that he had received over £25,000 from Natural Vitality for the sponsorship of my final fight. A sponsorship initiated by me. The agreement between the two protagonists included the clause that Natural Vitality would deal with me separately. As for a demand for a cut of the proceeds from the Sun; what can I say? Had I considered he had earned it or deserved it then I would have been more than happy for him to have a percentage of what was a 'personal tragedy'

I no longer had a secure job to fall back on. I returned to work and was placed on light duties. That meant office work, at the Fire Brigade headquarters until a decision regarding my future was made. I did not have to wait long – not fit for duty. I made initial enquiries through the Fire Brigades Union about appealing against the decision but the best they could suggest was two years special duties then a review. No way I thought.

I realised that unless I could make the money, I had, work for me then it would be a matter of time before it diminished. Taking bets had generally been a profitable exercise and with my earlier experience and with John's current experience, bookmaking seemed to be the answer.

We bought a shop in Romford. It was not a good business but it gave us a base from which to work from. It was not that long before we acquired another shop. John turned his job in as a betting office manager as did Billy when the second shop was acquired. The idea was to build up a chain of shops and then sell out to one of the bigger bookmakers. The shops produced a steady income but things were not happening fast enough for me.

I was still fairly high profile and I remember being invited to the Boxing writers' lunch. I was presented with a members' tie in recognition of my world title triumph. I said a few words of thanks and answered questions put to me. Two in particular caused some controversy when my answers were subsequently reported: What do you think of the idea of pensions for boxers?' and 'What changes if any would you like to see in Boxing?'
On the first question I emphasised the point that you can only get out of a pension what you put in. I made the point that in my first four years as a professional, I had only made £10,000. I emphasised that this was not a complaint, but a reality of boxing and I was not the exception to the rule. I was talking net they were thinking gross. It was a distinction that I did not really need to emphasize in the context of pensions.
Addressing the second question, I expressed the view that the then existing standard contract between the manager and boxer should be amended in favour of the boxer. I had my friend Shoey very much in mind. As it was then, taking the agreement to its letter, fighters were like slaves to the manager. I said, "The boxer could not pick his nose without the manager's permission." I made the point that options to extend the contract should not be allowed and questioned the wisdom of allowing managers to double up as promoters. I considered the conflict of interest too great. I made the point that this was a general observation about the sport and I was critical of the structure rather than individuals.
Colin Hart of the Sun wrote an article regarding the £10,000 in my first four years. Frank Warren issued a writ against the Sun claiming libel. There could be no dispute on my figures but the Sun made a settlement without contacting me.
Frank had also taken exception to my comments concerning the

manager's contract. I presume they were reported or relayed to him. He invited Harry Mullan the Boxing News editor and the 'Seconds Out' statistician to his office to go through the invoices that I had signed for payments received from Frank. An article was then printed penned by Harry Mullan.
It was on the front page of that week's edition of the Boxing News with the headline 'Slavery'. He referred to my comments at the Boxing Writers dinner although he was not there. Perhaps he was not a boxing writer. Nothing in his latest article suggested that he was. It was a million miles from being an objective article. To be fair when I made my response it was printed comprehensively. I produced my own figures to back up my statement of £10,000 in the first four years. It clearly differed. Part of the difference came from when the start date began. My start date began a month or so before my first fight, as I had to train for the fight and incur expenses in the process such as medicals, fares and equipment. Mullan put the start date as the day of the first fight. The end date therefore also differed. Frank had secured a fight in the four-year period, the European Title, and Mullan credited the subsequent payment within that period – creative accountancy.
The purses for all my other fights were also brought into the reckoning. It became an issue about whether or not I was appropriately paid. I had no issue with this. I was satisfied with what I had received, at that time. However, Frank was not the philanthropist Mullan was trying to paint.
What was interesting about Mullan's article was the presentation of purses. In the so-called initial four-year period, because of the relatively small amounts, VAT registration was not a requirement. VAT only arose after I became the European Champion. In Mullan's article the VAT on my purses was always included whereas when the manager's and trainer's fee was printed the VAT had been subtracted making the percentage deduction appear less than the reality. The presentation of the figures seriously compromised the Editor's integrity.
It was no slight on Warren. He only invited the Boxing News' editor to his office and presented him with documents. It was the Editor who was deceitful. Maybe he wanted to ingratiate himself towards Warren. Mullan claimed to have had sight of all the

invoices signed by me. No mention was made of the invoice signed 'M Mouse'. He quoted the correct purse, which leads me to think he saw the signature but chose to ignore it.
My comments concerning the manager/boxer contract and the conflict of interest of mangers *cum* promoters was also touched upon. Mullan wrote suggesting, that I was claiming unscrupulous managers exploited boxers. It seemed Frank Warren took it personally. When I made the comments I never mentioned Frank Warren and made the point that it was a general observation. In fact, I received a letter from the Boxing Writers' Secretary Frank Butler saying, "It was good to hear so much common sense being spoken." Mullan criticised me for making such remarks. Interesting enough a few years later a precedent was set by the High Court decision in a case involving boxer Michael Watson and Mickey Duff. The Court deemed that Duff's dual role as Watson's Promoter and Manager was a restraint of trade, as it denied the boxer's right to have someone to negotiate on their behalf. Mr Duff could hardly negotiate with himself said the Judge, Mister Justice Scott. "Every pound received by Mr Watson by way of purse or television receipts would reduce the Promoter's net receipts." I never got a apology from Mullan.
Frank and I had our differences regarding my retirement but the gap between us had now widened. He was allowed to respond to my letter and duly did. It was now about questioning my integrity. At that stage I had not made any public statements that could be potentially embarrassing for him but he was making the point and asking the question, how can I be believed? I did not think I was saying anything too contentious; I was keeping my powder dry. I replied, again addressing the numerous points he made in his letter. It was becoming a bit of a saga. On the matters of integrity I challenged him to a lie detector test. The editor's footnote at the end of my letter said that he would allow Frank Warren a response and a line would then be drawn under the matter.
Frank responded and made his points. He declined the lie detector test. The offer is still open. He made the observation 'how can machines be trusted. Machines had tested his [my] brain in various medicals and they had failed to highlight the

epilepsy. How can they be trusted?' What did he mean? Was he under the impression that epilepsy in all its forms would show on brain scans? Such an interpretation would leave one to believe that any form of epilepsy would be detected by such scans. Any, positively scanned boxer claiming epilepsy must be a liar and can't be believed.

The following week a few letters were published from the readers. The headline on the letter's page read 'Warren wins on points' I assume Harry Mullan was the arbiter. Maybe I'm a sore loser but I felt I was robbed of the decision.

The only occasions Frank Warren and I were to share the same arena again was when I was doing the commentating for the boxing. They were always his promotions. After three or four I still had not been paid so I sent some invoices into Thames Television for services rendered. I was asked by Thames to attend a meeting. They pointed out that they could not pay the invoices. They had an arrangement with Frank Warren and the payments were made to a company designated by him. There was a show due in Wales a day or so later and they said, Frank did not want me attending the shows and that they would not be able to use me any more. I asked for a letter to this effect and was informed one would be forthcoming. I did receive a letter from Frank Warren informing me that I would not be allowed entrance to any of his promotions but the letter from Thames did not arrive. I figured since they were my 'employers' I should show up; I wanted my presence recorded. I made my way to Wales accompanied by a Sun reporter posing as my lawyer. It was only a few shopping days before Christmas and despite Frank's letter I thought entry would not be a problem. I purchased my ticket but there was no peace or goodwill when I went to enter the arena. I was stopped by two of Warren's 'employees'. One was Leslie McCarthy. Leslie had always been a figure in the Warren promotions. His colleague I only knew as Bob, "You're not allowed in Tel."

I retreated with the Sun reporter in tow and back to the car for plan B. When a guy dressed as Santa Claus entered the building he was cheered and made most welcome. He showed his ticket before entering the main arena. He even went up to the ringside where Barry McGuigan was preparing for his debut on the boxing show as the new co-commentator. Barry was happy to oblige Santa with a photo and he and Santa posed accordingly. Santa then lowered his hood and discarded his beard to reveal yours truly. It was time for the Sun photographer and I to leave. As we approached the exit Leslie McCarthy and his colleague grabbed the camera. I went to the photographer's aid and we got involved in a very undignified tug of war. It was a question of upping the ante or giving up the fight I chose the latter. I would have been much happier choosing the former. They got the camera and removed the film.

That was certainly the finish of boxing, no more fighting, and no more commentating. I could handle the no more fighting. That was a decision I made but I did not like the idea of being dumped from the commentating. Particularly without getting paid. A letter was, in fact, delivered by messenger from Thames on the day of the Wales show but had been posted to the house next door. It informed me that they would honour the contract and pay the amount due in full. It was made payable to a company called Sports Network. I understand my former manager had a connection with this company but I had no such arrangement – highly irregular. A misappropriation of funds I thought. The money was not forwarded.

It was now winter and a relatively quite period for horseracing. However, Saturdays were always good days, it being the busiest day of the week. The turnover would be as much as the preceding five days combined. There was an intensity about it that would give me a buzz. The betting shops were very much a family business. Dad worked the board marking up the prices. Billy would run one shop and John the other. I was something of a floater. Every thing would be working steady under John's capable charge until I appeared with all my suggestions. I think John preferred it when I wasn't there. I had a disruptive influence.

John ran the show; I played at it. I was also playing the celebrity getting my picture in the papers. It didn't put any money in the pocket. It gave an impression of success but in fact it was the opposite. To make news you have to be original or do the unexpected or be different. So once you were in the paper for

something, the next time you need to make the news you have to be a little bolder until it goes to extremes and then you are no longer taken seriously. It was as if there was a tacit agreement between the press and us ‘celebs’. I had to be seen at all the 'right' places. I was there because it could lead to something. It seldom did but the fact you were there meant that you were still in existence - available for work. The showbiz events were glorified job centres for celebrities.
I did get work, guest appearances, on quiz programmes the likes of Blankety Blank and the occasional radio commentary on forthcoming fights. I made the prediction that Joe Bugner would beat Frank Bruno. I assumed Bugner would be fitter than he actually was. He wasn't and he lost. I vowed that should Bruno win I'd jump off Tower Bridge into the Thames. It helped to promote a premium rate phone line that I had an interest in. Bylaws prevented me from jumping from the bridge but I took a leap into the filthy river, photographed by a newspaper with which I was becoming synonymous.
The next day Frank Bruno was on the back page I was on the front wearing a tee-shirt displaying Natural Vitality. It must have been a bad news day. I tried after dinner speaking. I got involved in a Company called Amraf. I came across with my side of the deal they failed to meet their end of the bargain. They used my name and influence then avoided me.
I think I was going through a post celebrity traumatic stress disorder. I wasn't getting the same deference I had as champion. I was angry. Not at what was happening then but what had happened in the past with all those sycophants. This was the reality. Now I knew how the Emperor was allowed to parade in his birthday suit and I learnt how wise I wasn’t. I wanted to put the clock back and do things differently. I wanted that platform I once had. I still had things to say.
I received a phone call from Big Jon Robinson. Jon I had known from my amateur days when he was a reporter on the Hackney Gazette. He had seen me progress from a skinny 11 year old to a skinny 29 year old. He’d also worked with Frank Warren and was involved with the promotions and ticket sales before becoming the British representative of the IBF. Jon wondered whether I would like to get involved in some promoting with

Ambrose Mendy and Frank Maloney. It sounded to me like a re-unification of former Frank Warren associates. Why not? I thought if nothing else it would ruffle a few feathers. I did not know much about the finer details but what the hell. Tim Witherspoon was to fight in London. That was all I knew.
A press conference was held at the Tower Hotel next to the Tower of London. Maloney and I were present but Ambrose Mendy was missing. Ambrose was an integral part of the trio. His absence was a problem. I had no yet sat down with either Frank Maloney or Ambrose to talk about the finer details of what I was getting involved in. I was parachuted into this with a quick brief and played it by ear.
The boxing scribes of Fleet Street had gathered and they wanted their story. We kicked off with half a story. We had persuaded Tim Witherspoon to fight in Britain but the finer details were unknown. It was going to be met with scepticism by the hacks. Witherspoon was a former World Champion who defeated Frank Bruno in Bruno's first world title attempt a few years earlier. He was then still a better fighter than Bruno and this outfit of Maloney, Mendy and Marsh were going to promote Witherspoon in their first show.
It is difficult for any promotion to be a financial success without the assistance of television. Only with money generated from television can big names be attracted. To make a profit from the show on just the gate money is very difficult. We had not secured any television for the proposed contest nor sponsorship. The aim was to film the fight and then sell the rights to broadcasting companies around the World.
This was the role to be played by Ambrose. It was he and his brother Louis's company The World Sports Corporation (WSC) that was going to market and sell the rights of the fight. Maloney and I were to be the promoters. Mr Maloney already had a licence in his own right but this was going to be a Marsh, Maloney joint promotion under the WSC banner. Now that Tim had arrived it was time for another press conference. Now we had to be taken seriously by the boxing hacks. I went to see two brothers Panay and Gill the owners of the Phoenix Apollo, a restaurant I had frequented previously. I ran the idea around them about holding a press conference at their restaurant. When

I told Frank and Ambrose that I had arranged a venue for the press conference at Stratford Broadway I received some strange looks. Their caution was understandable. A Greek run restaurant in the East End was a contrast to the Tower Hotel and its prestigious location. As was the venue of York Hall in London's East End compared to Witherspoon's last visit to Britain - he topped the bill to a full house at Wembley.
On the day of the conference my two colleagues were impressed with what they saw, as was the press. The buffet was immense and appreciated by all. It was far superior to anything offered by the Tower Hotel. Unlike the Tower Hotel, it was free. From Panay and Gills perspective it was seen as an effective way of increasing awareness of the Phoenix.
The arrival of Witherspoon's Mexican opponent caused us a great deal of anxiety. In the boxing world Mexicans are seen as good fighters but they seem to diminish as you move up the weight category. He was around 5'8" and appeared to have a girth of similar proportion. We all feared the comedy of him being put beside Witherspoon, not to mention the tragedy of it all. We toyed with the idea of getting another opponent but it was too late. The guy was grotesquely fat. I don't want to be accused of body fascism but we were looking for an athlete to take on the former Heavyweight Champion of the World. After much consideration we decided we had to run with what we had, the show must go on.
The attendance was good but not great. The whole place was decked out with bouncers immaculately turned out in their suits led by Frank Maloney's brother Eugene who had been appointed head of security. The vast majority of the bouncers were 'brothers' and their smartness made them look more like a gospel choir. At the same time many of them looked like they would give Witherspoon a better fight than the official opponent. Not surprisingly there was only one winner but the Mexican showed courage and skills that belied his looks. He performed far better than many Adonis like bodies that have visited these shores. After the contest he got a standing ovation and we escaped any criticism from the punters.
Criticism did not totally avoid us. Frank Maloney and I found ourselves up in front of the British Boxing of Control. They

wanted to know what the arrangement was with Ambrose and World Sports Corporation. It was explained to us that WSC were on the posters and that they were not licence holders. They asked a few circumspect questions about WSC and Ambrose in particular. I got the impression it was Ambrose who was the fly in the ointment and I asked the members whether or not they knew something about Ambrose that Frank Maloney or I did not. Their response was that they were not there to talk about Ambrose Mendy. The issue was that WSC were on the posters and active in the promotion and that they were not licence holders.

I believed their argument to be completely fallacious. The role played by WSC was no different to that of a television company. Television companies are often active in promotions but are not licensed. Television keeps the business alive and their cash input dictates that they have a substantial role in the presentation of the promotion. That was the situation then and the trend has continued since.

We were informed our promoter's licence was to be on a temporary basis. No explanation was given for the decision. I suspect that their reasoning could not be substantiated in a court of law and thus there was this reticence on the part of the Board. In effect we were on probation. Frank and I were both annoyed at this but I in particular. Maloney, as mentioned, was already a holder of a promoter's licence from the Board. But Marsh/Maloney was not considered worthy. I interpreted this as a slight against me. We were also informed that we could no longer have Marsh Maloney in Association with WSC on our posters.

Up until then I had little dealings with the BBBofC. I just accepted their authority like many people accept Royalty. However, it made me see them in a different light. After all they were a self-appointed body. The way they impeded Frank Warren in the early stages of his promotional career suggested that they tended to the status quo. It may have been a fear of outsiders - better the devil you know. The real question was whether this conservatism was there to protect the sport of boxing or was it there to preserve their little empire? They tried to give themselves an aura of respectability by issuing 'licences'.

Despite this there was a *de-facto* legitimacy that could not be ignored. We were unhappy with the provisional licence as it made long term plans difficult. Yet we had to work within it. This was perhaps a time when discretion should have dictated a prudent approach but it was not in the nature of any of us. When we had our posters printed for our next big show they read 'Frank Maloney & Terry Marsh in conjunction with WSC proudly presents'. It was to feature John Tate from America, another former heavyweight Champion, against Noel Quarless from Liverpool.
After the show a journalist approached me, "What's it like being a promoter?"
"I don't know I'm no longer a promoter."
"What do you mean?"
"We were given a temporary licence for the show. It's over. I no longer have a licence so I am not a promoter."
"Why is that?"
"I don't know the board would not tell me."
"You must have some idea?"
"I don't know. They would not tell me, they didn't appear to be happy with Ambrose."
"Why is that?"
"I don't know. Perhaps they're racist? I don't know. It might be okay to have black fighters but not black promoters but I do not know because they would not tell me."
In the sports pages the next day reports were made, two of which I recall coming from the Mail and Today reading 'Black marks for Marsh' and 'Board Racist claims Marsh'. It was not long before I received a letter from the board asking me to appear at the next meeting on a disciplinary matter. I attended on this occasion with my solicitor John Marshall. Maloney and I had to go up there in any case to apply for another promoter's licence. The licence application dealt with, it was time to face a disciplinary hearing under the guise of bringing boxing into disrepute. Punching someone in the face is acceptable but expressing an opinion is not.
The Board expressed their concern about the alleged accusation and denied any racism. I now knew that the decision not to allow a full promoters licence was not based on racist motives. I was

getting somewhere. I was contemplating making other remarks to get further denials from the board. When the denials cease I'll know the real reasons for their actions. I stated that I had not accused the board of being racist but was quickly told by John Marshall to be quiet since he was representing me. So I sat there while he conducted my defence. He explained that I merely asked the question. Not having received a reason for being allowed only a temporary licence I was unable to give a satisfactory answer to the journalist regarding the board's decision. I was asked to speculate, 'perhaps they're racist... I don't know'.

I was asked to withdraw my allegation. I said, "It was not an allegation it was a question but in view of the boards denial that they are racist, I am happy to withdraw the question now I have the answer."

I received a reprimand. I considered any punishment a travesty. If anyone had brought boxing into disrepute then it was the board by their reticence. Their failure not to give explanations for their decision is what brings the game into disrepute. It makes matters worse when a Stipendiary magistrate, David Hopkin, acting as chair permits the session to have all the qualities of a kangaroo court.

Another matter had also been brought to the Board's attention. I had been sparring with 'licensed boxers'. It was pointed out that a licensed boxer must not box or spar another person whose licence had expired, been refused or revoked, in my case it had expired. The complaint was directed at the wrong person since it should have been directed at those who broke the regulations. I was invited by the board to apply for a licence to fight although in a somewhat limited capacity. It appeared to me again that the rules were there to protect their interest rather than the sport. The next day my punishment was reported and erroneously stated that I retracted my remarks.

I decided that I would take up the board's invitation and I approached the doctor who had made my original diagnosis of epilepsy. It had been many months since I had stopped taking the prescribed Tegretol and I was having doubts about the diagnosis. I was aware that I was challenging his professional judgement and the awkward position that put him in. I explained that I had considered the various episodes in isolation and relayed them to him accordingly. It was looking back with hindsight that the seizures had a pattern occurring short periods after major fights. I concluded that my 'epilepsy' was due to my post fight dietary indiscretions. The problem was not neurological but nutritional.

The Doctor stuck by his original diagnosis. I sought a second opinion. I made enquiries and booked an appointment with a Mister Fenwick from the Maudsley Hospital in London. I explained that I wanted to be allowed to spar and gave him the history. He concluded that I did not have epilepsy at that time and in his opinion it is unlikely that I had epilepsy when first diagnosed.

I was fit to take up my sparring practice. I then had to go to a couple of other clinics to undergo a series of tests that included a Magnetic Resonance Image (MRI). I asked Dr Fenwick to send the results to Dr Adrian Whiteson the medical consultant for the board. Whiteson was only a GP and not a Consultant in its medical sense. The MRI revealed a lesion to the brain but appeared as two-dimensional on the three dimensional MRI. The original MRI indicating a lesion was sent with the initial report. Fenwick pointed out that since the lesion had not appeared in the inferior brain scans, that the BBBofC insisted upon, perhaps it would be prudent to insist upon MRIs in the future. Another MRI scan had to be taken which gave the all clear. The first scan's output was put down to the machines sensitivity. The letter to Whiteson was in before the spring of 1989. It was not to be until 1997 that MRIs were to be used by the Board. The interim period saw the death of boxer Bradley Stone in Britain and a few others seriously injured all as a result of brain injuries. I still wonder if they were preventable and if the BBBof C were negligent?

Having got the all clear from Fenwick I thought I won't just apply for a licence for sparring but I will apply for a full licence. A twin track approach was taken. I applied to both the Board and the IBF UK. The IBF UK was affiliated to the IBF of which I was the former Light-Welterweight Champion. Big Jon Robinson a former commissioner of the IBF had set up the rival body. I had a medical and my 'epilepsy' history diagnosis was discussed.

The IBF doctor made the point about my post-fight dietary indiscretions. I was declared fit to fight and made the appropriate announcement that the fight was going ahead in Basildon two years to the day I won the World title – same time same place.
I knew I needed the licence from the Board of Control not because it was imperative but it would give a greater legitimacy to my promotion. Judging them as I have, I figured they would fear a rival domestic boxing authority and would placate me. Thinking it would be better having me in the tent pissing out... There existed various stewards but I had never sought to befriend any of them or really wanted to. So I never had their ear. My method of lobbying was through statements to journalists. Megaphone diplomacy if you like.

While John was away on holiday in South Africa I met up with Eugene Maloney. He was able to introduce me to some big punters. He was a big punter himself. We did a deal whereby he would get a considerable piece of the action. It was all on credit but Eugene had a way about him. Eugene was a featherweight at best but would scare men twice his size. Collecting was not going to be a problem. When John returned from South Africa we had a thriving phone business to complement the shops.
While all this was occurring, Mendy, Maloney and Marsh were making great progress. Ambrose teamed up with Nigel Benn who was formerly managed by Frank Warren before Nigel made a unilateral declaration of independence. Nigel joined what must have appeared as the Frank Warren 'appreciation' society. Nigel had knocked up an impressive record but wanted to fight bigger names. He was ambitious and eager and Ambrose was there to give him what he wanted. The arrival of Benn was a great boost for us. We had a fighter who could sell out a show and he duly did. We still were unable to secure a pre-fight television contract but Benn was making big noises.
When it came to getting Nigel noticed Ambrose certainly had a way. Along with Tony Shepherd, Ambrose's press agent, they were able to feed the press with numerous stories. It was easy being a boxing journalist while Ambrose was around. That blank sheet of paper they have the task of filling each day required no

innovation or inspiration. Just turn up at the World Sports Corporation press conference. Ambrose did it for them. He would build on a fact, add to it and then re-interpret.
Meanwhile Frank Warren was making representation to the IBF claiming that I was still under his contract. It was a load of bollocks. Ambrose alleged he was skint. I phoned him and arranged a meeting at his office. I thought if what Ambrose said was true, he might want to get involved. I was not getting anywhere with securing television for the fight and I figured with his contacts progress might be made. There was the other factor that having him on side would be one less obstacle. I went there under the pretence of chasing up the VAT money that was still due. I entered the building and sat in the reception area.
He had company, his brother Robert, and former gangster Uncle, Bob were there. "Watch ya," I said. They grunted back surprised that I spoke to them. I got the impression that their presence and my presence was not a coincidence. After five minutes or so I was summoned. I entered Frank's office and brought to his attention a small microphone I had in my left lapel. "For the record." It was a gesture on my part. Previous conversations between us had left us disputing their content. I kicked off, "Look there is nothing between you and I that twenty-two grand wont put right."
"There is the matter of your earnings with the Sun which I'm entitled to 25% of. I have a contract." Frank advised me.
I laughed it off, "I don't think so."
We spoke back and forth but no ground was being conceded. The conversation perhaps became more relaxed. My former manager left it with, "I'll think about it." I left thinking things were still open. "See ya." I said to the brother and uncle as I passed them. "See ya." they both responded and then reverted to type trying to suck the words back in as if they had been caught unawares and the words had come out involuntary.

CHAPTER SEVENTEEN
SECONDS OUT

When I got a phone call, the next day, from Thames Sport to appear on their Midweek Sport Special programme I couldn't help but feel my recent visit to Mr Warren and the invitation was more than a coincidence. They wanted to talk about my forthcoming promotion. It would probably help pad out the programme for that evening. The main boxing event was highly likely to be short. It was a British Title fight and the challenger was my mate Shoey. It was only two weeks earlier that he had the plaster removed having broken his leg. He had travelled to meet me the previous week and explained his plight.
On a previous occasion when he was going to take a fight and was not fit I paid him his purse, a thousand pounds, to withdraw. At that stage, I figured, he could not afford a defeat. It was a fight I was supposed to be commentating on in the Seconds Out programme. I was unable to help him financially this time. It was a good purse £5000. He needed the money so took the fight hoping he might get lucky with a punch in the early rounds. He never did, he finished the fight on the floor. Shoey was Liverpool based and his manager was based in London and would not have been aware of Shoey's leg injury and apparent lack of fitness.
My interview was pre-recorded to be broadcast on the same 'Midweek Sport Special' programme later that night. Nick Owen interviewed me. In fact very little was mentioned of my forthcoming promotion. Nick Owen grilled me regarding my claim of not having epilepsy some eighteen months after my disclosure of the condition. Owen said, “It is to say the least, fishy.”
He was right. It did have that appearance. Had I disputed the

original diagnosis contemporaneously then I suspect people would have had more sympathy with my situation. Had I wanted to continue boxing then I probably would have sought a second opinion at the outset. I had removed the microphone when Nick, receiving instructions through his earpiece, said he had a few more questions, which they wanted to ask.
"Why did you not tell your Manager that you had epilepsy when you signed the contract to fight?" Now I was beginning to think that this interview was also to say the least, fishy. I was being well and truly stitched up. However, one of the traits that had served me so well in my Marine training, went some way to destroying my credibility. Cheerfulness in adversity had me smirking and grinning throughout the interview.
I was deliberately evasive with some of my answers because I had a basic understanding of the law of libel. As far as I was concerned it was not a case of telling the whole truth but rather a case of telling what one could prove. The truth may prevail in the long term but it's proof that matters in the short term.
However, my evasiveness proved inadequate: a little knowledge is a dangerous thing. One of Frank's responses was, "If he said that and he said that to you, I'll issue a Writ in the morning."
Unbeknown to me, Frank Warren was in the studio waiting to put his point of view and BBBofC Doctor, Adrian Whiteson, was also going to make an input. Why we couldn't have a three-way discussion I don't know. The subsequent edited broadcast was presented in such a fashion. Warren and Doctor Whiteson were allowed to respond to my answers but I was not afforded such a luxury. Although the broadcast gave a different impression as it would cut from one to t'other and back again. To say the broadcast showed me in a bad light would be an understatement. Yet in my eyes I was an angel in comparison to the editors who I believed had conspired in the attempted assassination of my character. They did a pretty good job of it, with the help of my grinning demeanour; they distorted my case to millions of viewers. While I appeared shifty, evasive and jocular Warren and Whiteson were the epitome of seriousness and sobriety. He was claiming libel for, me saying or implying that I had said, 'I had told him that I had epilepsy before I signed the contract for the fight'.

I passed the writ onto Henri Brandman to deal with. I initially met Henri through Panay and Gill at the Phoenix Apollo Restaurant. The Phoenix connection had also brought Ambrose and Henri together. Ambrose was presently using Henri's services regarding a dispute between Warren and Nigel Benn. Henri asked me to give a complete detail of my version of the events.

It was duly sent for Mark Warby my Counsel to consider. He was not optimistic of the outcome for me. He suggested that I settle out of court. But there was no way I was going to yield. The advice I had received had been derived from an incomplete submission the final page of the transcript having been omitted in delivery.

While I was incensed with the television stitch up these lines of communication were not broken. I received a phone call from one of the Thames Sport's executives regarding Nigel Benn's forthcoming fight at the Albert Hall. They wanted to meet. It was arranged for the next morning.

The three of us met up with John Bromley, Stuart McConachie, and Trevor East. Trevor East referred to the earlier interview on Midweek Sport Special for which he was the Executive Producer. I made the point that I thought it was a stitch up. Ambrose made the pitch at £25,000 for our forthcoming Benn promotion. I thought that he went in too low. I told him so later. "I didn't want to give them a reason to decline us." he informed me. The deal done phone numbers and cards were exchanged. Frank Maloney and Ambrose both wanted to be the point of contact. I sat and witnessed the proceedings as a spectator.

What should have been the end of the beginning was, for me, the beginning of the end. As far as I was concerned we had now broken in to the boxing big time. That was the aim of the M-Squad and for me the winning post. I still had no joy in securing television for my own venture. It was ironic that I had secured a massive sponsor from a PLC but I could not deliver television.

The tent hire was around £20,000 and cash was tight. Business was not too bad though. I thought I'd release some of the equity on the house. I had paid £120,000 a year previous and put down a 25% deposit. I had spent a lot money on the house and a lot of work had gone into it so I anticipated that the £30,000 equity had swelled a fair amount. Following the inspection from the building society the house was valued at £105,000 meaning only £7,500 could be released. House prices were falling. I paid a visit to the bank but suddenly they became more cautious and were not playing. I had been living on 2 overdrafts for the last year. One account had been used to pay the £90,000 mortgage each month while the other was for personal spending – they were cancelled.

After one press conference promoting the comeback I was approached by a young reporter, claiming to be from the Sunday Times. He introduced himself as Kevin Mitchell and asked for an interview. I thought great I can now put the record straight. The problem with the tabloids was that everything had to be sensationalised and compressed. A complicated story like mine needed more explaining and paragraphs. The broadsheet was the place to do it. Arrangements were made for him to call at my house and I welcomed the opportunity to put matters right.
That Sunday could not come quick enough and I was up early in anticipation. The article was a hatchet job on me. It was attributed to Nick Pitt and Kevin Mitchell. I thought the two of them were a disgrace to their profession and took spin into a new dimension. I have never felt so raged about anything before or since. Nick Pitt it was expected of. I knew he and Frank Warren went back a long way. He was an acolyte of Frank but for Kevin Mitchell I had nothing but contempt. He was made welcome in my house any contentious issue he could have confronted me with there and then. But no he just let me talk and talk and talk. When it came to the story he just took what he and Nick Pitt wanted. I believe that even before hearing what I had to say the direction of the story was predetermined.

I was coming round to the idea of being more modest in my approach. The earlier pronouncements, about the tent and the specific date did not leave room for manoeuvre. I was beginning to think that the important thing was the fight the rest was superfluous. I'll have the fight, in a sports hall, the venue wasn't important and then retire. Jon Robinson had put me in touch with an agent in France as I was looking for an opponent. He came up with someone named Lofti Belkir. The announcement was made at another press conference. It was considered important to have all these press conferences to keep the attention of the public. That was a difficult task in itself, but was made even more onerous having to compete with a much bigger fight on the other side of the Atlantic between Britain's Frank Bruno and Mike Tyson. All the main boxing correspondents were in the States.

I eventually was up before the BBBofC concerning my application for a licence to box. An independent Consultant Peter Harvey had been invited to attend by the board. Also there was my consultant Peter Fenwick. The evidence was presented and the board members were then left to make their decision while I along with my mate Dartsy and the medical witness's waited in an adjoining room.

While awaiting the decision Peter Harvey spoke of once having to make an assessment for a journalist regarding a fighter who Dartsy and I both recognised as Frank Bruno. It was during one of his earlier contests against Jumbo Cummings. Frank had taken a good punch in the closing seconds of a round and appeared out on his feet. Mr Harvey explained that he was asked to make a medical diagnosis of what was happening to Big Frank at that moment. Harvey said he was having a seizure. In less than seven days time Frank was getting in the ring with the then awesome Mike Tyson. I was summoned to the room for the board's decision. My application for my licence was refused. They considered that I was in a greater danger than other boxers. That I presumed included Frank Bruno.

I was tempted to relay what I had just heard and see how the board would react. After all they were going to be receiving a big fat fee from the fight. But I did not want to deny Frank Bruno the payday. But the board smacks of double standards and hypocrisy. They have the audacity of fining boxers for bringing the sport or game into disrepute and they do that all the time. More recently there has been the case of Michael Watson who was badly injured during a fight. Rather than face up to their responsibilities to the poor man they spent tens of thousands trying to wriggle out of their obligation be it *de-facto* or *dejure.* Then they have the audacity to stand in judgement of others.

There was the occasion when Mike Tyson, a convicted rapist was allowed entry into the country following special pleading and lobbying to the Home Office. Mike Tyson behaved like Mike Tyson and the board accuses him of bringing the game into disrepute. It was the board that brought the game into disrepute not Mike Tyson. Similarly, there was also the example of female boxers seeking licences and the board taking a negative stance. More money wasted in legal fees and more ridicule brought on the sport. I don't see any board stewards or officials being charged with bringing the game into disrepute.
I did not need or want such a decision it sent out all the wrong signals. As much as I despised what the board stood for and the way it behaved I needed their seal of approval. It was a big set back.
The training preparation was nothing in comparison to what I had done in the latter part of my career. Now training had to be worked round everything else. Anyone can be a Christian in church just the same as anyone can be a fighter in the gym. The test for a true fighter was whether he lived the life of a fighter outside the gym. I wasn't living that life. There were too many distractions. I was letting things get to me.
I got a phone call informing me of a press report that my scheduled opponent Lofti Belkir was in prison. None other than Nick Pitt reported the story. The messenger pissed me off more than the message. I had received a fax confirmation from the agent that this guy Lofti was okay and I had acted upon that. I had seen such things happen in the past so I was not totally surprised but I could have down without it. There were too many negatives and it was having an adverse effect, if ticket sales were anything to go by.
I held another press conference and announced my new opponent as my odd sparring partner Sylvester Mittee. Sylvester was doing it as a sort of favour. It would have been a good fight. But things weren't happening. Well they were happening but not to my benefit. I left the press conference to find the car had been clamped.
Next morning at 6.30 I was getting ready to go for a run when there was a knock on the door. If there is a knock on your door at 6.30 in the morning it can only be one caller - the police. I was

arrested for suspicion of removing and stealing a wheel clamp. I was taken to Basildon police station where I would be detained until the arrival of two detectives from the Metropolitan police. Sledgehammer and nut were two words that came to mind. I was shown the cell and for a few hours I was kept occupied by the ranting of my neighbour. "Fucking Pigs. You're wankers. You're all a bunch of tossers. When I get out of here I'm going to fucking do you. Oi mate what you in for?"
I did not answer. I was trying to meditate to purge the stress that was accumulating. I knew I wasn't going anywhere until plod had arrived from London. Notwithstanding the moron in the other cell it was a time of peace and tranquillity. It was a moment to reflect and think things through. I had not done that for a long time I had been reacting to events and lacked any real direction. There was no strategy. Some would say too many irons in the fire. That wasn't the problem but the symptom. It was the symptom of not knowing what I was going to do with the rest of my life. Did I really want this fight? No. I had boxed myself in with my own rhetoric.
"Oi mate what you in for?.. Oi mate you deaf?
"Yeah."
"What you in for?"
"Conspiracy to murder."
"Who?"
"You if you don't keep quiet."
"Wanker. You're a wanker, I'm going to fucking do you."
When the Met boys arrived it was time for a chat. "Before we go on the record Tel, look, were getting it in the neck from above to clear this up. We have witnesses, if you admit it then you'll get a caution and that will be the end of the matter. Whadda ya say?"
"Put it in writing."
"We can't do that."
"Neither can I."
So it was into the interview room. The tape switched on.
"You have been arrested on suspicion of the illegal removal of a wheel clamp and the theft of a wheel clamp which is contrary to section one of the theft act." This is serious I thought I could get a criminal record.
"You have the right to remain silent but anything you do say

may be taken down and used against you. Do you understand?"
"Yeah. I will be remaining silent."
They then began to ask me some questions. After a few questions I interrupted, "I said that I would remain silent. Why are you asking me these questions?" Their monologue ended soon after. I was charged with the removal and theft of a wheel clamp. I thought it was great: a badge of honour. If you had to be nicked for something, I couldn't think of anything better. Despite making light of it, it was another distraction and something I could do without.
There were also problems on the betting side. The turnover was great but the credit control was very lax. Eugene was having us over. I got stung for over twenty grand. It slaughtered my cash flow and I found the situation extremely embarrassing. So John and I did what we always do when there is an impasse. We played chess to decide who was going to deal with Eugene. They were always close games. We had to wipe our mouths with the money but Eugene was put out the game for a while.
I got what I deserved in some respects. I had seen how, in the past, he had tucked up some of his so-called friends so I could not say I had not been warned - if he did that to them why not me. Why did I allow it to happen? It was greed on my part. The greed stemmed from the insecurity that I now had. It led me to conclude you can only con a greedy man.
When all seemed to be collapsing around me I received a reprieve in the guise of a phone call. A couple of blokes I had met on a previous occasion when I was looking to acquire some more betting shops were interested in acquiring one of mine. They had made a covert visit and were impressed with how busy it was. We had managed to build up the business in the shop to the point that it had potential for a buyout from a bigger firm. We had turned it around because we were not restricted to the rigidity of bigger firms.
Now the shop was a little goldmine and a prospective buyer was interested. The men were agents for Victor Chandler. A price was agreed at £130,000. That was a tidy profit and a boost to the cash flow. It also meant that the fight was on big time. The change over was to be a matter of weeks. Once the transfer of licences went through then the cheque would arrive. I had debts

outstanding and contacted my creditors to inform them that payment would be made in two weeks and everyone appeared happy. The two weeks passed the transfer went through but the money was not forthcoming.

The shop had not performed as well as they had hoped and so they weren't releasing the cheque. Their case was that we had misrepresented the business. We passed a tax deduction off the winnings of five percent whereas most firms chose at the time 9 or 10 per cent. They had based their figures on our turnover being comparable to others everything else being equal. They saw it as a concession and they claimed that we had said there were no concessions.

It was back to square one. The banks would not play and we were in the shit. Fortunately I was able to go to Mum for some cash and she took the place the banks had vacated. Throughout her life she has been thrifty and the family would make fun of her but now she was having the last laugh. The Gants Hill shop was still occupied by one of Mister Chandler's companies. There was a stand off; he wanted to renegotiate I took the view that the deal had been done.

When it came to putting the £5000 deposit for the tent there was none there. Mum offered to come across but it was the final payment that concerned me. The fight was off. An ankle sprain was the excuse. The reason was that I couldn't pull it off. In the past numerous injuries have not deterred me from fighting because it suited me. This would have been the case had the circumstances suited.

What do I do now? What does John do now? Now the money wasn't coming across the numerous creditors became understandably impatient. We believed that the money was only weeks away but you can only use that line for a few weeks. It became rather hollow and embarrassing. It was John who was at the sharp end taking the flack. I was always unavailable. That was part of the strategy. 'I can't do anything until I see Terry'. Terry meanwhile was having his mug in the papers and appearing on television. Enough times to give the impression he was a success - the boys doing well. I needed time and it was against me. If only I could be taken out of circulation for a while. Cash was so tight that most of the business was edged to cover our potential liabilities. We just kept the shop open to maintain the goodwill in order to find a buyer. One eventually came across after all sorts of problems and we were able to secure twenty grand at the back of November that would tie things over. What was important to me was that John should not have to cancel his round the world trip that was coming up. Also of equal concern was that I did not get too deep into debt with Mum. She was always coming across when cash was needed but she had spent years saving and I was consuming it in weeks.

Jacqui continued to be Jacqui. Another row ensured she wanted me to leave. It was probably a hormone imbalance - she was pregnant. I was only too happy to leave but not before I got it in writing. The note written I was out. It suited the situation. I had to find £1000 a month for the mortgage and it was a bloody struggle. Now I was off the scene she was able to claim benefits, which also entailed the mortgage payments. She was coping. There was more cash around now than what I was receiving when working. I had various options on where to stay so it was not a problem for me. However, I had not left Kelly, Jacqui had made the comment that she saw more of me now I was out the matrimonial home.

It was only a couple of weeks before our separation became public. 'Marsh dumps family', said the Daily Mirror. I was fuming. I was accused of numerous affairs that, regrettably, were untrue and it was presented as if I had packed up and left. Jacqui was quoted as calling me a Pratt.

I bumped into Henri Brandman later that week at a bash and he facilitated an interview with the Sunday People. A young reporter, Tina Weaver, called at the flat I was staying at and did an interview. I got ten grand. I did not want to bad mouth Jacqui but felt that I had to respond. I warned her that if she did not co-operate I would give my version. As it was I think the subsequent article served the purpose. It presented me as the victim of domestic violence. Being a boxer it was a good angle. I invited the reporter out for a bite to eat but she declined. Shame, I liked her.

Then I was asked to do an interview about the film 'Tank Malling' that I had played a very small part in. A reference was made to the separation but only marginal. It was a very neutral

reply. Two days later I am in the paper again. *'Let me come home begs Marsh': Marsh pleads to his wife Jacqui to allow him back home. "I still love Jacqui and I want to come home."*
It was a total fabrication. I felt it made me look a right dope and I was put in touch with these solicitors. I wanted to sue the paper for libel. The solicitors fired of a letter and a subsequent letter to the paper's reply. They did advise me that the article was not libellous. "Although it maybe untrue it does not represent you in a bad way." To be libellous it needs to be untrue and lower the opinion of you in the eyes of 'right thinking people'. It certainly lowered the opinion of me in the eyes of my friends.
I really felt outraged. I was due to attend the premier of the film in London's West End. Also there that night was John Conteh, another former world boxing champion, who played a part in the film. I asked Jacqui if she would like to come and gave her some money so she could glam herself up. For me it was a way of showing the newspaper report to be a load of crap. I could not have been that bad as she was out on the town with me.
At the after film party one of John Conteh's brothers approached me "Sorry Tel," he said in his thick scouse accent, "I didn't know it was your wife. I pinched her arse. I'm really sorry."
"It don't bother me mate she is only my wife in name."
I had got what I wanted which was the photo of her and me together. She looked quite good and was not recognised by the photographers as my wife. They were keen to get a photo of us both together. We relented. The pose made it into two of the red tops. The Daily Star had it on their front page. It read, 'Tel's new girl'.
I now focused my attentions on being a stunt man. I had my equity card, which was acquired while trying to achieve an acting career that was going nowhere. The membership to equity was also a pre-requisite for registration on the stunt register. I already had a few disciplines namely boxing, scuba diving, and a martial art. Seven disciplines were needed and I began working on swimming at the gold standard, which I quickly achieved, I took the test at a swimming club in Dagenham. I also began a crash course on the trampoline. Skiing and parachuting I thought I could bluff because of my time in the Marines. I was at

the silver standard on the trampoline when I attempted what is known as a lazy back. It is a back flip but without the tuck. You hit the mat on your chest. My instructor a young man, who I only knew as Alan, talked me through it. I was keen to get started and failed on my first attempt, I bottled at the crucial moment. I tried again and failed. It was lack of commitment to take the risk. I decided this time that I was going for it no matter what. I landed on my head. I heard a crack. The subsequent X-ray revealed I had dislocated the C5 vertebrate. In layman's terms I'd broken my neck.
Following an emergency operation I had to wear a surgical collar for the next two months It was the beginning of September and it was a frustrating time walking around with this restriction. I should have been grateful, it could have been a lot worse. The day after leaving hospital I had to attend Court to face the charge of, 'Theft and illegal removal of a wheel clamp'. There were several prosecution witnesses. I insisted on all the prosecution witnesses being called – it lasted all day.
The magistrates said they'd give me the benefit of the doubt as if they were doing me a favour. In fact they had a duty to find me not guilty if there is a reasonable doubt. However, I'd had a result with the verdict as it was at a Magistrates Court (formerly known as a Police Court). John and I returned to the car to find he had received a parking ticket.
A couple of weeks later I found myself back at the hospital I now had a son Karl. An additional mouth to feed was a further cost at a time when everything appeared to be working against me. The sponsors of my car decided that it was time to part company. A visit from the police investigating the wheel clamp was used as the reason or was it the excuse? Another car I had leased was repossessed. It was a period of retrenchment and sitting tight until a deal could be reached with Mr Chandler.
The need to respond to Frank Warren's writ also ate into my cash flow. Over ten grand had been consumed in no time. The legal defence did not look good to the lawyers but I was convinced of the strength of my case and would not yield. I spoke to Henri and I decided to act in my own name. My successful defence of the wheel clamp charge had encouraged me. It meant Henri having to formally withdraw as my solicitor.

John was getting into his tourist mode. He had an early evening appointment to have his various inoculations for his round the world trip. I was due to make a presentation that evening at a trampoline club. My instructor Alan had arranged but he phoned to say it was cancelled. There were a few matters outstanding that needed either John's or my attention. The chessboard was the arbiter. We arranged to meet up later that evening along with Dartsy. We met up in, Strings, a bar in Basildon along with Dartsy and an old acquaintance Mark Evans. We were having a bit of a laugh when we heard Frank Warren had been shot. We carried on, still having a bit of a laugh.
Several days later with Christmas approaching I attended Ambrose's office party. Ambrose had done a deal with the American promoter Bob Arum whereby Arum promoted Nigel Benn and his fights were sold to the UK television. Nigel, having gone into virtual exile, following his defeat against Michael Watson, had re-invented himself. Ambrose suggested I do the same.
Earlier I'd met with Victor Chandler. Mr Chandler was only too aware of my predicament. We could not reach an agreement following a meeting so I was off to the States to fight. The motivation was purely monetary. I had done some preparatory training before but not a lot. My neck muscles were still weak, as was my hand in making a fist, a result of the neck injury. I would occasionally get a pins and needles sensation. But I saw these ailments as ways of testing me to see if I really wanted it.

It was the eve of the flight to America. I was staying at Mums and had got back from the gym totally knackered. I had not done a lot but it was an indication of how out of shape I was. Mum informed me that we had a visitor. It was Kelly she wanted to be with her Dad and was constantly crying so Jacqui left her with my parents. She, by now, was fast asleep tucked up in John's now vacant bed. The phone rang at around 10pm and we all knew who it was going to be. Only one person phones at that time of night. It was my wife. She wanted to talk. She spoke in a manner I recognised as her drunken mode. "Look Jac, its too late and I'm too tired. I'll see you tomorrow before I leave." she beat me in hanging up. It was fifteen minutes or so later when the

doorbell rang. We all knew who it was going to be. I answered the door. She was holding the baby, Karl wrapped in a blanket. She was wearing just a short sleeve dress. "There you go you've got them both now." Karl was passed to me and I cradled him in a similar fashion to his Mum.
"If I can't have 'em you ain't." she said.
She had no coat and was lightly dressed but had done a good job of concealing the carving knife. As she thrust the knife at me I retracted the part of my body to which it was heading. My toes went up as did my hips and my stomach retreated. My head neck and chest were now parallel with her outstretched arm. I instinctively reached for her arm dropping Karl. The knife cut into my trouser near my groin, a brief struggle ensued. I was soon able to pin her to the floor. By now we had moved into the adjacent kitchen. I called for my parents. Karl was on the floor in the hallway. "What's going on?"
I nodded towards Karl and Mum picked him up. He was Okay. I had a few options, I could throw her out the house, but in her drunken state she would wake the whole street demanding that we return her children. I could knock her out, assuming of course I was capable. That was the preferred option but would play into her hands. So I took the third option. As I kept her pinned to the ground I said to Dad, "Phone the police let them sort it out."
"If you phone the police I'll tell ‘em you shot Frank Warren." Jacqui screamed.
"Dad, just phone the police."
It was several minutes before they appeared. I released Jacqui and left the kitchen with one of the coppers while his colleague remained with Jacqui. "She tried to stab me. I don't want to press any charges but it was a situation that needed your presence."
"Its not me you should be arresting its him. He shot Frank Warren." Jacqui kept repeating. Eventually she calmed down. It was clear that she was not in a condition to look after Karl who stayed with me while the coppers took Jacqui home.
Next day it was off to Gatwick. I toyed with taking Kelly, who was aged six at the time, with me, but decided against it. We kissed and hugged before I left for Miami promising I would soon return. Nigel Benn had a fight scheduled in Atlantic City but he

was based in Miami alongside former trainer Vic Andretti who had a house there. Nigel was knocking around with another Brit called Rolex Ray. I went to the gym and did some sparring against some tough looking Hispanic fighters. I handled them all comfortably. We hung around in Miami for a week or so before setting off to Atlantic City for Nigel's fight. It was an eliminator for a world title challenge. The fight was on the eve of the big fight between Gerry Cooney and George Foreman. Cooney confirmed what I had always assumed; white Americans can't fight. He got banged out by Foreman very early in the fight and seemed to have no shame about his defeat. He left the ring smiling. Nigel, on the other hand, in his fight the night before was not happy. He won but it was a pretty poor performance and gave no one anything to get excited over. His next fight was to be a world title fight against Canadian Doug De Witt.

Ambrose and I had a meet with Bob Arum and it looked as though business could be done. I was due to meet him again at his offices in Las Vegas. I was planning on that being my next destination. But I got a call from home. I had a date for the libel action against Frank Warren so I joined Ambrose, Nigel and their two wives on the flight back to London.

CHAPTER EIGHTEEN
NOTHING TO DECLARE

As we began to go through the green channel Ambrose and then Nigel were asked if they would open their cases. As I drew level with the final bay I called out to my travelling companions "I see the white man got through." I was then called over and asked if the entire luggage was mine and whether or not I had anything to declare.

The official then proceeded to go through my baggage. His method struck me as strange he seemed to be just going through the motions. I began to suspect that there was more to this. My first piece of deduction led me to suspect that it was Ambrose that they were after and I was merely caught up in their investigations. Ambrose was presently on bail, for which I had stood surety, facing a charge for fraud. The fact that he was allowed to fly back and forth to America suggested, to me, that it was not a serious matter. In addition, in this country we have a tradition of presuming innocence unless found guilty. Many people in the past have implied that a question mark hung over Mr Mendy. He did have form, his former acquaintance, Frank Warren, had made sure that everybody knew that. I considered his past was simply that - in the past. I liked him. It did not deter me from standing bail for him from my contingency fund many months earlier.

I was then asked by the custom's officer to accompany him with my luggage. I remember feeling quite tired and pre-occupied with the tasks that awaited me in the week ahead and sheepishly complied with the request. I was led through a corridor and asked to wait inside an adjoining room. "No way." I said sternly.

"Why not?" I was asked.

"There is no handle, it's a cell and I'm not going in there."
With that the officer asked me to wait and left for a few moments. When he returned several others accompanied him, whom unlike him did not display regulation Customs' uniforms. The group leader produced his warrant card and said, "Terry Marsh I am arresting you on suspicion of the attempted murder of Frank Warren. You were seen running away..." I was read my rights.

I was later to find out Ambrose was demanding that the Customs Officer allows him to see me. Some of the coppers went out to placate him. Following the arrest, the search of specific addresses was the next stage - secrecy was to them important. Ambrose, however, recognised one of the detectives from the press conferences that had been broadcast concerning the shooting. He phoned Henri Brandman.

It was not long before I was in handcuffs being escorted through the airport. I had been on the phone to Kelly less than twelve hours earlier promising faithfully that I would be home. The promise was now going to be broken and that angered me more than anything else. I had let her down. Paradoxically it was not a situation of my choosing yet a situation that I welcomed despite the risks. The financial pressures were building up around me. The war of attrition with Chandler was going to take up a lot of my energy. Once I got the money through, the banks and other creditors would be satisfied. However, that was months away and the world would not stop to allow Terry Marsh some breathing space.

The proposed comeback was a knee-jerk reaction to the financial difficulties. It was not a goal in itself but a tactic to give me cash to sustain the Chandler stand off. I did not want to fight and the arrest, assuming I was charged, would remove the ability for me to fight since getting bail to go to America seemed unlikely, although it worked for Ambrose.

The prospect of being remanded was quite appealing. I was unable to stop the world but the next best option was looking equally attractive: being taken out of circulation for the foreseeable future. I found myself in a strange situation. I was beginning to welcome the circumstances. It was beginning to be seen as the solution to all my problems.

It was not long before I was in a car with three coppers being driven towards London. The officer in charge, Detective Inspector Wiggins, was seated in the front passenger seat while I was in the back handcuffed to a Detective Twitchet. I questioned the necessity of them nicking me at the airport. They informed me they considered arresting me in the States but it did not get the green light from above. I detected a degree of disappointment, on their part, that a freebie to America was not sanctioned. I flirted with the thought of being 'busted by the Feds'.

It would have put a few extra grand on the exclusive newspaper story that, in my view, was now imminent. This was another positive factor about the arrest. Other than failing Kelly the only downside to the events was the concern over my forthcoming libel defence against Frank Warren. Being arrested for his attempted murder would be bound to prejudice a jury. Furthermore the disruption would do nothing to aid my preparation, which I now know to have been totally inadequate. Although, at the time, I was more than comfortable with my defence - ignorance is bliss.

I had made references to the episode with Jacqui on the eve of my departure, to which Wiggins expressed surprise. His surprise was met with surprise on my part, having concluded that everything had emanated from that night. If I accepted Wiggins implied ignorance of the night then I had been arrested for other reasons. I realised that I was perhaps saying too much. I had forgotten this was a war and I was fraternising with the enemy.

Wiggins had been waiting for verification as to our final destination; a police station had yet to be assigned to them. Eventually it came through that Hackney police station was to be our terminus. In the interim, search teams were sent to the former matrimonial home and my parents' home. Mum answered the early morning call. She cautiously opened the street door sufficiently to identify the callers. "We have a warrant to search the premises." to a man and woman they surged forward to enter but were stopped by the 64 year old. Not by her physical presence but by her demeanour. "Get out the way." piped up one of the WPCs.

"I will let you in but no one is going anywhere until you hear what I have got to say. I have a son in here that could find all this deeply distressing so I don't want you charging in here like the Sweeney. Now I'm going to secure the dog and then I will let you in and take your shoes off."

Mum & Dad where made to go into separate rooms. Mum felt uncomfortable in her dressing gown and went to her bedroom to get dressed. She was accompanied by one of the female coppers whose task it was to oversee her getting dressed. "I am not getting dressed in front of you. Out." The copper left and Mum dressed. As the search progressed so two of the team returned from examining the shed at the bottom of the garden, "Mrs Marsh, that's the tidiest shed that I have ever seen." This was a copper, either by design or accident that could not have given Mum a better compliment. "And I hope you left it as you found it."

Dad meanwhile sat down and let them get on with it quite distressed with the situation. Jimmy was confused but not distressed. There were lots of things being removed from the house in big plastic bags and dumped in the back of a police van. The numerous items appeared never ending to Mum and Dad and also the neighbours who were now witnessing the events. The more that was taken gave an impression of the greater the guilt. The reverse was invariably the case. The more things taken meant not that the case was strong but weak and more evidence was required to incriminate the suspect. So the search continued and the attic was the next stage.

"Found these in the loft." one of the search team said to his boss holding up a plastic bag containing red boxes labelled 9mm bullets.

"You never found them because they were not hidden." Mum responded being only to aware that the cartons had sat in a gun cabinet situated in the loft adjacent to the entrance.

It was in many senses a blessing since had the cartons and its contents not been there the search would have probably continued with a greater determination and thoroughness. Perhaps, plasterboards and floorboards being removed, the garden dug up or maybe the plumbing dismantled. As it was they had now found enough.

The journey from Gatwick was long and slow. It was good to be out of the car and stretching my legs. It made me wonder, whether or not this was by design in order to breakdown my resistance. In some respects I saw the situation as a challenge. When in the marines I had always wanted to undergo an escape and evasion exercise as well as a resistance to interrogation exercise. I was denied both but the opportunity had now arrived. The idea of escaping and having it on my toes gave me great excitement. I saw it purely as a test. The only thing that stopped me was it not being seen in that fashion by others.
I went through the formalities of being booked in by the Custody Officer. It entailed my property being confiscated. A big thing was made over my watch and that I wore it on my right wrist. Then as the many pockets were turned out on the ski suit, I was wearing, a key was found. I was asked about the key and I was at a loss, at that moment, as to its origin and told the coppers accordingly but they were having none of it. "What does it belong to?"
I reiterated my answer but to no avail. So, when pressed about the origin of the key, I told them what they wanted to hear. I let my shoulders sag, my head drop and consciously exhaled and exclaimed, "You win, it is a left luggage locker at Kings Cross. Its there you'll find the guns."
"What's there?" Giving the impression that I was glad to get it off my chest I ran off a list, "There's an Uzi, an Ingram, 500 rounds of ammunition and a white phosphorous grenade."
It was time for the prisoner to go to his cell. I picked up my watch that was sitting on a desk with the rest of my property that had been confiscated. It was a very expensive watch and I considered I would take more care of it than my abductors. My attempt was discovered and the Rolex was once again taken from me.
As I was being locked in the cell Henri Brandman was making himself known at the station's reception. He had acted on the phone call from Ambrose. Only a short while after his arrival several officers were preparing to leave and there was a degree of excitement. He heard shouts, "We've got the gun."
On seeing me he established that I was in good spirits, we joked about a few things concerning how events were unfolding and

what the initial impressions were about the manner and circumstances of the arrest. Following our conversation he was able to conclude that the excited coppers he'd seen earlier were on their way to Kings Cross. He informed me that it would be several hours before I would be questioned. I made myself as comfortable as I could by removing my ski suit and rolling it in a ball to take the part of a pillow. I would be left dressed in a pair of shorts and a white tee-shirt with the words 'WHO'S BAD' printed in black. The blindfold that I had from the flight helped shut out the light while I caught up on my sleep due to the jet lag.

Meals were provided but I refused to eat them, I wanted to choose what I ate. This was interpreted by some of my captors as a hunger strike. Being a lover of food it was something I could never do with conviction but they were not to know. I would eat only part of the food to give the impression none had been consumed. I would drink half the tea provided and then top the cup up with water from the toilet in the cell. It enabled me to occupy myself while awaiting the interrogation. It also gave extra work to the custody officers who had to monitor my 'fasting'. It led to a doctor being called to monitor me.

Being confined and having short naps, without the luxury of a watch, I began to lose track of time. This coupled with the effects of jet lag had a disorientating effect upon me. Three meals were delivered and later collected before it was time for questioning. I had been preparing for the occasion since my arrest. As the time moved on I became more convinced that the delay was part of a softening up process.

In order to relieve the solitude I would slip into a 'Billy Liar' mode. With poetic licence I'd see myself as a prisoner awaiting the interrogation and the ensuing torture. The real disorientation I was experiencing only served to give a degree of tangibility to the fantasy. A clanging of keys and the sound of footsteps was always the prelude to the cell door being opened. On this occasion when my keepers had no food I guessed it was time.

I was not kicked or dragged screaming by the guards. I was led with civility to the small interview room and joined by Henri. On the other side of the table, at which we sat, was Wiggins and

Twitchet. The politeness shown by the officers made it very difficult to get into character for the forthcoming scene. It was the beginning of a new act. The audience was in the form of an audio cassette. Two tapes were placed into the twin deck.

In front of my two adversaries were various hand-written notes. Wiggins left the room while Twitchet preoccupied himself with some insignificant task. This presented me with the ideal opportunity to see what was written on the various papers before me. The ease with which I was able to do this suggested to me that my inquisitiveness was something that was hoped for by 'Wiggs' and 'Twitch'. On their return to the desk and witnessing my surreptitious exploits their somewhat exaggerated attempt to block my view of the notes only confirmed my suspicions that they wanted me to see them. 'Bullets in the loft' was one note that struck a chord, but I was somewhat surprised to see written down, 'Wife's black boyfriend'. The comment both surprised me and amused me. The surprise came from my ignorance of any boyfriend. I was somewhat pleasantly surprised thinking it will be easier to offload her. The amusement came from the necessity for the colour of the boyfriend to be a factor. If, of course, any did in fact exist.

The bullets in the loft did not have any surprise element about it at first. I was aware of dozens of spent cartridges that I had retained in the loft of my parents home from when I had my guns. These redundant cartridges, I presumed, were the bullets referred to in the notes.

Wiggs made the introduction for the benefit of the tape and then read my rights, "...Anything you say may be taken down and used against you."

"Don't hit me again please officer." was my reply. I wasn't expecting fits of laughter from Wiggs and Twitch. I suspected that they had heard such words on frequent occasions. However, I was not expecting the response that ensued either, "Mr Marsh you have just made an allegation of assault would you care to identify the officer whom you claim assaulted you?" asked Wiggs.

"The good looking one." I replied.

"We now have to stop the interview while an investigation takes place by a senior officer concerning your allegation." I was returned to the cells. I did not welcome this outcome. I had been in virtual solitary confinement for many hours and I was looking forward to some conversation. I wanted to speak to them as much as they wanted to speak to me. There was common ground between us. Where we differed was on the agenda of the intended *tête-à-tête*. Eventually I was brought before a senior officer who informed me that it had been brought to his attention that I had made an allegation of assault against two officers. I rightly denied that I had made such an allegation. Shortly after, the interview recommenced.

"Is it true you were a fireman?"

"No comment."

"Is it true you were a member of the Royal Marines?"

"No comment." I was going to inform my inquisitor that the question compromises the official secrets act to which I had subscribed but I decided to retain my right of silence.

"Are you married to Jacqueline Marsh?"

"No regrets."

This strayed slightly from my intended path of no comment but I considered that such a comment to be innocuous and funny. It was not said for their benefit, it was purely an indulgent thought that contained sarcasm only appreciable to Jacqui and me. My marriage had been a continuous regret.

Further bland questions were put to me and each were met with 'No comment'. Then Wiggs asked me to give a brief description of my boxing career. The question caused great anxiety within me. Should I stick to my 'no comment' or should I talk. I felt I was back at a chessboard. The questions being put were merely preliminary moves in a bigger game. The initial questioning would appear innocuous, but designed to draw me into a false sense of security. If I talk now I have accepted the rules of the game, rules that I had no part in constructing. My continued silence would result in them giving up and I being returned to the cell and, I believed, eventually released. That, for me seemed too easy, it was an easy way out, I liked the idea of the predator and the prey doing battle. Staying silent would have been like the fox staying in his hole, safe and secure but fundamentally boring.

Out of the hole I came. "I could have been a contender Charlie." Wiggs appeared pissed off. He reminded me that this was a serious matter and that a man had been shot. I took the view that if he wanted my co-operation he could have invited me to the station and perhaps then I may have been more co-operative. As it was, I considered the whole affair as an unwarranted intrusion into my life. I had been handcuffed, my possessions confiscated, locked up and forced to renege on a commitment I had given my daughter and now this man wanted my co-operation.

When Wiggs was remonstrating it was like it was being recited. It was very monotone lacking sincerity. It left me to conclude that he was playing to the gallery - the tape. I then realised that the interview was not entirely about enquiry it was predominantly about presentation to a potential jury. It made me think about the rights that were read out to me. 'Anything you say may be used against you'. It says nothing about anything being used for you. So the interview was very much, one-way traffic. Prudence would have dictated that I should have kept silent but I was beginning to take a personal dislike to Wiggs. Perhaps the best way of getting back at him would have been to shackle the cackle and zip the lip.

It was not enough for me to beat him through silence I wanted to play about with him and expose his interview skills as basic. I had read somewhere that a detective who is capable of getting someone to 'cough' was highly regarded by his colleagues and I saw this as an opportunity to get back at the man who had arrested me. I wanted very much to be seen as the person setting the pace. I also wanted to belittle him when it was to be played to the future audience. I suspected that he was going to use this case as an opportunity to get noticed and advance his career. I was determined that it was not going to be at my expense.

It was prior to the second interview that Henri had informed me that I could write my own cheque regarding the newspaper exclusive. I thought it was time to be more candid and explain away the situation then get out and clinch the deal. But as the interview progressed it was alleged that live 9 millimetre rounds had been found in my Parent's loft. I was aware of spent rounds that I had retained but I could not account for the 10 live rounds allegedly found. I feared the ‘Old Bill’ could now justify my arrest since they could place a charge of possession of bullets against me. That would blight the exclusive and may prevent me getting out for the weekend. It was their trump card and would give a charge of the shooting Frank some credibility. Two totally different issues but that would not be apparent in the headlines. Once they make a pounce for you they have to make something stick.

Despite there being no evidence against me they persevered. In the interview I was asked whether or not a pair of trainers were mine. I found this funny and bizarre and for me confirmed what I had suspected. It was an attempt to build up a picture of me as the gunman. Why would they question me about these trainers? Could there be a footprint from these shoes? For some reason these trainers had pertinence to the case that I found hilarious. These particular trainers I had not acquired until the New Year and had irrefutable proof of this fact. Even if there was a link with the trainers there was no link with me. I was asked directly whether I was wearing them on the 30th November 1989.

Similarly there was the matter of a black woollen cap comforter that could be used as a balaclava. It had been purchased in Atlantic City along with five others to be worn by the 'Benn Team'. Much time was spent on this in the interview and my reasonable explanations were then twisted, in order, to be used against me.

More significantly was a matter regarding a green hooded Nuclear Biological Chemical (NBC) suit that had been retrieved during the search of the attic. It was a relic of the military days of either John or me. A witness had described the gunman as wearing a green hooded jacket. Wiggs made the point (referring to the seized jacket) and I quote, "Again stating the obvious, it would appear that this jacket is new and doesn't appear to have been worn. Have you another jacket that has been worn similar to this jacket?" Harmless words perhaps but later these words were able to expose the police case for what it was.

I was charged with attempted murder and possession of ten 9-millimetre bullets. Despite this I slept well in the cell that night and was transported to the court early the next morning. Some of the investigation team welcomed the early start because of the overtime they would draw. As we approached the court cameras began to appear against some of the windows of the van in which

I was transported. The van was backed up against the court building and the doors opened and I had to navigate a short space before entering the court building.
I was taken to a cell and left not knowing what the next stage in the procedure would be. I didn't have a clue what time of the morning it was I guessed it was early because of the absence of traffic during the journey from Hackney. I retraced the interview. The inexplicable points both puzzled and haunted me. I kept repeating them to myself hoping I'd make some sense of it all.
"In fact certain members of your family believe that you were about to shoot Warren...Statements have been taken...A number of persons have been interviewed and will state that you have been seen jogging in the Basildon area in a green anorak jacket, with a hood with the draw string pulled tightly around your face tied underneath the chin...So in effect Mr Marsh this completely destroys the alibi you gave us yesterday...We have three independent witnesses, plus a photograph. On the face of it...it would appear that you were lying yesterday."
I was beginning to feel vulnerable for the first time. They had three independent witnesses to say I was somewhere that I knew I wasn't. There was more than one witness saying I had this green anorak that I had been seen wearing while out running which I knew to be untrue. And then they claimed that family members believed I had shot Frank. Throughout the interview these were things I had no explanation for other than to dismiss them as total fabrication. I have to assume that Wiggs was only the messenger.
Other memories of the interview replaced the uncertainty with amusement "Because we know you lied already. You alleged that this officer sitting to my left, Detective Twitchett had assaulted you...We go on from there to another example of lies you told yesterday. You said to a number of officers, referring to a key with a red tab on it, that it came from a left luggage locker at Kings Cross. You also said that you had left a gun in that locker...You also stated that in the left luggage locker, you deposited an Uzi sub Machine gun, 500 rounds of ammunition and I believe a phosphorous hand grenade. Again that was another example of your lying...three occasions that we know for

a fact that you lied."
Henri appeared and gave me the run down on events outside and where I was, Barking Magistrates Court - I should have been able to work it out. He mentioned that we would be applying for bail but added that I shouldn't expect to get it.
On being summoned I entered the packed courtroom and was directed to the dock. I saw ahead of me the three magistrates seated behind a raised platform. "Stand up lad." one of them ordered and I complied slightly agitated at the term lad. I was unable to ascertain whether it was meant in a friendly manner or an address less respectful than Mister Marsh. I confirmed my name and address described as 'no fixed abode' and the hearing commenced. The charges were read out and we asked for bail.
The prosecution objected claiming that they had over ninety witness statements and that I, the defendant, had been proved to have lied. Furthermore during searches no gun was found so the defendant still had access to a gun and witnesses' lives were in danger - in their opinion. The bail was denied and I was remanded in custody to reappear in seven days time. I gave a smile and a wink to the family and friends before being taken down to the cells. As for my 'lying' it was deceitful of the prosecution to present it in that manner and the 'lying' had no pertinence to the case. I only lied when they refused to accept the truth.
I was beginning to get totally confused and troubled. Ninety statements against me, who were these people? Then there was the matter of the gun. Because they had not found it, it was assumed that I 'still' had it so they could not give me bail. Following such logic if a gun had been found would bail have been permitted? As for witnesses I never believed any existed.
It was not long before I was collected from the cell and back into the police van for delivery to Wormwood Scrubbs. As the police van sped away from Barking Magistrates Court it was pursued by a number of reporters and cameraman. However, with the van's two tones blaring and the blue light flashing it was not long before the pursuing pack were shaken off. I then noticed that we were privileged to have an escort both front and rear. The time of transit appeared to coincide with 'rush hour' style traffic and Wormwood Scrubbs was on the other side of London.

I remember how the convoy went through the traffic like a hot knife through butter. One of the younger detectives could not hide his excitement at the dash across the Capital. I found the whole thing unnecessary. It left me to question the necessity of both the convoy and the speed.
The handcuffs that I had to share with one of these rookie cops really pissed me off. I felt that since I was wearing the handcuffs and, in my view, treated in an uncivilised manner. I should do something to give their treatment of me some justification. I wanted to hurt them badly so that it would not go away so that they would not forget it. One of them, I overheard, in conversation implying that he would be telling his girlfriend and mates down the pub that he was in the van taking Terry Marsh to the 'Scrubbs'. I enquired, "Would you like something as proof?"
"An autograph would be nice." came the reply.
I was an angry man. I was thinking of something along the lines of removing a part of his nose or lip. However, it would play right into their hands and give them another edge in the case that they were now going to attempt to build against me. I realised that I was going to be in the system for many months and that I should use the time productively. The last five years had been in many respects like a prison sentence. I seemed always to be doing something for somebody else and never doing what I wanted to do. It meant that I was never free. I never had time to think, to reflect and enjoy any of the moments. I was always too busy.
As the convoy approached the Scrubbs I recognised the twin towers that flanked the huge gate. I had seen them many times in black and white films on the television. My recollection was one of a former inmate coming out of the prison with a brown paper package under his arm being greeted by a gangster in a Rolls Royce. On this occasion someone, yours truly, was going in. The prison had been built in 1875 and it looked like not much had been done to it since, other than periodic layers of paint. Although physically I was confined, I felt relaxed yet very angry. Was that possible?

CHAPTER NINETEEN
THE SCRUBBS

On entering the reception area there was a sign displaying white lettering on a navy blue background informing of the aims of the prison, it read:
'Her Majesty's Prison Service serves the public by keeping in custody those committed by the courts. Our duty is to look after them with humanity and help them lead law-abiding and useful lives in custody and after release.'
It gave all the right messages for the incoming guest. When the prison warden said to my rookie escort, you can take them off now, pointing to the handcuffs. I regretted that I had not taken a chunk out of his face. Documentation was exchanged and I was now in the care of the prison warders. I was prepared for some sort of confrontation but their demeanour and manner undermined any rebellion I was contemplating. The actions of the police allowed me to take the view I did, but the prison staff at the reception did not warrant such a reaction. Their requests seemed reasonable and I felt obliged to conform.
I was given a slip of paper, written on it was 'MARSH T PMOO11'. I was given a plastic bowl and plate that in turn was filled with 'food'. Under normal circumstances the food would not have qualified as edible but my quasi-hunger strike was beginning to have an effect. The grub was quickly demolished. I was unaware, until my feast was consumed that the small dining area that accommodated me was a cell. I was unable to detect any activity beyond the locked door and resigned myself to waiting to see what happened next.
It was the first opportunity that I had since my arrest to assess the situation with some objectivity. My thoughts on the situation at face value lacked consistency. I liked to think that the script

had been entirely of my choosing but I knew that not to be the case. If it was the case then I would be able to stop it at will. Yet it was becoming increasingly obvious that I had no power whatsoever. Even if I wanted to fight back I would be easily contained. I felt superior to all my captors both physically and mentally but they had the upper hand. They were free and I wasn't, yet I believed one on one none could match me. I think it was this that made me hostile towards them.

At the same time they were, from another perspective, saviours. I could avert the return to the ring and the otherwise imminent financial disaster. Up until then it seemed as though it would not be possible to avert both. That was until the newspaper deal was on the table. The production of the bullets deprived me of what I thought would be my imminent release. But only for the moment, the paper deal would be there later after the trial if it ever got that far. Would any sane person contemplate such things in such a precarious position? The consequences of a guilty verdict could mean a life sentence, which I suppose was in the long term. In the short term other pressures were dictating my actions. I could only play the hand I'd been dealt.

I was no longer able to stop it. I believed that at the initial stages I could have brought an end to it all, by being more co-operative, but that would have not served the purpose. It was necessary to go further into the system before I jumped off. I had now reached the point of disembarking but realised I was unable to. Not only would it not stop, the momentum had increased.

My thoughts were disturbed by activity on the other side of the door. It was becoming a regular pattern. Many thoughts emanate from ones mind when in solitude. The brain becomes hyperactive and creates many permutations on even the simplest of issues. Then a disturbance or intrusion brings you back to reality.

I was asked to move a short distance to where the showers were positioned. I was met by what I thought was a store man who threw a towel at me, "There you go Royal, that's for your shower." It had been on the other side of the Atlantic Ocean the last time I'd experienced the luxury. A radio was playing in the background the upbeat music breached the stolidity I had imposed on myself. Another notice caught my attention. 'Prison

rules required prisoners to keep themselves and their cells clean at all times'. The hourly news was reporting my trials and tribulations. It accurately reported that I had been charged with attempted murder and possession of 9mm ammunition. The store men on hearing this began to show amazement. The latter charge had, as far as they were concerned, along with many others, been sufficient proof that I was guilty. "You silly bastard why didn't you get rid of the bullets?"
My response to this was mixed. I knew that at face value the bullets were incriminating but, considering my firearms background, felt their alleged presence could be easily explained away. Still their emergence was both a surprise and, while in prison, a source of embarrassment.
I then realised that the store men were themselves prisoners. The esoteric address from one of 'Royal' I had not responded to at first. Seeing him as one of my keepers, I had no desire to strike up a conversation. Now having found common cause, the relationship being one of peers rather than warder and prisoner, the conversation flowed. As I had surmised, he had been a Bootneck while his colleague had been in the Green Jackets.
A warder informed me that my civilian attire was not suitable. Despite the regulation, that un-convicted prisoners were entitled to their own clothing, my ski suit was deemed a security risk because it had a hood. I accepted the position and discarded the clothing. I figured that it would have been uncomfortable anyway. So I was left in my tee-shirt and shorts. This I considered much more comfortable and appropriate. However since the prison physical training instructors wore such items, it was explained, I would not be permitted to wear them to avoid the risk of being mistaken as a PTI. I had already pictured the scene of me walking into the wing displaying 'WHO'S BAD' on the now smelly tee-shirt. I thought it would have been a source of amusement.
Prison rules meant I had to forgo my civilian clothes and don prison dress. This comprised of a thick cotton blue striped shirt and a pair of brown denims. I had asked the lads in the stores for the blue denims that I could see on the shelves and what they were wearing but it was explained, they were for convicted prisoners only. I had surrendered my ski suit willingly and my

tee-shirt shorts and socks reluctantly, but with a degree of resignation. I could see the other point of view. But when it came to them insisting that my training shoes be given up I felt my contempt for the system resurfacing. The warders concerned did not take any pleasure in the rule implementation. It helped restrain my rhetoric but it was an example of rules just for the sake of it. Since I was in prison dress it had to be 100%. "No split rig." said one of the warders. So I was issued with a pair of black prison shoes. One of the store men gave me a new pair, most found themselves with a pair previously worn. I sensed that the term 'split rig', a phrase I had come across often in my marine days, was a surreptitious way for the warder to inform me that he had some military service under his belt. From first impressions it appeared that everyone in the nick had some sort of military experience, prisoners and warders alike.

Time was moving on and more prisoners were arriving, each going through the same induction procedure as I. Each, I had concluded, had been remanded from the various Magistrate Courts. Unlike I, they, I presumed and later was to confirm, did not have the dubious pleasure of being driven across London at what seemed like 100 mph.

Another warder had arrived and he gathered up six of the prisoners and escorted them out of the reception area. They trooped out struggling to hold all their possessions. There were prison blankets, plastic plates, cups and cutlery. In addition to this all appeared to have either a box or a plastic carrier bag with their personal possessions in. I became conscious that I had no personal possessions. I also noticed that I was one of only a small number who never wore civvies. I felt comfortable with this because it appeared to me that those better dressed and possessing personal belongings gave normality to the situation, which suggested compliance on the part of the prisoner. From my perspective this seemed perverse. People were being incarcerated before trial, so by definition innocent, resigned to their predicament. There appeared to be no fight in them. It then occurred to me that I was not as vociferous or as rebellious as I was expecting my fellow inmates to be.

When my turn came to be escorted over to C wing I could not help but feel intimidated by the locking and unlocking of several gates. The procedure was something that I was to encounter for many months. While in the reception snippets of information, from overheard conversations, suggested that I had drawn the short straw. B wing was the better of the two options for remand prisoners. C wing was a shit hole and this was confirmed on my arrival.

It was a Victorian building with Victorian sanitation within the cells, comprising of a bucket. The building was long, tall and narrow with a transparent roof that allowed light to come into the edifice. The view of the glass roof was slightly obscured by a wire netting that stretched across the length and breadth of the structure at the first floor level. It was assumed by me that it was to stop inmates from throwing themselves over in a fit of depression. On the ground floor cell doors could be seen running uniformly down both flanks yet as we walked further into the building it could be seen that some of these cells had been converted into offices plus a serving area for meals.

The large void in the building was broken up by two iron staircases, which led to the landings above. Each landing, like the ground floor, had the cell doors facing into the middle of the wing. As one looked over they could get a birds eye view of the activities on the ground floor partially obscured by the wire netting. I had been assigned to the 'threes this was on the second floor. This I found confusing. For the benefit of prison the ground floor was called the 'ones', the first floor was called the 'twos' and so forth. Positioned on the landing by the stairs was a small office with a 360-degree visibility where the warders responsible for that landing would hang out and drink their mugs of tea.

The cell allocated to me was the closest to the landing office. Displayed upon the brown metal door was painted a large letter 'A' in white. The inmates were referring to the warder in charge of the landing as 'Guv'. Some would address him as Mister followed by his surname. I would do neither I would hope to get his attention by some other means normally by gaining eye contact. I, like all the inmates, was referred to by surname only. I found it very provocative. I took the view that since I was an un-convicted prisoner I should be shown some degree of civility and I would demand they address me as Mr Marsh. It was fortunate for me that I was not holding my breath waiting for a

civil address. I would have ended up as another prison death statistic.
Having been allocated my cell I was locked in it. Yet outside there was still much activity and it appeared that I was the subject in a peep show. To get a glimpse of me the inmates were using the spy hole normally used by the warders. As each inmate looked in they would give words of encouragement. The idea of crashing out and getting some sleep was futile. In order not to appear a miserable bastard I had to acknowledge each and everyone. It did not occur to them that I might have been tired. At the same time I did not want to be seen as just sitting on my bed like some lost soul.
I did what I always do when stuck for something to do. I began to exercise doing my ton ups. It was a circuit of ten repetitions of ten exercises repeated until I could not go on then I would try to do one more. Ironically when it was seen through the spy hole that I was training I heard one of the prisoners say, "Leave him alone he's training." Whoever he was he must have had some influence since the verbals stopped although the voyeurism continued. This did not particularly bother me since I am always able to squeeze out a few extra press-ups when I have an audience. I had pushed myself hard in the workout, which, without a watch I could only guess, lasted around twenty minutes. The exercises complete I laid on my bed breathing heavily, my heart racing, high on endorphin and purged of anger.
It was, I thought, important not to worry too much about what others were doing while banged up. I had made my bed and it was time to just lie in it. While in here I should just concentrate on my immediate surroundings. I glimpsed out of the window to see the exercise yard below. There must have been over a hundred prisoners walking around in an anti-clockwise direction. I looked down upon them all literally and metaphorically it was not for me I was above that sort of thing.
As before the door being unlocked and pushed open distracted my thoughts. I looked up but saw nobody standing there as expected. The open door seemed to be a cue for various prisoners to make themselves known to me. The first guy was called Dennis. He asked me if I needed anything like tea bags or

squash. He also asked me for an autograph, as did a number of others subsequently. Almost every one of them told me not to talk about my case. I interpreted this as them suggesting that I don't make any confessions or admissions to anyone. My reply always had a similar theme. I was not worried about talking about my case, I had nothing to worry about or hide and I was not the slightest bit worried about the case against me. I believed it to be spurious.

The issue of the bullets arose frequently in greater numbers *vis-á-vis* the autograph requests. It really pissed me off being seen as an idiot in the eyes of everyone. It was no good pleading innocence because that was expected. After all everyone in the remand wing was pleading innocence and fit up. So I had to just explain the history of the alleged bullets. I got the impression that my explanation from their perspective was an admission on my part to the veracity of the case against me. It seemed as if I would have been received better if I had claimed the 'Old Bill' had planted them. At least that way I could have put the blame on my arrest upon another party. As it was, I deserved to be banged up because of my 'carelessness'.

I felt uncomfortable with all these strangers coming into my territory yet I did not want to close the cell door. So I ventured out onto the landing. A guy called John came up to me and asked if I wanted a job as a cleaner because he would be able to sort it out. The way he approached me suggested that he considered such a position to be advantageous. "They let you out the cell, no bang up." he said with a degree of pride as if he had been able to work the system. I saw it as an act of collaboration and I did not want to be a collaborator. Furthermore, this was a remand wing and by definition all the prisoners were un-convicted. To entice people to work for them to be spared endless hours behind a cell door, in my view was tantamount to nothing short of slavery. I asked rather sarcastically about the hours, whether or not it was a 5-day week, only to be informed it was a 7-day week and you had to perform on bank holidays. Realising the terms and conditions were not endearing me to such a responsibility John quickly spoke up like a salesman spinning his final desperate pitch, "You get extra money as well." Dennis reappeared and asked for another autograph. This time it was for someone who worked on the hot plate down below on the 'ones'. He asked if I could dedicate it to his girl friend Jacqui. So I signed it, 'Your a cracker jack...Terry Marsh'.

It became apparent that I was 'on the book'. This meant I was a Category A prisoner. When I had first got sight of the A painted on the cell door I assumed that it meant that the adjacent cell had a 'B'. When the prisoners made the reference to 'Cat A' prisoners it always appeared to be tinged with a degree of deference.

The 'Cat A' was also the reason why I had been given a cell on my own. This the other prisoners saw as a perk. I took the view that it should have been a right. It was explained to me that the inmates had to double up two to a cell. In some prisons, it was pointed out, it was a case of three to a cell.

John the cleaner was still trying to get me a position. My enquiries about the terms and conditions he must have interpreted as interest. Another prisoner quickly put him down, "Don't be a dickhead, he's a 'Cat A' he's on the book."

"Don't worry," said John, "I'll keep it open for you."

Quite a crowd was beginning to gather round. Each made some suggestion that enlightened me a bit more about the prison routine. Also, I no longer needed to explain away the bullets. Enquiries were still being made but by now John amongst others were sufficiently versed in the circumstances. They were explaining away their presence on my behalf.

I was now beginning to get lots of sympathy now my explanation about the bullets was spread around the wing. Their perception of me was beginning to change. It was more a question of I being caught up in something that was nothing to do with me and I was merely a fall guy.

I was ostracised from the ensuing speculation about my innocence or guilt, as it was time to go back behind the door. It was then that I remembered what I needed to do. I spoke to the warder about my necessity to attend the libel hearing on Monday and he assured me that he would look into it. I got the impression that he would have agreed to anything in order to get me behind the door. The Terry Marsh debate continued but the opinions were restricted to those carrying mops, brooms and buckets.

Arrangements were made for me to attend the Court on Monday. I was eager to prepare for Monday's court appearance. I had not been able to liase with Henri but I envisaged he being alongside to assist me in the conduct of my defence - that was always the plan.

When the door was next unlocked it was time for tea, I wandered out and joined the flow of bodies moving along the landing, descended the stairs and queued for food. I declared myself a vegetarian and ate accordingly. Those serving behind the hotplate I mistook for civilians. However, an abrupt order from one of the prison officers to his hot plate delegation served to correct my misapprehension. They like the cleaners and store men were inmates.

If all the prisoners were to refuse to do these tasks then the authorities would not be able to cope. They would have to start letting people out. The prisoners, in many respects, were their own jailers. With the food slapped on the tray it was time to fill the plastic pint mug from the choice of three urns labelled coffee, tee and water. I chose tee indifferent about the incorrect spelling.

"Aint you got any tea bags?" It was John the cleaner, "Don't drink that. They put that stuff in it."

"What stuff?"

"That stuff... you know...stops you have a sherman."

"What's a sherman?"

"A wank."

"Oh bromide, a sherman tank."

"I'll get you some tea bags." and off he went.

I filled my mug with the 'tee' and returned to the threes and my cell. The door was slammed and locked behind me. I tucked into the food with my plastic knife and fork. Both the food and tea was marginally above the ambient temperature. The good point was the cell was warm despite being January. The warmth emanated from a thick hot pipe that runs through the cell. It was the only endearing feature.

The most repulsive feature was the brown bucket wearing a white plastic lid positioned in the corner. I won't be using that I thought to myself. No sooner had the thought left my head then the feeling hit my bladder. It was the consequences of the food

and tea. I'll have to remember not to fill the pint mug in future. The bucket remained dry I did not yield but made a quick exit out the cell when the door was next opened. I headed along the landing to the toilets that were open plan and an extension of the landing. There was much activity around the toilet area, with prisoners relieving themselves, emptying and cleaning their buckets along side others cleaning their plastic cutlery, others were cleaning their teeth, while some were filling washing bowls with water that was being taken back to their cells.
Having visited the toilet I aped those chores, I had just witnessed, and returned to my cell for another period of what I now knew to be known as 'bang up'. I figured that was it for the night and made myself comfortable and worked on the case awaiting me on Monday. It was a bit inconvenient not having all the necessary papers but I figured that I was sufficiently versed in the details. I didn't have a brief to learn. I knew it because I had lived it.
To my surprise the door was unlocked one more time, "tea, coffee or water?"
I took the tepid tea "Goodnight" said my servers and it was finally 'bang up'.
I dozed off and, with no watch, was unaware for how long I had slept when I awoke. I could not get back to sleep, my mind wondered and considered the tea that I had earlier consumed. I thought I'd test the theory. I was disturbed when the spy eye situated on the door received an occupant who persisted on the voyeurism. "Do you mind? I am trying to have a Sherman." I shouted out to the eye on the other-side. They obliged and I was able to confirm that bromide is not put in the tea. I'd got through the first night okay.
I was awoken by the sound of the external bolt being retracted on the other side of the door although the door itself was not unlocked. It was like an alarm call. It was followed by further activity, which I knew to be the cleaners or collaborators. I guessed correctly that the next time the door opened it would be for breakfast and without bothering to enquire I made my way to the hotplate. I had no intention of doing porridge, I chose the cornflakes, an extremely hard boiled egg and very brittle toast. I returned to the cell and it was again bang up time. As with the

tea, the previous evening, the food consumed and digested, the cell doors were opened. Time for cleaning and slopping out and it was bang up again until dinner and so the routine continued.
When it came for my landing to be opened up for exercise I was asked if I was going out by some neighbours and felt it rude to decline. Beside although I did not need the exercise I would welcome the fresh air and a break to the routine. I was now doing what 24 hours ago I considered beneath me. As we entered the exercise yard we slipped into the slipstream of those already circling. C Wing was to our right, four yards away, separated by very high fencing with razor wire sitting at the top and also protruding at mid-height. The gap between the fence and the building was littered with rolled up newspapers that had been thrown from the windows of C wing. There was several tangled in the razor wire. "They're shit parcels." I was informed by one of those in my company.
"Better out than in." said another as if to excuse the unsightliness. Not that a justification was needed. I was amongst a group of four other inmates walking round. One said, "Don't talk about your case."
"I can talk about what I like, I've got nothing to worry about. It can all be explained away." That was my thought and response.
The group would continue in its anti-clockwise direction.
"When you up before the Beak?"
"Who?"
"The Court."
"Friday."
"Your best to have a lay down."
"A what?"
"A 'lay-down' you go up before the magistrates every twenty eight days. It's less hassle than going every seven days."
"What about your committal?"
"Go for the old style, section one, that's best. Keep your cards close to your chest."
I was getting a crash course in criminal law. Also on more immediate matters I was getting enlightened. I learnt that you receive pocket money each week. It was around 75 pence with which you could purchase items from an internal 'shop'. You did not receive the money physically but it was credited to you. The

shop sold various toiletries and food with long shelf lives. For those who were working there was a couple of quid on top. The cleaners got paid around two pounds for a seven-day week. Then there was tales about the dreaded block. It was described as the prison of last resort. It was a much harsher regime than C wing. None of the present company had been a guest but they had heard of the horrors there.
There was also a gym. Sessions were held every morning. Being limited to 18 you had to get your request in early. "You put an app in." An 'app' was an abbreviation for application which was acquired from the threes' office. It had to be completed and returned. Anything you wanted had to be requested through an 'app' which was always addressed to the prison Governor. The exercise over we was herded back to our cells. It was bang up time but not before I had acquired an 'app' from the threes' office.
I filled in an app for the gym and then while I had a pen in my hand wrote a letter of complaint to New Scotland Yard regarding the manner in which I was transported from the court to the prison. I believed that the driving was too fast, dangerous and a risk to the public. I'd now completed my first full day in prison it contained no surprises. It was a repetitive sequence of eating, bang up, slop out, and bang up with an hours exercise sometime during the day.
On the first Sunday the routine was interrupted when the cell door opened unexpectedly. This must be for the gym, I thought wrongly. There was no gym on Sundays and the app was returned because I had not put my prison number on it, "Marsh visit."
I ventured on the three's landing and was directed onto the ones to join a dozen or so other inmates. There was a head-count before the prison officer began putting his keys to use. Eventually we entered a building and into a small passage. There was, ahead of us, a locked door and behind us a locked wrought iron gate. We were locked in and left there unsupervised but going nowhere until the door ahead opened. Apart from the occupants it was bare of any furniture and decorated with 'HM Government paint' a paint that is hard to describe but you know it when you see it. I was one of the last in

and next to the iron sentinel. I looked through the bars familiarising myself with the prison layout should the opportunity arise to escape. To get a wider peripheral view I placed my face sideways against the bars pressing hard and with my hands clasps round the bars pulling in an opposite direction. In the four or five days since I was arrested I felt that I had been treated like an animal on various occasions. As my flesh pressed against the cold iron it was to be the first time that I felt like one - caged.

We waited in the 'cage' for around twenty minutes before the door ahead opened and we moved forward into a large space.

There were a couple of prison officers, one with a clipboard calling out names and numbers. "Marsh seventeen." I followed the route of those called before me and found myself in the visitors' section being directed to the seat seventeen. Mum and John where present. John was tanned from his round the world excursion. It transpired that we were within eighty miles from each other when in America - it's a small world. It was such times Mum was made for. Its as if she thrived on it. She would take everyone's problems on her shoulders. The funny thing about it was that at this moment there were no problems, financially anyway. John would simply say to the creditors "Can't do anything until Terry gets out." The cash flow or the cash demands were now all put on hold.

Kelly spent most of the time with my Mum and Dad. While Karl was cared for, primarily, by a neighbour Sharon and her husband Bob. They were not friends of Jacqui and I barely knew them but they were concerned about the kids and they admirably took on the task unsolicited. It was not that my parents were unwilling or unable to care for Karl but there was reluctance on the part of Jacqui. Karl, only a few months old, unlike Kelly was unable to express his preference.

Mum informed me that they had been in contact with Henri and filled me in with events that had transpired. While under arrest they had a visitor. On answering the door one evening the caller spoke to Billy saying that he was from the West Ham area and he was concerned about me and wanted to help and whether there was anything he could do. He was invited in. As well as Mum and Dad, Dartsy was also present.

It was bizarre: the visitor introduced himself as Steve Farrell. He spoke about his mate waiting outside in the car and having to give his wife house keeping and being in possession of a cheque for two hundred and fifty quid that he wanted to cash. Dad asked him about certain people he knew of in his manor but his answers were evasive. The visitor referred to a time he was in company when someone said to him, "I know I can always rely on you Dave."
Mum interjected "I thought you said your name was Steve."
"I'm called Dave as well...You know he was involved?" the guest proffered
"His what?" asked the matriarch.
"Not involved, on the borderline. We can help. If he walks though money will have to be paid."
He was shown the door, no car could be seen outside. They figured there was one of three options. He was a journalist, a con man or police. John concluded he could not be a con man since he was too stupid. Nor was he a journalist, he was not asking enough questions. It was concluded he was probably a police officer.
The events had dominated the news media and I was aware of the news value but had not seen the articles. Jacqui had done an exclusive with one of the Sunday red tops and I hoped that she had been aware of its commercial value. It was a story that was worth a minimum of thirty grand at the time. I now considered myself an 'expert' on such matters. Anything less than this meant she was being cheated.
Papers are commercial operations, designed therefore to make money. Her face on the front page with a quote and the exclusive tag makes them tens of thousand from both circulation and advertising. I was just hoping that they suitably rewarded her.
Mum had informed me that Journalists were queuing at their door but they maintained a dignified silence. Of course such observations by me implies my philandering with Fleet Street or Wapping was undignified - although profitable.
"What about clothing would you prefer your own? We can bring them in."
"No I don't want to put you out. They've locked me up let them do the laundry it makes their job harder."

"We'll see you tomorrow."
"What?"
"We'll be here tomorrow your entitled to a visit a day so we'll be here."
"Don't be silly. It ain't as if it's round the corner."
It was agreed that someone else would visit; there were plenty of people wanting to make acquaintance and give support. The visit over all was well. I felt I was back in control.

CHAPTER TWENTY
THE PRISONER

I was handcuffed to one of my two prison escorts and transported by a car booked from a local minicab office in Shepherds Bush. There was no police escort, no blue lights flashing, no speeding and no going through red lights. What a contrast it was from the transportation from the court to the prison three days earlier. What had changed to justify such a downgrade in security precautions? Or was it the case that the earlier transportation was a serious misjudgement?

I was sat in the back flanked by my escorts. The front passenger seat was empty. Not withstanding the handcuffs there was a normalcy about the whole thing. I was allowed to dress in my civilian attire that had been left at the prison reception and my escorts seemed quite relaxed considering, if you believe the prosecution case, that I was a danger to witnesses and the public.

Still handcuffed I met up with Henri in the Court and he gave me a draft of a speech that I was to read out. As I was a defendant in person for the libel Henri could only assist as a friend and not in a legal function. With my free hand I read through the three sheets of A4 paper and realised that the other side was making representations to get the libel action adjourned.

When the court was ready to sit the escort was ordered to remove the handcuffs and the hearing began. The Crown Prosecution was first to make representation. I thought, what the fuck are they doing here. It has nothing to do with them. They of course argued otherwise saying the hearing could prejudice the criminal trial and therefore sought an adjournment of the libel action until after the criminal trial. Counsel acting

for Frank Warren then followed with their submission. They argued that Mr Warren was not at this moment in time fully recovered from the shooting in order to undergo the event. It was time for me to make the submission.
The main point of my submission was that the police were using the libel action as a motive and therefore it was necessary that this should go ahead to expose this theory as groundless. The speech complete I sat down Henri passed a note which read 'very good' It may have been good but was not enough. The judge found in favour of the Crown Prosecution and Frank. It was ordered that the libel hearing be heard after the Criminal trial.
It was now back to the handcuffs, minicab, prison and cell. I was to wait a further 24 hours before I was to get a visit to the gym. I amongst seventeen others was issued with prison shorts and vests. Those in civvies invariable wore trainers and preferred them to the dirty white prison pumps that had seen many other prison feet before. I decided to forgo them both on hygiene grounds and because I had a decent pair of trainers in my property box stored somewhere in the reception area. I opted for training in bare feet until noticed by the prison officers. 'Plimsolls or cell?'
"Its unhygienic to share shoes. Give me a new pair and I'll wear them."
I was taken back to the cell and an 'apps' was submitted for the gym for the next day.
I was mustered with the gym coterie and approached by a 'screw', I no longer saw them as prison officers, "Are you going to wear the plimsolls?" he asked.
"No it's unhygienic."
"You can't go."
On a brighter note my trainers arrived and at gym the next day I was there in 'split rig'. I would work out with a South African guy – another collaborator. He claimed to have been in the South African Special Forces. His performance in the circuits we did together did nothing to question his authenticity. I had something to aim for now. I had only started training around Christmas having been restricted because of the broken neck. I was still well short of being fighting fit but now I was to have some healthy competition. The training complete a shower would

have been welcomed but it was not to be. There were shower facilities but these opportunities coincided with the gym that also coincided with the exercise period. I soon got into a routine. The gym was my highlight of the day. Visits were also appreciated and many heads of inmates and their visitors were turned as numerous well-known people visited expressing their support.

The spare time I had was taken up with reading. It was mainly newspapers and some books that I had got from the wing library. The library comprised of one shelf in an aluminium cabinet. There stood a collection of well-worn paperbacks by Tom Clancy, Frederick Forsyth and Wilbur Smith and very old hardbacks. The age of the hardback books were betrayed by the yellowing of the pages. They otherwise looked as though they had never been touched. It was not surprising because it was a hassle just getting access to the books.

The screws were always claiming to be too busy. Yet they seemed to spend most of the time drinking mugs of tea, on the rare occasions I was out of my cell. It was not as if they even had to make the tea themselves. It was made by one of the collaborators designated as the tea boy - invariably a 'white collar' prisoner.

I was generally getting really pissed off with the screws. It was not so much what was done to me but their treatment of other prisoners. If prisoners were wearing prison clothes as opposed to civvies they were constantly being told to tuck their shirts in. There was no please or thank you about it. If there was a disagreement it was always the prisoner who was at fault. In no time at all the prisoner would find himself jumped on by half a dozen screws and wrestled to the ground.

There was always at least one screw that had to go too far. It only served to exacerbate the problem. It resulted in the need to use more force to control the situation that was escalated by their incompetence. There were some decent screws that understood what their job was all about regarding respecting the prisoner and treating them as equals but these were the exceptions to the rule.

I now understood the routine and prison life was becoming predictable and monotonous. That routine was broken when I

was awoken several times in the middle of the night by a combination of the light being turned on and the screw banging on the door shouting, 'Marsh'. I'd lift my head off the pillow to see what was going on. The cell would darken and the screw moved on. It puzzled me but not to the point that the puzzlement was preferable to the sleep. When morning arrived I was taken to see the Wing Governor.
"I have received reports that you are contemplating suicide."
"From where?"
"I received a call from a newspaper. Therefore I am going to send you over to B wing to see the doctor."
I am in the prison's hospital waiting room along with some pretty sad cases. One introduced himself as Spider. No introduction was necessary since he had a web tattooed over his face. He was seeing the shrink as well. He informed me that he was pulling a flanker and on one occasion pretended to be a budgie and began perching on the end of his bed.
"Wouldn't it be better to pretend you were a spider?"
"No that's too rational can't be mad if its logical coz its coherent."
There were others who sat there in a vegetative state. I wasn't sure whether this was drug induced or a severe state of depression. I don't know which was more horrific. I arrived after Spider but saw the shrink before him, which was a relief. I think he was going to be taking up a lot of the shrink's time.
"Do you know why you're here?"
"Where?"
"Here."
"Where's here?"
"Seeing me."
"Because I have been brought over here."
"Have you ever contemplated suicide?"
"No."
"If you had would you tell me?"
"No."
The conversation continued and went round in circles.
I was pissed off that I missed the gym that morning it was enough to make you want to top yourself. Friday soon arrived and it was back to the court. It was a big inconvenience because you had to vacate your cell and return all prison items and do a

leaving routine at the reception. By now I had acquired quite a lot of papers, books and correspondence, which, as part of my possessions, had to go with me. I had acquired a cardboard box from somewhere along with a number of carrier bags which were very handy for carrying my papers. I had received many letters some of which struck chords with me and implied empathy. One in particular was from a woman who really seemed to be inside my head. I made the assumption she was a copper, as I did with every letter I received from strangers.

The police who drove me to the court in Barking picked me up early. The conversation was flowing both ways and by now I was only too aware that there was no such thing as small talk. A few references were made to Henri and they were quite dismissive towards him. They didn't see Henri as a specialist in criminal law *per se* normally they would only have contact with such solicitors because of the nature of their investigations. Henri was there to serve a dual purpose, which would become apparent, but they never had the brains to see that.

I was remanded in custody again for a further seven days and after the hearing sent back down to the cells and there I waited. When it was time to leave I was escorted into a prison van where I was locked into what is effectively a cupboard with a seat and a window to view the outside world during the journey. The journey confused me since it was going on a tour of East London stopping at various courts picking up more prisoners. The prison van full I wrongly assumed that it was off to the Scrubbs. We were taken to a dispersal centre near Waterloo Station where we were unloaded and banged up until reloaded into vans going to the various prison destinations. The journey was very uncomfortable and long. I would have welcomed a police escort with the sirens blaring and blue lights flashing along with the speeding that I complained of seven days earlier.

On arrival at the Scrubbs a joining routine was carried out. Nothing had changed from the previous Friday except that I was allowed to take my trainers with me to the wing. I also managed to smuggle a couple of pairs of boxer pants, which became my only attire when in the cell.

It was a stroke of luck that I had got the cell I vacated earlier that morning. I began to realise that a lot of cells were shared. In

fact two to a cell appeared the norm. I began replacing the pictures I had removed from the cell walls earlier that day using toothpaste. It makes a pretty good substitute for glue. I made my bed, organised my papers and books and generally personalised my space. I was not looking forward to the appearance at the court in a week's time. It was uprooting, mundane and protracted. It was a massive inconvenience. I was beginning to understand what prisoners meant about taking a lay down where you make another appearance after 28 days.
I was somewhat resigned to not getting bail and thought I could use the time productively. Mum had sent in a language course with a Walkman and earphones. I opted for Italian, as there was an Italian on the threes. In fact he was from New York but of Italian extraction. He was in charge of the three's or should I say in charge of the collaborators on the threes and was in effect a collaborator himself. He was charged with some conspiracy involving the Mafia. I wasn't impressed but I figured he could help with my pronunciation.
While I was studying Italian I also took the opportunity to learn English. Dartsy had sent in a dictionary *cum* thesaurus and I began to go through the words that I had heard the prosecution use. I was both impressed and alarmed by the use of the words and how they were delivered and twisted to the point that they served to deceive. I felt pleased with myself finding an appropriate word to describe this phenomena 'prevarication'. I found myself using it quite a bit in conversation. There were lots of opportunities to use the word in prison. I also began to write poetry or more precisely rhyme. I enjoyed it.
My thirty-second birthday had arrived. I was unaware of this fact until I was greeted with a chorus of happy birthday from those serving breakfast. It had been announced on some radio programme that had a birthday spot for the famous or, in my current light, infamous.
Court appearances came and went and then it was time for a lay down. I then realised what I had been missing. The Friday court appearances coincided with the weekly film. It was now the highlight of the week having really enjoyed the first film aptly called 'Her Alibi' I really enjoyed it and laughed long and loud. I don't know whether it was because of the film or having been

starved of such entertainment my demands were easily met. It could have been the pleasant smell in the hall that had evolved during the film. 'Odourama' I thought to myself. The penny dropped when I received a nudge from the guy next to me and a burning rolled up cigarette was stuck in front of me. The best films to watch were those involving cops and robbers. When a copper got shot everyone cheered including me.
The gym sessions became a mixture of circuits and indoor football and both were enjoyable and satisfying. I felt good. Both my mind and body where benefiting from my 'sojourn' - another word I found in the thesaurus.
I was really pissed off when informed that I would be changing cells and having to share. I questioned the legitimacy of two beds to a cell and discovered amongst other things, when reading the prison rules, that doubling up needed Home Office approval and a certificate that I requested to see - to no avail.
I also noted that prison Rule number 49 stated, *'A Prison Officer must not act in a manner that will deliberately provoke a prisoner'.* That was a rule that I saw being breached everyday. Generally, I had reached an accommodation with my environment and was prepared to take the silly shit dished out, like being a number, tucking in your shirt and answering to Marsh. In return I could have my own privacy with my own cell and improve myself both physically and mentally during the stay.
I was relocated to a cell further along the threes which was identical in all respects to my previous accommodation only there was two of everything with the one exception of prisoners of which, I was presently the only one. I knew my solitude was not going to last, A young lad remanded that day had the dubious pleasure of being my cellmate. His mattress was both ripped and soiled and his bed minus numerous springs. The state of which had deteriorated greatly since my occupation and it was dubious whether both the mattress and bed could be described as such or function in the manner designed. The new boy Kumbi, looked towards the screws while pointing to the bed.
"Its broke."
"We'll sort it out tomorrow."
I sprang to his defence realising that his complaints were being

dismissed.
"Send him back to the court and tell them you can't accommodate him cause you ain't got a bed."
"We'll do it tomorrow."
"And how's he going to sleep tonight? Prisons are supposed to operate twenty-four hours a day. Get him a proper bed or send him back. Just because it's inconvenient and you want to knock off early." The door was slammed shut.
"Thats it walk away. Only doing your job. Sorry about that mate, bastards. They expect you to obey the rules but they won't themselves...What you in for?"
"Conspiracy to steal a bag with persons unknown from persons unknown. Do you mind if I smoke?"
"I'd be a liar if I said no. Oh fuck it, go on but don't kick the arse out of it."
"Thanks." Kumbi pulled out his 'baccy' and Rizlas and started to roll a fag. He was dressed in prison clothes and appeared to have been living rough. It is mainly the case with most prisoners wearing prison clothes that the prison's clobber is better than their own. You do of course get cases like mine where the civvy clothes were not suitable but friends on the 'out' quickly supply replacement clothes. So those in prison clothes are seen as the second-class citizens on the wing. I was often asked, "Why are you wearing prison clothes?"
In fact prison was very hierarchical. As well as the two-tier system concerning clothes there was a pecking order depending on the charge you were facing. At the top stood the armed robbers, the 'blaggers' as they were referred to, those doing security vans as opposed to someone holding up the local newsagents. At the bottom were the sex cases. It stemmed from sexual assault through to paedophilia. They were all referred to as 'nonce cases'.
Because of this pecking order it was customary to enhance the charge you were facing. However, if anyone suspected that you were bullshitting they would ask for your charge sheet or 'deps' this was abbreviation for your depositions. The 'deps' were the statements of the case against you. I was still awaiting mine. The high profile of my case meant I needed no charge sheet or 'deps' and found myself at the top of the pecking order alongside

the blaggers being a 'Hit man'.
There appeared to be a paradox about the prisoners thinking. There was this unanimity about the coppers being institutionally bent and fitting people up but they appeared to accept the charge sheet as a bona fide reference to the status of the prisoner particularly if it was a nonce charge. The alleged nonce would get bashed up if found out. Which often occurred as a screw would give the nod. There was always someone eager to stand in judgement and double up as the executioner. Hot water from one of the urns or a heavy battery placed in a sock were two of the preferred weapons. Both of which would be directed at the face. I saw a couple of such attacks, against alleged 'nonces', and it was telling how slow the screws were to react.
The most disconcerting part of sharing a cell for me was looking at Kumbi. It was seen as a reflection of myself. The room had two of everything laid out symmetrically. As I sat on my bed and looked across I saw an image like me sat on a similar bed with similar furniture and he looked a pretty sorry sight.
Next morning he got a change of mattress but not a change of bed. I hit the gym again for some indoor football and twisted my ankle in the process. It put me out of training for a while. It had the effect of giving me more time on my hands with nothing to look forward to in the day - the devil makes work for idle hands.
I submitted an 'app' for a change of clothing and waited. No clean clothing was forthcoming. On the following day I submitted another app. No change of clothing was forthcoming and the same applied the day after. I put an app in to see the governor complaining about the situation. I got an audience with him.
"Its no good you trying to be some barrack room lawyer because frankly you have not got the intellect." I was advised by this prick sitting behind a desk. He was right. Nonetheless the response did not say much about this governor. I was making a reasonable request for a change of clothing as my present prison clothing was dirty and my three previous requests for a change had not been met. It was them who insisted that I wear the prison clothes on my arrival. Furthermore, there was this rule about prisoners keeping themselves and their cells clean at all times.
I made a request to see a prison visitor. These were people

described as outsiders who could hear prisoner's grievances. I made my representation only to find the 'visitor' making excuses for the prison service. I decided to abide by the prison rules on hygiene. As I was wearing dirty clothes I figured it was best that I have my shirt out over my trouser rather than tucked in. Teatime arrived and as I proceeded down the staircase one of the screws put his arm across my path blocking my descent, "Tuck your shirt in Marsh."

"No it's unhygienic and a prisoner has to keep himself clean at all times. Furthermore you are acting in a manner that is provocative which breaks prison rule number 49."

"Tuck your shirt in or get back to your cell."

"The only place I'm going is to get my tea. If you want me back in my cell you take me."

His outstretched arm grasped the railing and he called for assistance "Mr Bowater, Mr Everson, Mr Williams." or something like that. Several screws came charging up the stairs.

"What's the problem?" asked the senior screw.

"He won't tuck his shirt in."

"Get back to your cell."

"If you want me in my cell you take me."

"You are disobeying a lawful order I will give you one last chance. Are you going to tuck your shirt in?"

"No."

By now there were around a dozen screws on the stair looking up at me. It was a stand off and I was resigned to holding my ground knowing I was in for a kicking. The silence was broken from behind me.

"Hold your ground Tel, they're shaking, their bottles going."

The voice I heard was right. The screws were shitting themselves and some backing off. I believed I was on my own and from where I stood all I could see was the dozen screws. The screws saw me at the head of a mass of prisoners who where up for it. The senior screw gave the command, "Let him through."

I made my way past the screws that stood aside on the steps at various levels and headed towards the hotplate while being inundated with pats on the back.

"Well done Tel."

"You showed them."

"Let's kick off while we're on a roll."
"Don't gloat." was my response to one and all.
I returned to my cell ate my tea and waited for slop out in anticipation of further praise from my 'comrades' on the threes. The cells on either side were opened but ours remained firmly shut. It remained that way until all prisoners were locked up including the collaborators and then the door was unlocked and opened. I was escorted to the ablutions to clean my cutlery and get water for washing and cleaning my teeth. Kumbi did likewise unescorted. It was a moment when I saw the advantages of sharing a cell. Kumbi, I felt, was my security against any threat of beatings since he'd be a witness.
Nothing untoward occurred that night but the next morning the isolation routine continued. When it came to breakfast I was given an escort to accompany me to the hotplate. I went to join the queue at the rear when my screw escort ordered those in front to make way for me.
"Fucking celebrities," said one indignant prisoner, "this preferential treatment is all wrong."
"This is meant to be a punishment." I tried to explain as I was getting stuck into the cornflakes.
Back at the cell it was explained that I was to be charged with disobeying a lawful order contrary to some prison regulation. I was given a sheet of paper informing me of my rights. I was told to gather my possessions and then escorted to the block where the adjudication would take place. Before entering the adjudication room I was instructed that I should give my name and number to the Governor. I was marched into a room flanked by two screws and directed towards a chair that faced whom I presumed was the Governor. I noticed it was always a matter of seeing the Governor and it was described as the definitive Governor but every time I had seen the 'Governor' it was always someone different.
"Good morning. What is your name?
"Mr Terry Marsh?"
"What is your number please?"
Why did he have to say please? It was the first time I had heard the word from the prison regime and it totally disarmed me. I was prepared for confrontation but such intention melted.

"I've yet to learn it."
An issue was not made of it and it made me question the need for it in the first place. "You are charged with disobeying a lawful order do you understand the charge?
"No. I note that I am entitled to view the Adjudication Manual I'd like to see it."
"Do we have the Adjudication Manual?"
There was fumbling and shuffling by the screws as it became apparent that they could not supply me with an Adjudication Manual.
"Case adjourned until the prisoner examines the Adjudication Manual."
I was escorted back to C wing along with my possessions in the box that by now was in the process of disintegration through all the upheavals. A minor victory, I had been seen taken down to the block but returned within hours. It was to be two days before I got sight of the Adjudication Manual and given twenty-four hours to examine it. It was very informative and I noticed that as much as it was a guide to the prisoner it was also a guide for the screws and governor or governors. Not only was there guidance, there were also rules that had to be adhered to by the screws and governors. This governor seemed a reasonable bloke and I expected to get a fair hearing from him and looked forward to the reconvened adjudication.
The screws were as predictable as ever. "Marsh, when you enter the room give your name and number to the governor. They marched in I ambled, "Good morning."
"What's your name and number?" He asked abruptly.
I should have guessed it was another governor. No please, from this guy.
"Mr Terry Marsh."
"What's your number?"
"I think it is on the papers in front of you."
"You are charged with disobeying a lawful order do you understand the charge?"
"Yes."
"How do you plead?"
"I never disobeyed a lawful order. It was necessary that I keep myself.."

"We'll hear what you have to say later I take it you are pleading not guilty."
"Yeah."
"Is the officer present?.. What happened?"
"I was situated on the stairs when Marsh passed me with his shirt hanging out and I told him to tuck it in and he refused"
"What have you got to say about this Marsh?"
I made my case but was wasting my breath.
"We cannot have such ill discipline within my prison. You are found guilty as charged. You will be sent to the block and be restricted all privileges for a period of three days and loss of remission take him away."
Until then I had a sort of faith in the system in the sense that at the lower level there was the expected ignorance and disrespect but I had a faith in those higher up whom, with a better education, could and would take a rational and even handed approach. I believe he sided with the screw as a show of solidarity that in the short term may have advantages but in the long-term adverse consequences. It perpetuates the feeling of distrust and dislike that prisoners have for screws and the system in general.
I had now written many poems during bang up and this situation was an inspiration for some lines:

'the sentence passed, I was amazed.
It met with disrepute.
He's just like all the other screws,
except he wears a suit.'

CHAPTER TWENTY-ONE
THE BLOCK

The cell was bigger than my previous habitat. I noticed the bed was less a mattress and the only furniture was a *papier máchê* style chair and desk. The screws were smarter in dress and posture, shoulders back, stomach in, chest out sort of thing. Shirts and trousers were neatly creased in all the right places and the shine in their shoes was something I had not seen since my military days.
Two of these screws followed me into the cell and one produced a clipboard and read from it, "You will wake when the bolt is withdrawn from your door. You will be out of your bed when the door opens and you will remove your mattress from your cell and place it in the storage cupboard. You will then fold your blankets like so." pointing to a pile of blankets on the bed frame. "You will be entitled to one hours exercise. In the evening when ordered you will retrieve your mattress from the store and take it to your cell. Do you understand?"
"No."
They turned and left the cell. "Shut the door please..." they kindly obliged. "..and make sure you lock it." they obliged again.
So this is the block. The bed had strong plywood where the springs would normally be and its legs were bolted to the ground. I tested it for comfort. It failed miserably. I examined the *papier máchê* table and chair. The desk came in two parts. The parts dovetailed together. Whereas the top part of the desk took some ingenuity to create, it even had an incline; the lower section was more simplistic. A sheet of cardboard about 2 metres long by 0.75 metres was divided in to three equal parts with the aid of two creases along its width. It facilitated the base on which to slot the top of the desk with ample leg room.

By dismantling the desk I was able to unfold the bottom part and lay it on the bed and place the inclined top at the head of the bed and be in a relatively comfortable slumber. So comfortable I refused to hear the banging on the door and shouting from the screws. "Marsh get off that bed... You're not allowed...That's against the rules."
The door did eventually open for my exercise. As I went to exit the cell a screw blocked my exit and held out his arms crucifix like and gave me a nod. What do I do I thought to myself, then inspiration. I began to frisk him. He went apoplectic. "What you doing? Don't you ever touch me." he raged as he pushed me away.
"I thought you wanted to be searched." I said unable to hide my laughter.
"Put your arms out." he demanded of me now having gained his composure. I complied. "No, to your side." he was flustering again.
"I was only doing what you told me." I said, repositioning my outstretched arms from in front of me to the side of me. I tried to excuse my laughter by claiming I was ticklish as he was frisking me. It was a funny moment.
Returning from exercise I noticed the desk had been replaced with a sturdier model. How petty I thought. I positioned the desk onto the bed and sat in the recess that would normally be for legroom and read my books and learnt my Italian. I missed out on newspapers, which were deemed as a privilege.
These newspapers were ordered from the local newsagents by my family and delivered to the prison along with hundreds of others by other families doing likewise. It must have been a good business for the newsagent concerned. I only hope that he or she was not an ex-screw. Other matters, seen as privileges, included being able to buy food and toiletries. I was allowed to retain my small transistor radio. It was difficult to get a reception and the only station I could receive that was audible was radio four. I only managed this by resting it on the metal pipe that run through the cell. In addition to being a source of heating it was an admirable aerial. Being an un-convicted prisoner I was still entitled to my visits everyday.
The good thing about the block was you knew where you stood;

there was consistency. They did not engage in conversation with me nor I with them. I got my change of clothing regularly I got showers regularly and the food was also warmer as was the water from the urn to the point I was able to give my face a steam bath each morning. I would catch up on the news on my small transistor radio and listen to the early morning news programmes. It was a time when many things were happening throughout the world and this period in the block was an opportunity to take in these global changes and have some sort of understanding of the dynamics behind it all.
I began also to give serious thought to the system that I was now a prisoner of. The relationships: between the courts and prison, the police and the courts and the law in general. Then there was the relationship between the state and its subjects. I was only too aware that I was staying in Her Majesty's prison and acts whether right or wrong were done in her name. I could not lend my name to some of the iniquities as she does. Training was difficult due to my ankle injury but I did what I could. Three days in the block complete in was time to go back to C wing.
I was back in the gym and the temptation of the indoor football was too much to resist and my heart ruled my head when it came to playing. The foot still hurt but it was worth it. While playing I was summoned for an unexpected visit. 'A legal', I was advised. I thought I would be receiving my 'deps' as I was eager to see all these witness statements that the Crown Prosecutor implied were against me. Henri advised me that the police wanted to interview me about matters unrelated. Henri and I entered a room and faced two detectives. Buy now I had been well versed on the way to meet these interviews and wishing that I had taken such an approach at the beginning of this saga. My approach was to be 'No comment.'
"Did you take out a second mortgage with Western Trust?"
"No Comment."
"Was this a joint mortgage with your wife?"
"No Comment."
"Do you recognise the signatures on this application form?"
"No Comment."
"Are both the signatures yours?"
"No Comment."

The questions continued, as did the "No Comment." The interrogation over I was taken back to the wing. I went to the wing welfare office on the 'ones' explaining that I wanted to contact Jacqui regarding the mortgage that the police were questioning me about. I realised that it was all getting too much for her. The phone was answered by one of the neighbours, Sharon, who had taken Karl under her wing for the initial week following my arrest. "Is Jacqui there please?"
"No Terry, Jacqui has been taken to the hospital. She's taken an overdose." The visit next day informed me of the developments and Jacqui's recovery and filled me in on the details that had not been mentioned in the Sun Newspaper that morning - it made the front page.
I'd learnt that the Mortgage Company had sent a representative to the matrimonial home protecting their interest of course. Jacqui was the only one to greet them. She erroneously denied all knowledge of the loan, which explained why I had the legal visit. It was a good move. It kept the mortgage company at bay and prevented them from foreclosing.
While getting stuck in during another football session the ankle injury re-occurred and I had to hop back to C wing, hop up to the threes and hop down again for dinner. I had a bit of help on the return trip. It became apparent that I could no longer stay on the threes while my present disability persisted. I was moved to the 'ones'.
On the ones were the wings various administration offices along with, as we know, the hotplate and the bulk of the collaborators, other than the landing cleaners on their respective floors. I had a double cell but was the only occupant. I was the only cell on the ones getting bang up. I was easily forgotten about and on a few occasions overlooked.
The constant detour of having to unlock and subsequently lock up for meals and slop out was a bind for those screws on the ones and so my cell was left unlocked most of the day. I was not allowed out the cell but I had regular visits from the collaborators. As individuals I had no problem with this but I still had my reservations about them as a caste. I learnt a few of the advantages of prison regarding dental and optical benefits. Lots of the prisoners used it as an opportunity to sort out

matters in these departments. I followed the advice and booked a check-up.
While in the waiting room I got talking to one of the convicted prisoner a few years older than myself. He had a lot of advice to offer regarding committals and the system in general. "What you in for?"
"I'm a lifer."
What did you do?"
"Nothing."
"Am I missing something?"
"I was found guilty of a shooting a bloke outside a cafe."
"How?"
"Cell confession."
"There must be more than that?"
"Nah, that's all that's needed."
"He said to the police, I told him, that I shot the guy."
"It's scary, on the word of one person."
"So don't talk about your case. The facts of your case can be used to give support and credibility to a made up confession."

About a week had past when I got another legal. I was not sweaty this time and my teeth had received a scale and polish from the dentist. I was even able to grab a shower. The 'deps' had arrived. Henri had two piles one for each of us. He brought to my attention the so-called incriminating evidence against me. There were a few statements by a man named William Hawes. In the first statement he described the gunmen as mixed race. His second statement gave a description as over six-foot and 5 weeks after the first statement, he described the assailant as, looking like Terry Marsh. In that five-week period Christmas and New Year had passed before the realisation had come to William Hawes, a boxing fan, that the gunman looked like me. The other piece of evidence was from a Mrs Jacqueline Ann Marsh. She had stated that I had said that if Frank Warren wins the libel action then I would shoot him.
"That's it." said Henri.
"Henri, are you saying that I have been locked up for all this time on the strength of this?"
Henri repeatedly nodded in a slow deliberate manner looking at

me over his spectacles with an ironic smile. I was also laughing perhaps for two reasons; firstly, at the ridiculous case that was against me, secondly, at relief, that it was not a fit up. I returned from the 'legal' with mixed feelings but my elation surmounted my frustrations. Now with my 'deps' and back in my cell I quickly scanned through them. It was not until bang up that I went through them studiously. The statements, from the various witnesses were, principally, in my favour – I knew many of the witnesses.

One name I did not recognise was Peter Harris and as I initially scanned his statement I saw my name and focussed on it and the surrounding text. The words that leapt out at me from the statement was hotplate, Wormwood Scrubbs, exercise yard, Frank Warren, shooting, gun, brother, blood and guts, autograph, At first I thought it had been some bureaucratic error after all Henri had not drawn my attention to it. But that lasted only an instant. This appeared deeply worrying and I began to read through it impatiently. I got to the end and realised that this did not look good. It was obvious Henri had not had sight of this statement. I began to go through every word and sentence systematically and it was damming and enough to put me away for life. It finished with; Marsh had a dislike of Warren and said, "When I shot him there was blood and mess everywhere. My brother was getting rid of the gun that I had."

Prior to that meeting with the lifer I would not have realised the precarious position I was now in. When I did touch base Henri informed me, the statement had only been in one of the two bundles supplied to him. It clearly added to the case for the prosecution. In some respects the statement was too detailed from the prosecution's point of view. On further examination the statement contradicted the statements made by witnesses on the night. Nevertheless, what was without doubt was that 'confessional' evidence saying I had shot Frank Warren now existed. It became apparent to me on examining the depositions that prior to my remand there was not a case against me. No wonder they were keen for me to be remanded. I suspected that the guy was a plant and put in the prison with the purpose of doing what he'd done. I thought back to all those prisoners who had given me the advice, 'Don't talk about your case'. By talking about my case I was able to give information about the case against me. My words are then repeated with the added confession. The truth then supports the lie.

During a later visit from John and Dartsy they relayed an incident that had happened over the preceding weekend. My parents had received a phone call from a strange woman asking to speak to 'Terry's brother'. John wasn't home so they took her number. She gave the contact name of Mary. On phoning Mary, John was informed that she had information about a person whom was looking to dig up some dirt on the Marsh family. This obviously raised John's interest and he arranged to meet Mary at MacDonalds in the Town Centre.
On route to MacDonalds John made a slight detour to the pub where he met Dartsy and his friend and drinking partner Dave McLeod. John told them about the strange telephone call and they agreed to assist John.
"Remember a strawberry milkshake means everything's Okay." John joked as he departed. John arrived before Mary, as did Dartsy and Dave who sat a safe distance away. On her arrival Mary informed John that a few years ago a free-lance journalist made her life hell. She went on to say that this person was now trying to dig up dirt on me. According to her this gentleman had given her so much grief that she wanted to kill him. She then asked John if he knew where she could get a gun. John flippantly referred her to the local pub. This pub's perceived prerequisite for entry, at the time, appeared to be a criminal record. My brother thanked her for the information and offered to buy her another coffee, which she accepted. While queuing for the beverage Dave and Steve queued behind him, "Follow her and I'll see you back at mine." he said whilst looking straight ahead.
John gave Mary her coffee and departed for home. Steve went to get his car whilst Dave initially followed her on foot to her vehicle. Playing the percentages they had a pre-arranged pick up point. Dartsy was an old hand at this sort of thing having driven for the military in Northern Ireland.
By the time Mary left a light drizzle had started. Dave followed her. After seeing her get into a white mini-bus he quickly made

his way to Steve's waiting car. Within moments Mary had passed.
Their journey took them to the same roundabout on three occasions before terminating on a local estate where she disembarked. They tried to follow her but lost her in the maze of back alleys that made up the estate. Returning to the car park they waited for a little while to see if she would return. Suddenly another mini-bus pulled up where upon six large built gentlemen got out. There was uniformity in their plain clothes and they displayed an abnormal interest in Dave and Steve as they followed in Mary's direction. It was felt that an opportune moment to depart had arrived.
John informed Henri of this event and reported it to the police, supplying the registration numbers of the vehicles. They asked John who he thought it was, to which he replied, "The Police." However he was advised that the Police didn't do things like that. They later informed him that they had made enquiries and that the woman was a local nutter.
John concluded that it was the police acting on the statement made by Harris. He had made references in his statement that I had said my brother had the gun and was going to leave it behind on a robbery. The scam was an attempt to check out the veracity of the statement and more probably to give some credibility to the statement. It made us conclude that the police were not working with Harris but that he was manipulating them. They were keen to hear stuff that would enhance the case against me. Harris a career criminal knew the system and knew how to manipulate it to suit his own agenda, which was getting bail and reducing the sentence. The question that puzzled me was that how a person so devious and manipulative could allow himself to get imprisoned in the first place.
Financially, matters were looking good. John had reached a deal with Victor Chandler and was able to satisfy the immediate creditors and more importantly pay back the money borrowed from Mum and Dad.
There was a statement made by Mr Chandler to the police. It referred to the meeting we had and described it, rightly, as civil. There was a reference to two attacks on his shops subsequent to our meeting that I am sure Mr Chandler only mentioned

through questioning by the police. However, it was placed in the statement.
It had been explained to me, by the lifer, how things work. Once they get you in their sights the subsequent enquiries are purely about making a case against you. If what is heard from an enquiry is in the suspects favour then a statement is not taken. If the reverse occurs a statement is taken. The incriminating matters are then the aspects that are worked on in the statement producing narratives that fits their case. In the Chandler statement the attacks on his shops were referred to although it had no relevance to the case or me but it left another lingering doubt. Another feather added to the 'scales' weighing the case against me. My concern was that these feathers insignificant in themselves were becoming a weight barring down upon me.
John had pointed out that the attacks might have been a factor in an agreement being reached and the lump of money £115,000 forthcoming. This coupled by the Harris claim that John had been intending to leave 'the gun' on a robbery was building a picture of Godfather proportions. We indulged in the fantasy, John was Michael Colleone, I was Santino and Steve wanted to claim the part of the Consigliore. However, John and myself vetoed it. Both of us saw him, because of his bulk, as the character Luca Brasi. It was amazing how despite the gravity of the situation visits always ended on a happy note - cheerfulness in adversity. I'd then limp back to the cell. The injury had by now healed but I persisted with the limp. It helped when it came to smuggling papers out of the prison. The swollen ankle [sic] would be the excuse for removing the laces that facilitated more room for hiding the papers and easy removal of the footwear. The visit complete I would produce the papers and ask the screw if I could take them back to the cell.
"No it's not allowed they must be sent in. You'll have to give them back." It worked every time.
The drugs within the prison were becoming more apparent. Until I became a resident of the 'ones' drugs was something that I had only heard of notwithstanding the spliffs while watching the Friday film. The frequency of discussion made the talk more probable than fanciful. Now I would witness the stuff and its

use. I become an unwitting catalyst to many acts. My stash of Kit Kat bars had caught the eye of a few of the visitors to my cell and they were keen to get what they referred to as the 'Jimmy Boyle'. It was the foil wrapping on my chocolate. It was needed to act as a receptacle for heroin. The 'jimmy' would be heated until the yellow powder placed on it evaporated and the vapour could be inhaled. It was known as 'chasing the dragon'. The more ingenious would devise elaborate constructions but they all needed 'jimmy' and at the time of need I was the only person who had a supply.

It was less than a week before I was to have more permanent company. I was not the only inmate with an 'injury'. This guy was recovering from a broken leg. I wasn't happy with the situation. I was only too aware of the reality of claims of cell confessions and I did not want another. I kept reassuring myself that I could not be convicted on the word of this Peter Harris but should there be another claim then it would be the word of two against one - highly dodgy.
He had long greasy hair and wore prison dungarees. The collaborators now aware of my 'cell confession' began to check out the new inmate with what they saw as probing questions. "I dunne ha' te take this shite." was his eventual response to the inquisition. When banged up introductions were made, "Bill McCoosh, call me Schoosh."
"My name's Terry.."
"Yeah I know who your are?"
"I'm sorry about all that earlier on."
"Nae to do with you mate. You wer'ne asking questions."
"I know but it looked like they where ganging up on you."
"Fucking cleaners and hotplate boys that's all they are. Dunne be taken in by any of them. I bet they've all said they have a Rolls Royce on the outside."
The look on my face must have shown that it had stuck a chord.
"Most of them are Walter Mittys telling you they have thousands outside. Dun ne believe any of 'em."
"Now you come to mention it there are quite a few like that."
"I'm nae one of them. I'm in for a stupid robbery because I was talked into it by a mate. Then he fucks up and through helping

him I'm sharing a cell with you. Listen I got the gist of your problems and you be sure I wonne be making nae statements about you real or fabricated."
"Don't matter someone has already done it."
"Make sure you let everyone know that. It will discourage anyone one else getting the idea thinking that someone has beaten them to it. Could be a blessing."
"Its a fucking ridiculous case they've got against me anyway. If it weren't for the cell confession they've nothing."
"Nae just you. It happens all the time. Every prison I've been in and I've been in a few."
"What is the worse?"
"Barlinnie"
"What about here?"
"This is a shit hole from what I've seen and this is worse than B wing. I was on the hospital wing there for my leg."
"How did you do your leg?"
"Helping my mate. He's a big lad and a bit slow and when we had it on our toes he was struggling and while helping him I busted my leg. I shouldn't be here. I wanted to get away from all this and he, my mate, needed money and I let him talk me into it."
He seemed on the level there was no side to Scoosh. I was to discover he was an intelligent guy. Always able to finish off the crossword that I struggled over. He had taken and passed A level English while doing some of his earlier bird and had planned to go abroad to a sunny climate and make a living teaching English as a foreign language. He knew the law, or more accurately, how the law worked. It was not long before a trust had developed and I gave him sight of my 'deps' and watched him dismiss each as nothing more than superfluous to the case against me. Had things been different he would have made a fine Barrister.
The man was a walking contradiction he had intelligence and yet had a record of petty crime that he admitted was deeply embarrassing. Yet he described it in such a manner that it was amusing. There was no pretence about him, "You should use your time to write a book."
"I did and when leaving Barlinnie the screw said that I was not allowed to take it with me and threw it in the dustbin."

"What did you do?"
"Nothing. It wer'ne his fault, he was a screw."
On the first of April it kicked off at Strangeways prison. The inmates had had enough. It understandably created interest and as the Strangeways phenomena spread throughout the country so there was expectations and anticipations that it may kick off here. At the time there existed a tension that seemed based on race lines. Those on the hotplate pointed it out to me. There was not a black face behind the server. As I looked around me on the ones there were no black faces at all. There were plenty on the twos, threes and fours. A few of the screws seemed to be encouraging the divisions. Of course we had the backdrop of Strangeways and it was perhaps a policy of divide and rule on the part of some of them. Other screws just wanted it to kick off. As much as they presented a united front to the prisoners they were not without their internecine factions. "If it does kick off make sure you get Mister so and so."
It seemed that the prison officers would lose nothing by such a riot. They were presently involved in an industrial dispute and Strangeways had strengthened their hand. The prisoners of Strangeways were not the only ones kicking off. The preceding day saw protests in London against the Poll tax it resulted in some 341 arrests. Some of those arrested got charged and found themselves as fellow inmates. Some describe it as a riot other referred to it as a popular uprising. What cannot be disputed is that the conditions at Strangeways improved and the Poll tax was sent back to the drawing board.
I had Scoosh for company for a couple of months before his trial. He was pleading guilty and therefore had something of a fast track judicial process. I was pleased for him when I heard that he effectively walked free from the court. The sentence he received had been served while awaiting trial.
Once again I was alone in the cell. It resulted in me having a stricter routine. I had noticed, when sharing, how unproductive the days became regarding the betterment of mind and body. Cellmates were for me a distraction. By now my ankle had made a recovery, but it was expedient to feign a limp since it kept me from the three's and sharing a cell, in the immediate term anyway. I was excluded from gym as a result but did my ton ups

twice a day. I regarded it as a trade off and took comfort in the fact that in my own small way I was beating the system or so I thought.
Because of my circumstances I did not have much occasion to have much interaction with the screws, apart from the routines of visits and the weekly film. They were both routine and did not require much interaction from me nor discretion on the part of the screws. One screw with whom I did come across regularly, although indirectly, was Cherub, as Scoosh and I would refer to him. He was no angel and responsible for the collaborators on the hot plate. He was not a very pleasant person constantly threatening the collaborators with the sack. He had all the attributes of a bully.
Were it to kick off in C Wing this guy would have been first on the list of many prisoners seeking 'retributive justice'. My own view was that they would have trouble finding him. He would be cowering, with his eyes tightly closed, in some dark corner.
Easter was now approaching, I'd made further trips to the court and remanded again and again. The committal hearing was now scheduled for May. I was looking forward to it since I assumed that after the hearing I would be out and ready to pick up on things. The money problems had now corrected themselves. I was worried that I would not complete the Italian course and although the committal was still many weeks away it appeared to me to be a short time because I still had so much to do before then. Anyway I no longer had to share the cell and feel obliged to strike up conversation with the cellmate. Perhaps I could finish the Italian in time and also work on my fitness.
Good things come to an end and so was the case now. When I saw a prisoner standing at my door resting on crutches I knew that my isolation was over. Now being wary of plants or opportunists I politely asked him questions. He informed me that he was charged with a nonce crime. I took no position on my new cellmate, but was not happy with my present circumstances and decided a change was required.
It was now Easter Sunday it was no better or worse than any other Sunday. Dinner was relatively early as always. The earlier the dinner the earlier the subsequent tea the quicker the lock up and the sooner the screws can get home. The same would apply

to Saturdays. With the new inmate I found the bang up more frequent and in turn the unlocking.
When it came to unlocking for lunch, it was a senior screw that performed the task. He suggested that I get the food for the cellmate because of his temporary disability before getting my own. At the hotplate I found myself behind a prisoner who had been picked up from the streets. He smelt awful and I realised that I had not joined the end of the queue but unwittingly jumped into a space that had emerged due to smell. No one complained about my pushing in. He was an elderly bloke and had a look in his eye like he had won the pools. Prison must have been better from whence he came. Under the glare of Cherub I requested the beef on behalf of my cellmate followed by potatoes, vegetables and gravy. I was aware of the gaze from the screw. I knew it was a matter of time before a comment was made. "Right Marsh," noticing the beef on the plate, "you are, no longer entitled to vegetarian meals." I feigned horror at being caught 'bang to rights' and then tried to wriggle out of it, "Er, er, its not for me, er, er, its for my cell mate."
"Well, he should get it himself."
A defeatist attitude I gesticulated only to then salvage a riposte, "But he has, er, er, a bad leg."
"Then someone from the hotplate will take it to him."
That was good enough for me. I placed the tray on the hotplate gave him a smile and said, "That's fine by me you can take it to him." I turned away to return to my cell. He screamed out, "Come back here and pick up that plate." I gave him a two-fingered salute. That was my way of showing the collaborators that he was a man to be ridiculed rather than feared. I approached the same senior screw, who had suggested that I get the dinner, to explain that I was not permitted to get the dinner for my cellmate and that despite my explanations, was not allowed to collect it for him. Cherub was not far behind blustering, flustering and wobbling. "He was vegetarian and he took meat and now his left the tray on the hotplate."
“I tried to explain to the officer that I was collecting the food for my disabled cellmate but he insisted that I could not do so."
"He’s twisting it, it weren't like that." Cherub pleaded to his superior officer.

I sported a grin that I neither wanted to nor could contain which annoyed him even more. I was instructed by the senior screw to get my own food. I was greeted on my return to the hotplate as a hero and made the point that I wanted the vegetarian dish. I'd won the moment.
Slop out time the door was, as usual, unlocked but on this occasion pushed wide open to reveal Cherub standing there like some big time Charlie potato. Behind him stood six other screws "Get your things Marsh your moving to the threes."
"Its Mister Marsh to you and did it really need seven of you to tell me that?"
"Marsh, Marsh, Marsh." Cherub spat out. I fell back on my bed laughing and mimicking. I was given a brief respite from my imminent move when called for a 'visit'. The shortage of staff over the Easter weekend meant that such processes as visits were delayed regarding the transit to and from the visiting block. It was to be over a couple of hours before my return and now it was time for tea. The move would have to wait. I left the hotplate with my tray piled high with lettuce, tomatoes, cress, beetroot, very hard boiled eggs, cucumber, cheese and bread plus a fruit cake and mug of tea. I made myself comfortable in my cell and began my feast. Half an hour past and I was told politely by another screw it was time to move.
"I'm still eating my meal and will move when my meal is complete and sufficiently digested. It is Easter Sunday and this is the one time of the year that I have a substantial feast. Please allow me to finish my meal and then I will move my things."
"I'll come back in twenty minutes." The prison officer replied. He was very reasonable about the whole matter, which made the position I was taking harder to play out. Twenty minutes passed and I was still nibbling and genuinely enjoying the leisurely pace of consumption. Normally my food hardly gets time to touch the sides of my mouth. The officer reappeared. "Still haven't finished but getting there. As you can see the food has diminished."
"I'll be back in ten minutes."
I was to receive a few more visits before the tray was cleared of it's contents. "I just want ten minutes to digest my food then I'll move." It was going to take a couple of trips to the three's to move all my books and papers. As I entered the cell I recognised

the smell that I had earlier experienced in the dinner queue. I was to be sharing with the old man. I looked at the screw he gave a grin which suggested that my intended cellmate was no accident.
"No way." I said and went to retrace my steps when my path was blocked. I turned and made my way in the other direction down the up stair and my path was again blocked. I jumped over the railing and joined the twos and then negotiated the stairs and then avoiding a couple of tackles made it back to my cell.
Immediately I shut the door and made a barricade against it with my bed. I then stripped naked and grabbed the Johnson's baby oil and covered my body with its contents. The cellmate sat there stunned at what was happening. I removed the barricade. The door opened the screws were out side mob handed but did not come into the cell. The cellmate was removed and the door relocked. Some of the collaborators had witnessed the chase and now were using the spy hole to see what was going on in my cell. I sat naked on the bed poised in anticipation of the door bursting open and being rushed. I figured that I was safe while the collaborators were still out of their cells. When it went quiet outside I knew that the confrontation was close. I grabbed the piss bucket and stood on the bed in a corner furthest from the door.
When the door did open it were at least eight against one. "You are not going to be silly about this are you?" I was asked.
"I'm not being silly. What is your problem? I thought I was remanded in custody to be kept secure. I'm in a cell going nowhere what's the problem?"
"What you doing with that?" pointing to the piss bucket
"You give it to me for pissing and shitting. I can't apologise about its contents."
"We are not going to get violent are we?"
"I'd just like to go on record that the first mention of violence was from you. I've made no threats to anyone."
"What about that?" pointing at the bucket again.
"I told you about that and I'm not oblivious to the lot of you creeping closer to me."
I quickly removed the lid from the bucket and retaining the handle swung the empty bucket in the enemies' direction. The

mob floundered, panicked, ducked and dived. Having regrouped they grabbed me by my arms and legs in a futile attempt to pin me. I withdrew my limbs that simply slithered from the grasp of the screws. "Send for towels." ordered the senior screw.
When the towels arrived the screws eventually wrapped them around my wrists and ankles and balanced my body on other towels like a harness.
I was then carried from the wing. There were a few screws that definitely seemed up for it but I wasn't going to give them the satisfaction. I would have played into their hands. I would have taken a beating without getting paid for it and given some of them an excuse to feign injury in order to get time off with pay. I began to realise if you have a problem with someone in authority, abusing their position, the worst thing you can do is hit them. You are doing them a favour. They get compensation, time off work with pay and you get slaughtered.
One screw in particular would need to readjust his grip that resulted in me being jerked upwards. He seemed to need his knee to assist on each occasion. Whether it was meant to be provocative to me or therapeutic for him I don't know. It fucking hurt though but I was not going to give him or anyone else the satisfaction of knowing.
I was now outside the wing and in the open air. The screws voices carried and bounced off the adjacent building that we had just left. The noise brought inmates to their windows. They saw a naked man spread-eagled being carried away by several screws. The cheers and jeers began. I assumed the former were for me.
"Go on Tel."
"Leave him alone you wankers, he's a straight goer."
Being Easter Sunday gave a religious edge to the whole affair and I was beginning to a get a feeling of *'déjá vu'*, forgive them they know not what they do.
On arrival to the block the reception committee was there to greet me. The cell door was already open in anticipation. I was delivered into the cell in a slingshot fashion followed by a period of sliding. The corners of the several towels were still in the grasp of each of the respective screws. They wiped their hands free of the baby oil and off they went leaving the block staff to

lock up.
"I've seen it all before," the senior screw of the block said to me shaking his head as he looked down at my naked body sitting on the cold floor, "you can't beat the system."
I replied, "If you don't win then you lose. If I don't lose then I win."
He paused before banging up, "I haven't heard that one before."

CHAPTER TWENTY-TWO
COMMITTED

When the bolt went back that morning I turned over. When the door opened I feigned snoring.
“Marsh get up.” ordered some Neanderthal.
“What time is it?”
“Seven thirty.”
“And you expect me to be up at half past seven on a bank holiday Monday. You’re having a laugh.” I put my head back down on the pillow.
The sheets were pulled off me and I pulled them back over me. He pulled the sheets again. My point made, I jumped up out the bed and was quickly out the cell still naked. The speed of my rise startled the screw. I think he thought I was going to chin him. I sauntered out as if it was the most natural thing in the world. I had a nice dream that night so my blood pressure was high in some parts of my anatomy. It made the screws feel uneasy.
The Adjudication was again a farce I was 'condemned' to the block for about a week. I got into a good routine and every moment was productive be it mentally, spiritually or physically. Both the screws and I knew where the line was drawn and each of us did not trespass over it. When it came to the final day I was told to pack my things in preparation for returning to the wing.
"If its all the same with you I'm happy where I am. I'm staying here."
"I am giving you a lawful order to pack your things."
"I'm quite happy where I am thank you."
So I found myself in front of the Adjudication panel again. Now there was another Governor. How many governors has this place got? I was sent to the block for a further two days as punishment. This was fun I had beaten the system. The two

days up I was ordered to prepare for leaving. "I'm quite happy where I am thank you very much." I envisaged the scenario whereby this was going to be my home until the trial.
It was time for a visit and I was duly escorted over to the visiting block. Visit over I was escorted back to B wing were my possessions awaited me. B wing was more sedate and smaller than C wing. The screws did not have the same aggression as those on C wing. Things on B wing seemed less oppressive. I could not put my finger on it but I did not like it. First impressions? I preferred the shit hole. I may have been deluding myself but I believed I was now something of a hero over there and would have liked the opportunity to have another stay there. I felt I could have caused a lot of lawful destruction. Having now been a student of the Adjudication Manual I knew enough to make life difficult for the screws. I'd been assigned a cell on the two's although I did not enter it. I remained on the landing looking down below on the ones waiting for lock up. At lock up each of the prisoners, on the arrival of the screw, would enter his or their cell.
When it came to my turn I remained looking over the balcony.
"Ok." said the screw.
"You talking to me?"
He gesticulated towards the cell
"Its ok, I'm staying here."
"You've got to go in your cell."
"Why? I mean I'm not going anywhere and the wing doors are locked and you'll only be opening up again in another hour or so."
"You've got to."
"Why?"
"Because if you don't go in of your own free will we will have to make sure you do."
I sat down, "Away you go then." The one screw now became three.
The task of man handling me began. It was over in seconds as I was thrown into the cell. My possessions followed.
"Hey mun lee d'mun lone. T dun na tin," said my new cellmate. He seemed to like my entrance, “spect mun wha ya name?”
“Paul.” I replied. He didn’t know of me or recognise me. I liked

that. For the first time for ages I had anonymity and I didn't have to worry about a cell confession. He was from Holland. We shared a spliff which chilled me but not enough to placate me concerning my badly torn mattress that I was expected to sleep on.
The next opportunity to get out the cell was for the evening meal - late afternoon they did like knocking off early. I didn't have an appetite – despite the puff. I got to the hotplate and the food was piled on my plate. The boiled potatoes were grey with flashes of black while the custard was like yellow water. The food never served the demands of the palate but was sufficient to satisfy the stomach but today it surpassed itself in its vulgarity. I thought it would be of better use to the floor than my stomach and so the tray spun 180 degrees. "Sorry," I said to the screw "don't suppose I could have some more?"
"Pick it up."
"So you can give it to someone else. In your dreams."
He wanted to take it further but I walked off back to the cell. The 'accident' caused some distraction and a few others also had spasms resulting in the 180-degree tray spin. He was pulled between dealing with those still there and me walking off.
I put the excuse for a mattress outside the cell door. The screws were right behind me. "What's the problem?"
"There's no problem."
"What you doing with your mattress?"
"I haven't got a mattress."
"What's that?"
"A large sponge."
"It can't stay there."
"Well it's too dirty to remain in here."
"Its a fire hazard."
"Ok, I'll sort it out."
I picked up the mattress and threw it over the landing.
"Right, down the block."
I had a good routine down the block. Now back there again I hit the ground running. I was knocking out the ton-ups, which was now something of a misnomer. It was now 30 reps of twelve exercises. Exercise complete I would give myself an improvised shower with the jug of water, as I stood in the bowl. The

mopping up was done, utilising a prison vest. The arms by now where tired and the wringing of the wet vest was another exercise which was only complete when the floor was dry. I was once again high on endorphin. The physical excursion also helped me sleep like a baby. The adjudication the next morning was becoming routine. Different governors but of one mind. It was all becoming very monotonous even my kangaroo impression. More loss of remission and I had not been sentenced. The exercise period proved informative. I was one of several. However, I stood out because of my lack of facial injuries. These lads had been transferred from other prisons where it had kicked off. They must have lost the battle. When the punishment period was over I stayed fast but another visit allowed them to move me back to B wing.

I was returning to my previous cell and anticipating the Dutch Rasta and another spliff. I was disappointed when I saw my cellmate was a middle aged grey haired overweight red neck. Time to move I thought. This time I tried a different approach. I put an application for rule 43, a prisoner protection scheme. I stated that I was in fear. I found myself up in front of another Governor and was asked if I had been threatened. I said no and explained that I was in fear that false confessions could be made against me by other prisoners. I thought the best way to combat this was through rule 43. It was bullshit but I wanted my own cell and own privacy.

A couple of hours later I was summonsed from my cell and told to pack my things. I found myself being moved to another prison, Pentonville. Being situated on the eastern side of London I recognised how much better it would be for my family when visiting. It was built in the mid 19th Century and was officially a local prison. I still had to go through the reception procedure on arrival. There was a couple of the inmates working there handing out the clothes who both knew me from my amateur boxing days in the East End. "Got any gear Tel?"

"Nah I wasn't allowed to bring anything with me I had to leave behind all my tea bags, chocolates, tins of fruit and breakfast cereal."

"I'm talking about steam, steam tugs - drugs."

"Oh nah I ain't."

"There you go." he surreptitiously slipped it to me. It was easier to take it than reject it. The latter would have drawn attention to us both. I did not know what I had wrapped up in the cellophane. I assumed it was puff?
I was assigned my own cell that was in a much smaller wing than I had been accustomed to. A few inmates made themselves known to me. One in particular was noticeable because of his smashed in teeth. An injury he received down the block after it had kicked off.
I'd been in Pentonville a couple of weeks when Nigel Benn became World champion beating Canadian Doug De Witt. He and Ambrose were due to make a visit. A more important visit was the meeting I was to have with Henri and my Barrister Judith Nutt. The committal was now only a week away and I had lots to go through. I had gone through the many depositions dozens of times analysing every word. There were many points that I wanted to highlight. The main points were the so-called confession, the green jacket, that the police had found with gun residue on the chest and cuffs and words that had come from Frank Warren's own mouth, after being shot, implying the shooting was a collective act rather than the act of an individual.
With the formalities of the introduction to Judith out of the way it was down to business. Fifteen minutes had been booked which became apparent when the screw kept entering, "Times up."
Fifteen minutes was enough for Judith but not for me and I still had not made my input. I had the same statements to go on as her and being a professional she must have noticed what I had and perhaps much more. But it was a ridiculous situation. I have an important day in my life and all I'm given is fifteen minutes. The whole thing stinks and I was angry. Judith and Henri had now left. I got up to leave with the screw. He told me to stay where I was. "What was the rush for if I now have to wait?" I asked.
He locked the door returning several minutes later. "Ready?" he asked.
"Nah. You fuck me about I'll fuck you about. I'm not moving."
"I'm ordering you to move." he said in his Yorkshire accent. I did not like this screw anyway. He had an arrogant manner about him against other prisoners as well as myself. I wouldn't need

much provocation to subject him to a piece of offal removal. In fact at that moment in time I would have enjoyed it but he was a distraction to more pressing matters.
"You better get your mates because you ain't capable on your own. You're fucking inadequate. You can't back up your hard man image one on one."
He left locking the door behind him and went for re-enforcements.
He returned mob handed, "Come quietly or we'll use force."
"I'm not moving."
So each limb was grabbed as was my head and I was lifted and carried. My hands were bent inwards towards my wrist and, as before, one had to be more enthusiastic than the others which caused serious pain. I tried to blank out the pain. I closed my eyes and bit my lip to prevent reacting to the sadistic act. "Down the block." one of them said.
As I was being carried through the prison wings so I could hear the other prisoners being banged up. At the same time the screws were removing my clothes until I was naked. I was carried head first into a cell. I expected to be dropped but was pinned face down on the floor by several screws. Both my arms were bent up my back while my legs were bent so the soles of my feet were touching the cheeks of my arse. My head was held in a protective manner unlike the rest of my body, which was being aggressively restrained. One screw was giving the instructions and the others were dutifully obeying. I opened my eyes. I could not see what was going on, the palms of the hands cradling my head acted like blinkers. Systematically screws began to extricate themselves from the cell until only one remained, his weight being all that was now pressing down on my bent limbs. On the command he made for the exit and the door was slammed shut.
So this was the block. It was a lot more Spartan looking than the Scrubbs. Nearby was some excuse for clothing. It was a one size fits all top and bottom. It was made of a heavy nylon that appeared designed for life's unfortunates. It appeared indestructible, easily washable and incapable of being used as a tool to do harm either to the occupier or their captors. It was back to the ton ups.

My training was interrupted by the arrival of the screws en mass. They told me to put the indestructible clothing on. I donned the trousers, which were like a baggy pair of shorts. The bottoms on I began to question myself. Why did I conform? What was I doing? It was them that stripped me naked. If they want me dressed then they should do it. It was not a big deal having no clothes on. It had also happened in the Scrubbs but I suppose the difference then was it was on my terms not theirs. Perhaps they had a psychological edge this time? I balked at wearing the top. I was able to restore some sense of rebellion. My manhood covered up a Governor entered, a female of the species. She informed me that I had a visitor and that if I didn't misbehave she would allow me the visit.
The visitors were Nigel and Ambrose back from America with the championship belt in tow. Outside the prison was a gathering of press who recorded the new World champion's appearance. The next day I was taken to the block in preparation for a further adjudication for disobeying a lawful order. I spent a couple of hours studying the manual, which held up the proceedings a bit. When I was first summoned I complained that I had not had sufficient time to study the manual. I was allowed to remain in the cell for longer.
Eventually I was up before a governor. It was the same governor whom had 'allowed' the visit from Ambrose and Nigel. It was the usual routine, "You are charged with disobeying a lawful order do you understand?"
"No, I wish to have legal representation."
"Denied. How do you plead?"
"I can't plead because I don't understand the charge."
"We will assume that you are making a plea of not guilty. Call the witness."
The screw gave his account, which I did not disagree with. Then I was asked if I had anything to say.
"I would like to question the witness."
"Why?"
"Because it is my right."
"Go on."
"You say that I disobeyed a lawful order. Could you define what a lawful order is?"

The Governor interrupted, "I'm not allowing that."
"Hold on, you deny me legal representation then question my right to question a witness and now forbid me from asking him if he understands what a lawful order is. After all, he is saying I disobeyed a lawful order. I want to know if he knows what he is talking about."
She relented, "Ok."
"Er a lawful order is er, er, er that given by my superior officer." The screw flustered. Heaven forbid if what he said was correct but it was not a time to gloat. The arrogant screw had shrivelled to his rightful place in the pecking order of life. Even within the prison room at this stage my status was elevated above his.
"He doesn't even know what a lawful order is. How can he accuse me of disobeying something he don't even know the meaning of?" In true lawyer fashion I went on, "I move that the case be dismissed..."
"I know what a lawful order is." interrupted the Governor.
"You won't mind telling me then seeing as I have been denied legal representation."
She prevaricated. I interrupted, "A lawful order is best described as that given by a prison officer or official in the execution of their duty be it construed as a fair and reasonable order to give to a prisoner. He doesn't know what a lawful order is. You don't know what a lawful order is. How can you form a judgement?"
It did not stop her from reaching a verdict of guilty. Although there was not much she could do. The committal was very soon. My punishment was a further loss of remission.
I got a visit that afternoon from Jacqui and Karl he was now approaching seven months. She seemed to have got herself together with a little help from her 'friends' - the police and the press. She also was still getting loads of help from my family. Mum Dad and John were the *de facto* parents of Kelly and Karl. That was perhaps why she was looking so well, everyone was at her beck and call.
I noticed that there had been a few exclusives some genuine while others fabricated. One was with a Sunday paper, which had been done by a freelance, promising her £40,000. He ripped her off as he did with me on a previous occasion. Still deals had been done and money was not a problem for her. The irony of it

all was that the stories were about how hard up she was. She wasn't.
Her other 'friends' were the Police. She had a couple of female Met coppers helping her out. She had them running around doing errands and everything. She needed help and they gave her it. Emotionally she was very delicate and I suspect that they knew this and were keen to keep their 'star witness' on the right side of sanity. At one stage it had looked as though the children would go into care because of Jacqui's disposition. However, Mum was the predominant carer and when the social services came to visit, the children would be looking 'spick and span'. The social services would leave happy that she was coping. I think the police would have liked to see Kelly and Karl go into care it would have made their job easier in 'grooming' their witness.
Jacqui's sanity was a key issue in this. I had not made any claim on this but she had her problems. It was not her fault but it was not mine either. These things happen and I just took the view that I had made my bed and had to make the best of it. I did not love her and never did but felt an obligation to protect her and when Kelly arrived my fate was sealed. I knew that without me she would fall apart. The police were doing their best to help her keep it together purely to serve their own ends. One thing that I found despicable was that one or some of the coppers had bought Kelly a present for her birthday. How low can you get? Buy a kid a present while trying to put their Father away for twenty years on dubious evidence.
The most damaging part of Jacqui's statement was her claiming that I said, 'If I lost the court case I would shoot Frank Warren'. However, all this was hypothetical because there had been no court case. During the interrogation the police put this to me and I put the statement in context. They never pursued it. I considered they were satisfied with my answer.
I was surprised to get a visit from Jacqui. The last communication I had was from her solicitor who had served divorce papers on me. I signed them leaving the blanks to be filled in by her solicitor. It could have been seen as an unconditional surrender, but I was not going to go crawling to her. As a wife she was not a compellable witness. That meant she could not be subpoenaed to give evidence. Had the divorce

gone through, so I understood, she could not refuse to testify. It would have added a few more of them feathers to the prosecution's case. It was a bizarre affair a 'key witness' visiting the prisoner.
It became so apparent that she was my reason for being remanded in custody. The line spun that witnesses were in danger and feared for their lives was based on this one person who was now visiting me. Still I made allowances for her. It was not an act of altruism on my part I had a 'reputation' to restore. Much of the crap written about me, by the newspapers, had emanated from her. None of it would stand up to proper scrutiny and her time in the witness box was going to be the moment to do it. The many phone calls she made to my parent's home were taped and sitting with Henri. I felt sorry for her, she really was a lamb to the slaughter, but it was not my shout. It was not me who was moving this. It was now the police or the Crown Prosecution who were the driving force. They felt that they needed her. It was them that were using her and I suggest without an ounce of concern for her future well being.
I was pleased to see that she appeared to have got herself together, but I knew it was transient. The question was how long before she fractures again? It was a difficult time in some respects because I could not do anything to help the kids. However, I was comforted that family and friends were there to pick up the pieces when that time arrived.
It was the eve of the Committal hearing when the cell was opened early. I recognised this as the start of the leaving routine. I got breakfast early and was told to pack my things ready for leaving. I made the point that the committal was tomorrow not today but the screws insisted that they were right. "I was at the court when the date was set so I should know."
"No it is today." insisted the screw. I did not want to go on a fool's errand because leaving and then joining a prison is a big disruption. All your items have to be taken with you. It was always the case that your personal items exceeded the capacity of plastic bags and tattered boxes that somehow you manage to acquire. Then you have your depositions. Ninety-six witness statements in my case. As far as evidence was concerned it was just one statement. That being the statement of Peter Harris,

the so-called 'cell confession'. Harris was his pseudonym. He had to hide behind a non-de-plume because prisoners don't take kindly to people who grass. I did not see him as a grass but an opportunist. I mean the grass can cover the spectrum of motives from conviction to expediency and be either honourable or dishonourable. Peter Harris went off the spectrum. He was a storyteller. I was looking forward to meeting him just so that I could put a face to the name. Until I was able to do that he could have been one of many. I had spoken to many and parts of the conversation could have easily have been one of those many meetings I had in those first few days.
It was comforting to have a name that was supplied by him. Otherwise, it would have been necessary to refer to him, as Mister X. It would have been too much of a risk to assign him a conventional name. In case by coincidence it was his actual name. That could then have been used against me. The chances of getting his forename correct must have been in the realms of 100 to 1 but it would have been another of those fucking feathers added to their case in the hope of tipping the scales. I was hoping that his name was Pinocchio. Along with the depositions was the transcript of the police interview, which was a great read that ran into 300 pages (www.terrymarsh.info).
I now found myself sharing a large cell with dozens of others. Systematically prisoners would be summoned until I was the only prisoner remaining with a couple of screws loitering. "The Court have changed the date," they informed me.
"Don't tell me let me guess. Tomorrow?" the shrug of shoulders and embarrassed grin confirmed I was right. I was lead back to my cell and the screws helped with my possessions.
I was fairly upbeat about what approached. I expected to be home very soon. I had now built up a good understanding of what a committal was. It was not about innocence or guilty but the integrity of the evidence. Was there a '*Prima Facia*' case? As well as Italian I was picking up a fair degree of Latin phrases. It meant, was there a case to answer at face value? I was confident the answer was no.
That night after bang up I laid on my bed thinking it was my last night in captivity. I drank my tea and ate my bar of Kit Kat. I had got some baccy and rizlas in anticipation of having that

spliff passed to me on my arrival. On unwrapping it I was disappointed to see it was yellowish powder.
As the night progressed so I became restless and could not sleep. My mind was active and much was running through it. I thought about the discarded Kit Kat wrapper and the 'jimmy'. I also thought about that powder which I presumed to be heroin. They were separate thoughts but it was not long before I was thinking of each in concert. Before the night was out I was chasing the dragon.
The Committal began with the prosecution giving a brief background to their case. I had a terrible headache that day and found the proceedings difficult to follow. The light seemed to exacerbate my suffering and I would intermittently close my eyes and cover the lids with my hands to allow some reprieve from the pain. They called upon a Mr William Hawes as their first witness. He described himself as a pensioner who would sell a few boxing tickets and with the commission purchase a ticket for himself. Were he a defendant he would have been described as a ticket tout. He was a keen boxing fan. As he stood in the witness box, his story unfolded. He had both his hands out grasping the front ledge of the witness box displaying an array of gold rings. He explained how on the last day of November he was waiting outside the Barking Theatre where a boxing promotion was taking place. He was waiting outside for a friend, Scotch Peter whom he was holding a ticket for. He then heard a bang and then saw a hooded man running towards him. The man he described as mixed race. He then told of how five weeks later he made a statement to the police saying, the gunman looked like Terry Marsh.
Later in the day Peter Harris appeared in the witness box. It was good to see him in the flesh and put a face to the name. There may have been a 'meeting' between us but I had no recollection. Harris informed the court of the alleged conversation that he had with me. It included how I confessed to shooting Frank. The police then produced the green hooded jacket. It had begun to look quite worn and the police made much of this jacket. However, Judith Nutt somewhat stumped them when she made the point of the distinct lack of badges on the item. Witness statements showed that the gunman had

badges on his coat. Still the prosecution case was enough to persuade the Magistrates that there was a case to answer and I was therefore committed to trial. I would be tried at the Central Criminal Court - The Old Bailey. The Hawes statement and the green jacket were merely padding. Evidentially all that was pertinent was Harris's statement.

I was astounded how I could be imprisoned on the strength of this bloke Harris. Okay perhaps it was not for the Magistrates to decide whether he was lying or not. I'm at one with them on that but I was to be imprisoned for several more months before trial solely on the word of this guy. Magistrates can only give a maximum of six-month sentences but they were effectively exceeding that term by committing me for trial. Innocent until proven guilty? What a load of bollocks. I really began to question the mindset of these three people stuck up there on the bench. They seemed very much to be guided by the Court Clerk and took her advice. Why did they not just stick the Court Clerk up on the bench and do away with the facâde that I was being committed for trial and denied bail, a euphemism for imprisonment, by so called members of the community. I would love to be inside their heads just for a few minutes to try to understand the motives of these people in volunteering for the task and then doing the states bidding. Generally they must have a pretty high opinion of themselves to think they can be dispensers of the State's justice. I only hope they have no skeletons in their own cupboards. Still I would be sleeping well that night. I hoped they couldn't and shame on them if they did.

CHAPTER TWENTY- THREE
POLICE CUSTODY

I was sent down to the cell and knew I had to wait a few hours before I would be picked up by the prison wagon and taken to another prison. I had been overlooked when it came to lunch but Tina Weaver, from the People newspaper had somehow used her journalistic skills to get to see me in the court cell. She had brought a burger, fries and milk shake for the prisoner. I fancied her the first time I saw her when she had done the story for the People newspaper. Our paths had crossed on a couple of occasions since our meeting but this was the first time I had butterflies in my stomach. For the brief moment she was there my headache ceased.

Much to my surprise I was not taken to Brixton there was an intermediary stop somewhere in Westminster. I noticed we were now in the charge of Coppers. The van unloaded, the human cargo was led into a hall that was effectively a massive cell. There was around sixty of my peers sitting on the integral benches that hugged the walls. I met a former opponent Vernon 'the entertainer' Vanreil. We did not get the chance to say much he was leaving as I entered.

It is easy to go unnoticed in such an environment but there was one person who stood out. It was because of his demeanour rather than appearance. He was a little boy inside a man's body. He was confused and worried because he had lost the money that his Mum had given him. The gist of it was that he had it clenched in his hand on arrival but it had now gone. Some bastard had nicked it. The next occasion the door opened the simpleton approached the copper, "Mister Policeman I've lost my money." The copper wasn't interested at all. He was more concerned with getting the new arrivals in the hall and shutting

the door behind them. The poor thing was getting a bit of stick from some prisoners. Those who were giving him stick did it out of ignorance and insecurity. He or them that stole his money did it out of pure wickedness. There was not a lot I could do to help him but I shamed those earlier teasers into keeping silent. The next occasion the door opened I tried to help him, "This lad has had his money stolen and I want to report a crime.."
The door closed before I could complete my sentence. It was not the intention to bring amusement but it brought smiles from many as if to say, we could have told you that would happen. Still it got a bit of sympathy for the simpleton and hopefully it would assist him in some way whatever prison he ends up in. When summoned I, with a few others, was led through a labyrinth of corridors and each assigned a cell. This was quite a big building and appeared like a prison but I did not know of any prisons in Westminster. I assumed it was purpose built to cater for arresting demonstrators. It seemed too close to the seat of government to be a coincidence.
I was placed in one of many cells that lined the corridor we were in. These cells were a fraction of the size of what I had been used to. It was about the size of a disabled toilet. My headache returned. The bright light in the cell did nothing to alleviate the pain and seemed to exacerbate it. Even when I closed my eyes the light seemed to penetrate my lids giving me a sheet of amber rather than the blackness I longed for. I persevered until a copper passed. "Can you turn the cell light off please. It's keeping me awake."
"In a minute."
I waited a minute. I waited two minutes. It became five and then ten. I pressed the button in the cell to summon the coppers. I waited and waited and fucking waited. "Fire, fire, fire, fire," I shouted.
I heard the sound of racing footsteps and shouting. I then saw several coppers some with fire extinguishes at the ready.
"Now I've got your attention. Will please turn the light out."
"That's not fucking funny" said one copper.
"It was not meant to be fucking funny. I just want the light out."
The light stayed on and the headache continued. I could not even pace up and down my cell - it wasn't big enough. I felt like a

The winner in Manila; having just won the Gold medal at Welterweight.

The passing out parade for the King's Squad - I'm centre, front row.

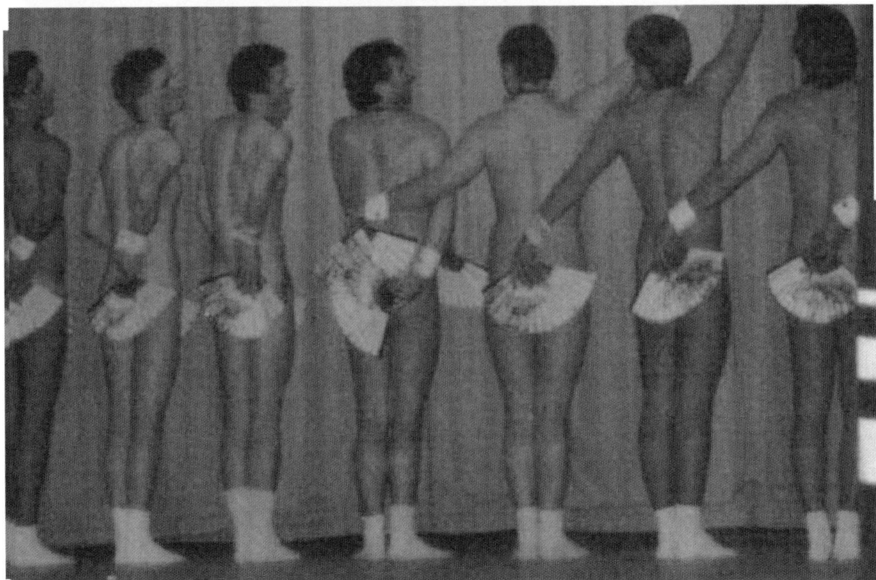

Top: Playing the Commando with actor/friend Glen Murphy. Bottom: On stage with White watch Tilbury at a firemen's concert.

Top: Manley v Marsh in the Big Tent the fight begins....
Bottom: Ouch.

Top: I'm loving it.
Bottom: Not very pretty but effective.

Top: A rare occasion where there was light between the two protagonists.
Bottom: Joe Frazier can't help you now pal.

Top: Nearly there.
Bottom: *Quod Erat Demonstrandum*..

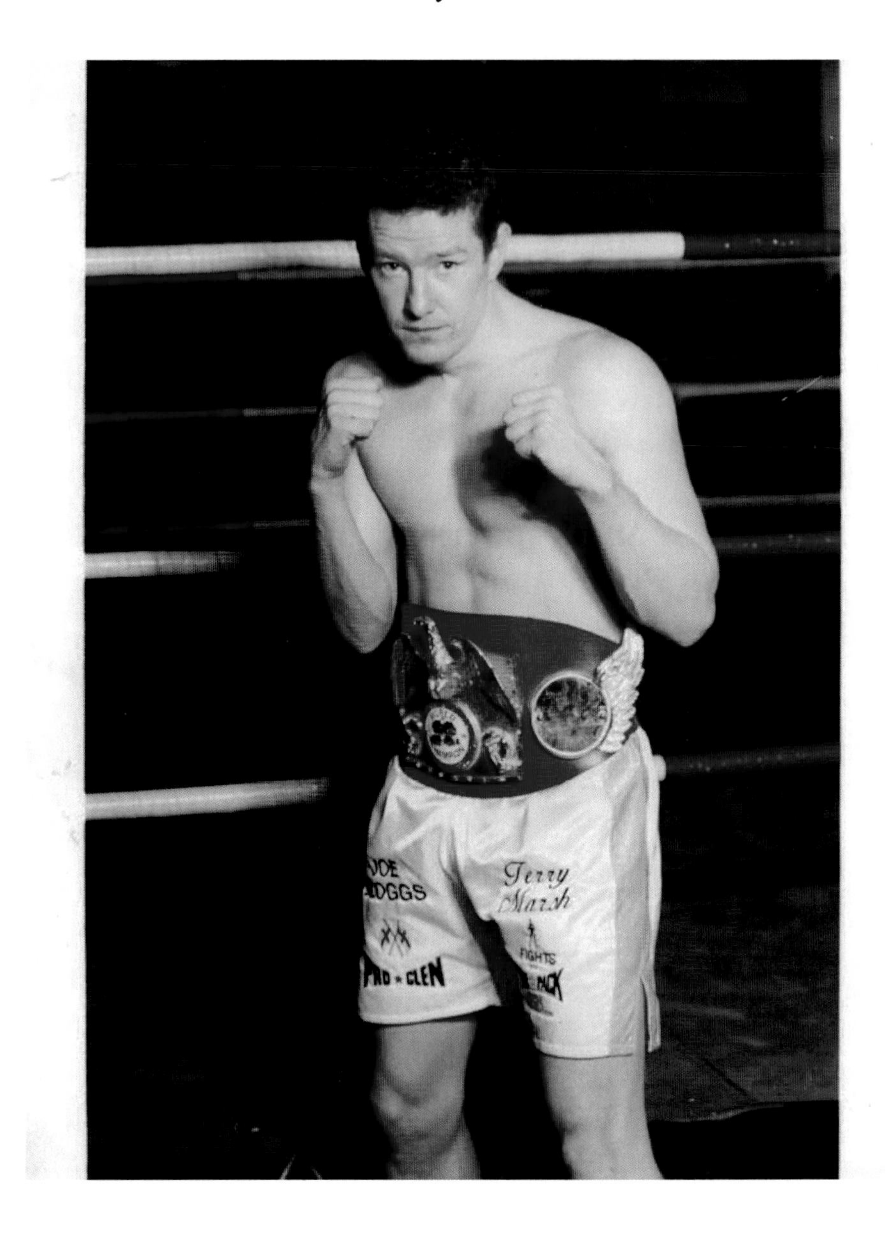

Undefeated

caged animal and whether the bastards knew it or not they were subjecting me to torture. I eventually wrapped some clothing round my eye and must have gone to sleep.
When awoken I was loaded onto another prison van. We were not going to Brixton by the most direct route. We stopped at numerous police stations en route. I expected more prisoners to be picked up but they were being dropped off. After what appeared an eternity it was my time to be unloaded, I with two others, one of which, was the simpleton. Like those before, the drop off was a police station. This one was in Hayes. It became apparent that there was industrial action by the Prison Officers Association (POA) and the prisons weren't accepting any more prisoners for the moment.
I remember reading a report about the Prison Officers Association complaining that they never had enough manpower and were concerned for the prisoners and overcrowding. My experience suggested that their words and their actions were at a variance. Double their money and they'll be willing to have six to a cell. It was the first industrial dispute where I have had no sympathy for the Union.
Anyway I was now going to get a taste of being a custodian of the police. It was clear that our accommodation had been improvised. We entered what looked a cosy room from which three cells could be serviced. It did not have the impression of being a place of work but one of leisure. There was a few cushioned chairs, presently empty, facing a television. There was a also a coffee table with a few newspapers resting on it. I had heard stories, when in the Scrubbs, about prisoners being held in police cells; a legacy of past industrial disputes. Those involved always referred to them nostalgically. The new regime, on first impressions, suggested a change for the better. I was shown my cell and the door closed behind me. The television and home comforts were for the police.
I managed to get into reading numerous books during my stay both fiction and non-fiction. I would get consumed in the book and it would take me over for the duration. I was also still plugging away with the Italian.
My jailers seemed to welcome their new duties. All they seemed to do was sit and watch telly all day with their feet up. It was

more overtime, extra money. The food would come from the police station and was simply 'canteen food'. It was appreciated for the first few days but then I began realising this was not a healthy option. I requested salads. The only tasks for my keepers were to accompany me on my hour's exercise, which was a bind for them. Initially they had each of the three prisoners handcuffed to a copper and we would 'exercise' on a section of ground adjacent to the police building. That lasted for a couple of days then they tried to pair me off with one of the other prisoners. "No way" I said when they tried to pair me of with the simpleton.

Notwithstanding that he was not very mobile and acquired an unpleasant smell I was not going to do their job for them. The poor thing should not have been locked up in the first place. He needed care and attention, what the fuck he was doing there I didn't know. I mentioned it to the coppers. They felt uncomfortable with the situation but they were only doing their job. Despite that pang of guilt they had a cushy number. Visits were more relaxed and you did not have the overbearing presence of screws. I even got a visit from Tina Weaver, the friend or the journalist? She was clearly a journalist of that I was only too aware. I had a story to sell after the trial. However, I hoped and wanted her to be more of a friend than a journalist. Letters were exchanged and I found myself being seduced by the correspondence. Were her letters written to lift me or lure me? They served both purposes I felt great after reading them and I wanted her more. She was the person I wanted to be with after the trial.

Occasionally, at the whim of who was on duty, I would be allowed to make a phone call. I would phone my parents to speak to Kelly. If she wasn't there I would phone her at her Mums. Jacqui and I would obviously talk but I would steer clear of talking about anything legal, suspecting that the phones were tapped. After a couple of occasions the calls to Jacqui's were forbidden. "Orders from above." one of the coppers said. It was not long before she phoned me and was told that she was not allowed to speak to me. The copper informed me that she had called and what the situation was. I was amused at what I suspected would happen next. It was a Saturday night and fairly late. She probably had a few glasses of wine, which was a contributory factor to her making the call. I imagined that she would be on the phone to the Metropolitan police demanding that she be allowed to speak to me. The Met keen to keep her on side would capitulate. They, so they thought, needed her so much.

It was about fifteen minutes before I was informed that there was a call for me. "Its your wife." said the copper amused by the about turn.

Jacqui told me how she got on to the Met and used her influence. She had them on a piece of string. It was a simple ploy, if you don't do what I want I won't do what you want. A *quid pro quo* seems fair enough but she would insert the trade off at a time when you were at your most vulnerable. Such tactics had plagued me all through my marriage.

That night Jacqui was at her best getting the Met flapping around making up rules on the hoof. It was a strange situation; the matrimonial home was in Basildon Essex, some fifteen miles from the 'Mets' limits, but for the duration the address was under the jurisdiction of the Met and not Essex police. John had been told this by some Essex police whom he knew. Another reliable source of information was from the Freemasonry community.

From both sources John had been warned that he was a suspect. If that was the case I was only too pleased to take the heat from him. For that theory to fit it would have required John to have had a stand in during the gunman's initial loitering while he was at the doctors. John would have been clever enough to do that but the police would not be clever enough to work it out.

While confined to the police cells I got a visit from some 'lay visitors'. These are people who call at police stations to see the prisoners. I don't know what the intentions of these visits are but in practice they serve as a check on the police. They had little, if any, authority and perhaps their potential presence, served a beneficial purpose. I was asked whether I was comfortable or not. I made the point that I was uncomfortable about the simpleton being here. It was clearly wrong and that they should be doing something about it or contacting someone who could. His departure a couple of days later made me feel good about myself. I don't know whether the move was connected to my protestations. I just hoped that there was a little compassion and understanding in the system to cater for the irregular occurrences and that he was moved to a suitable place. It also needed compassion and understanding on the part of those within it. On this occasion the police showed a lack of both. I hope the prison visitors compensated for the police's shortfall.

Police cells did have some advantages. When they sent out for a takeaway you could also make an order and the occasional curry was appreciated. It very much depended on who was on duty. On a few occasions I was invited to join them watching the television but I always declined. I felt uncomfortable about taking something that could, at a whim be retracted.

Now having seen this Peter Harris and heard his evidence I was keen to find out more about him. I had asked around and had been given a name of an inmate who worked on the hotplate around the same time as Harris. This guy, I was told, was now at Brixton prison. I wrote a note to John giving his name and details so that he could pay him a visit and find out what he knew. I suggested that he leave a tenner for the bloke's cash account to keep him sweet. I also had instructions for John to give Jacqui seven grand so that she could pay off the second mortgage that she claimed she knew nothing about. The police were trying to make an issue of this. It was quite comforting that they had their sights on other matters since it suggested to me that they had a fall back position. As was the case with all the letters this one was scrutinised, unbeknown to me this one was also copied.

The timing of my note to John could not have been any worse. It coincided with Henry making another appeal for bail at the High Court. In the hands of a prosecutor the note was presented with all sorts of connotations. Interfering with witnesses, perverting the course of justice and bribery were implied. Henri informed me, in his usual understated way, "It does not paint a good picture."

Suspecting that Harris had done a deal with the police, meant, he needed to be investigated. It seemed it was all right for the police to go around questioning anybody they liked, leaving some witnesses feeling extremely intimidated, but I was not allowed to

investigate witness's making allegations against me. It was blatantly obvious that there was an ‘understanding’ between this Harris and the police.
One inmate had said to me earlier on in my incarceration, "They lock you up to fit you up. Then when you try to undo the fit up they accuse you of interfering with witnesses and perverting the course of justice." They can investigate you but you can't investigate them. It is not as if they are objective about the whole matter. If they were objective you would never get police complaining or feeling disappointed about a verdict. They should see every verdict as the right verdict. If it is good enough for the jury it should be good enough for them.
I did have some fun with my letter writing. I wrote to my cousin, David a coded message. He informed me that he had not received it. I assumed the police were busy trying to decipher it. It was returned to me six weeks later. I don't know why it was retained for so long. The coded message when successfully deciphered read: 'Once upon a time there was a bunch of wankers who had nothing better to do with their time than waste it on deciphering codes'.

CHAPTER TWENTY-FOUR
HMP BRIXTON

The industrial action lasted a month or so before I was transported to Brixton. The prison had been built in 1819. From 1898 it was a trial and remand centre for the whole of Metropolitan London. Joining routines were much the same wherever you went. However, there were slight deviations dictated to by the layout of the building and timing of your arrival. I was taken aback when asked my prison number. I pleaded ignorance. "What number?" Being in police custody had eroded the need for numbers.
"The number you were assigned when you first entered prison."
I could not say that I had forgotten it. I never made the effort to remember it. So I made one up.
I got there late morning and was fed at the reception area. On tucking in I quickly realised that I was going to have to re-adjust my culinary expectations. As the day progressed so more prisoners arrived and the dining area was becoming increasingly cramped. It soon became standing room only. The tea I had drunk with my food had now worked its way through my system and wanted to leave. On the next occasion the door opened I informed the screw that I needed the toilet.
"You'll have to wait."
I unzipped my trousers in preparation for a piss.
"Ok, ok you can go." the screw relented.
A cheer went up. It was early evening before we were systematically taken over to a wing and assigned a cell. I was sharing a cell with someone who described himself as a former Tory Councillor, which was more than likely as he faced a charge relating to escort agencies and pornography. He claimed his only crime was not paying the police enough. I was to discover that

the cell assignment was temporary and the next morning was assigned a cell with another new boy Mickey Freilander.
Mickey was from the East End and lived very near my former East London home. At around 22 he was ten years my junior. But had a much greater experience of prison life and its culture. On the first occasion I went out on exercise with him he met up with a few of his mates from 'on the out'. They acted as if the incarceration was the most natural thing in the world. The conversations were about the state of play of their respective positions in the legal cycle. Arrested, released, arrested, released, arrested, charged, bailed, arrested, released, arrested, charged, bailed, arrested, charged, remanded, tried, verdict, probation. Spiced in all this was the mention of drugs. Drugs seemed the driving factor in it all. Mickey did not appear hooked on anything chemical but he seemed to have become part of the system or the system had become part of him. He had, to use his coin of phrase, been 'captured' on or following a burglary. I felt comfortable with him and suspected that there would be no fabricated cell confessions. He was a petty criminal and seemed to enjoy the life style. The language he used made it sound like a playground game. It was like he had not left school and the police and prison officers had replaced the teachers.
He seemed to mix with the druggies but not get drawn into it other than the puff, which was not regarded by anyone as problematic. He pointed out to me how to spot those on heroine. 'Their teeth shrink'. I don't know whether it had any scientific basis but I started looking at people's teeth and also gave mine a check because of my indulgence. He had been captured fair and square and would be copping a plea of guilty. He figured that he would do a few months in 'Wanno' (Wandsworth prison) then be out. He didn't see the point of taking his chances with a not guilty plea. "If you are then found guilty they lump you off."
"But what if you are not guilty?"
"If they fit you up and you are calling the police liars. You are questioning their integrity; they can bring up your previous. Who are the magistrates going to believe?
"Plead guilty put it down to drugs and go for a drug rehab."
"Why don't you do that?" I asked.
"Already done it. Run by a bunch of fucking weirdoes. I would

piss off for a couple of days then go back and say I was feeling depressed and needed time alone. They swallowed it every fucking time."
This was a new insight. Mickey went on, "The joke about it all is when you are accused of something you have actually done you are prepared with excuses and alibis. When you haven't done it, it is harder to defend against unless you can be certain what you were doing at that particular time."
As we walked around the exercise yard daily so conversations flowed. Few admitted to being caught through there own stupidity. It was always the case that they had been grassed. Whether this was factual reporting or a case of being in denial only they would know. These guys were marked men and much of their time was spent on remand on charges real or imagined. They were not big players but the police must have seen them as the 'usual suspects' and things were made difficult for them with the help of grasses.
"It's pretty straight forward." said Mickey. "They threaten to remand you unless you give 'em something."
"What money?"
"Nah, info. It becomes crazy because you get pulled in for questioning for something you know something about but did not do. You then worry about being released because your mates might think you have grassed. So you are hoping to get charged and remanded in custody for something you have not done." he laughs again.
"How come all these big time gangsters can get away with it then?"
"Work it out."
I couldn't but one of Mickey's mates put his theory forward, "These big firms are operating because they are allowed to operate. If the police wanted to close them down they could. Why do they allow them to operate? Because police get something from them, it's a trade off. The bigger the crook the bigger the grass. It was the only way they could get away with it."
He had a point if I could be remanded in custody with no evidence why couldn't these big boys?

The whole routine of prison visits I found disturbing. The

visitors were treated like shit. It was particularly short sighted where children were concerned. Kids were not allowed to interact and play with their Dads in a natural way. The kids were the real losers in this and nobody seemed to care. A case in point was when Kelly came to visit. I had a bar of chocolate for her but was not aloud to take it on the visit. I gave the screw a look of pity. "I'm only doing my job." To be fair to that screw he was not happy with what he was doing. I had some sympathy for him but there were other wankers who seemed to revel in the position.
This was particularly hammered home during the Brixton visits. One such screw who resembled a power lifter was monitoring the visits. The task could be justified on security grounds but the main aim appeared to be the prevention of drugs coming into prison. As visitors and prisoners embraced or kissed so drugs could be passed. When one such oral transaction was suspected so the big blob pounced. In the hope of preventing the prisoner from swallowing the suspected evidence the screw grabbed the prisoner around the neck. The prisoner was restrained from flapping his arms and legs by two more screws assisting the lump that had the prisoner trapped in a neck *cum* headlock. It was quick but violent and for all to see. I was taken back by it and just glad that Kelly was not present to witness it. Sadly other children did.
I understood it was a common occurrence but it did not deter people bringing drugs in. There were always plenty of people clucking. Which suggested the demand outstripped the supply. Clucking was a symptom of dependency on heroin. It was described as doing 'cold turkey'. Mickey only did puff which he managed to easily acquire.

Screws, referred to, as the 'spinners' would search the cells frequently. Your cell would get ‘spun’. On one occasion I was reading a book, To Kill a Mocking Bird, when the spinners appeared. It meant leaving the cell and waiting outside on the landing. Engrossed in the book I treated the invasion with indifference. I left the cell before being told and sat against the wall on the landing. One screw ordered me to stand up. I continued reading. "Get up." he persisted.

I looked up at him to acknowledge I had heard him and went back to reading the book.
"I said stand up."
"I heard you the first time but I'm alright here thank you very much."
"You are disobeying a lawful order. Stand up or you're down the block."
"Come on lets go then." I said.
Up I got and two screws escorted me to the block. I had now been in three prisons in less than five months and I had been down the block in each of them. I was in the block for half an hour or so when the screws came in mob handed, "Has he been searched?" asked the screw in charge. On hearing the negative I was searched. The routine was that you remove your upper garments then put them back on then you remove your lower garments. I did not like that so I removed them all and stood naked, stripping under my terms, in front of them with a big grin to compensate for deficiencies in other areas, notwithstanding it being late spring it was a particularly cold day.
I was then ordered to squat. I had seen this routine pulled on numerous prisoners. It's designed to find out those prisoners who have stuck drugs up their arse. I also knew by reading the prison manual that it was not a lawful order.
"It is not a lawful order." I informed them.
"Yes it is." they informed me.
"Okay put it in writing and I'll do it."
They relented and left me alone to get dressed. They returned half an hour later explaining that the screw who brought me down there was new and a bit eager. I was allowed to return to my recently spun cell and continued reading my book. Mickey had a spliff waiting for me.
The block was not the most intimidating section of the prison. The view from the cell window presented a more hostile looking residence. There was an exercise yard about the size of a tennis court. It had the pre-requisite of high fences like the other exercise yards, but unlike the others covered with wire fencing giving the impression of a cage. It was a prison inside a prison. I would notice on occasions the cage being put to use by the

residents of that particular block but the numbers were never more than half a dozen. Most times it was two or three. "That's where the IRA boys are." Mickey informed me.
Apart from the one episode with the spinners the regime in Brixton seemed less aggressive than the Scrubbs and I did not have many opportunities to make a stand on principle. One instance did occur though when Mickey wanted to go to the toilet. Again through reading the prison rules, I learnt that the bucket was for night time purposes only. Mickey had a call of nature and sought permission to go to the toilet. His request was denied, "Do it in the bucket." was the suggestion.
I made the point that it was his entitlement. Furthermore, I did not want to be subject to seeing him crap in a bucket and have to put up with the smell of the deposits. Mickey laughed it off but I was not going to take this lying down. So I took it squatting. I dropped my trousers and sat over a piece of opened up newspaper and did a shit on the problem page. It was duly wrapped like it was a portion of fish and chips. Mickey passed comment on the smell. "Sorry mate but this is a point of principle."
When the doors next opened I exited the cell with the parcel and headed towards the screw's office. I released my grip on the parcel but still pinched a corner of the wrapping with my thumb and forefinger. The paper unravelled and the contents hit the ground at speed and at an angle. The timing and impact was perfect, as was the exit strategy. I'm sure I could not have done a better job had I tried another hundred times. Mickey thought it was hilarious "You've got some nerve." It was as if he would not dream of such recourse but then I would never have the nerve, even if I had the inclination, to do some of the things he had done. It was not long before we got a visit from the screw. "Can I have a word?" he was looking at me. Why me I thought it was Mickey who wanted the shit. "That was a bit extreme."
"What?"
"It doesn't bother me. It's your mates who have to clean the shit up."
"They're not my mates, they are collaborators. They're more your mates than mine."
After Mickey had his court appearance he was shipped off to

'Wanno'. I now had a cell to myself but felt uncomfortable with the situation. I had a degree of stability with Mickey. I trusted him but now there was uncertainty about what awaited me concerning the next cellmate and those after.

I really did not want to take the chance of running the risk of another 'cell confession'. The trial was estimated to be some four months off. I did not see that as a long time. After all I had now been banged up for 6 months so I was well into the second half. I also needed every day of that remaining four months to complete my 'Italian in three months' course. It was probably more of a reflection on me than the course. What it did serve to do was alter my concept of time. Four months to wait for a trial would be for most people an eternity but for my purposes the time was barely enough.

I decided that I was going to create and I needed some pretence for doing so. It was easy in the Scrubbs and Pentonville the screws gave you every opportunity to have genuine grievances. At Brixton apart from a few indiscretions a fairly straight game was played.

I made my concerns known about being exposed to another opportunist prisoner looking for a way out. I also implied that should my concerns not be addressed then there would be disruption. I did not know what I was going to do but I was going to do something.

CHAPTER TWENTY-FIVE
CATEGORY A

I was taken to the high security wing. I was stripped searched before entering and allocated a cell on a landing with only six cells. There were four other prisoners on my landing. The so-called landing doubled up as a recreational area as there were some tables and chairs. Two prisoners were much younger than I in both looks and attitude. From my perspective they were kids. Darren was still in his late teens while Lee was barely out of them. Both had been charged with murder. Darren's resulted from an interrupted burglary in a shop. He mentioned unashamedly that the deed had been recorded on the in-house video. "A legal first." he added.
Lee, following a high society burglary got a black cab home. An ingenious getaway I thought. He informed me that the Cabbie got suspicious of his young fare and was driving him to the police station. When he did not yield to Lee's threats, Lee shot him. Perversely I felt safe, they were both resigned to the fate that awaited them and would not be able to do any deals with the police.
Lee was hooked on heroine and despite the high security was able to get the stuff in although there were times when the supply dried up. The other two, Luke and Steve, were also my juniors. Luke was in his mid twenties while Steve was somewhere between Darren and Lee. However, Steve was more reticent which I suspect was a combination of caution and maturity. He kept his cards close to his chest. He also had the distinction of being restricted to wearing a blue, prison issue, bib and brace with a yellow vertical stripe running the length of the clothing on one side. This was to denote that he was an escapee or depending on your view some one who failed to escape despite

trying. Luke on the other hand was very vociferous, claiming the police had fitted him up by planting drugs and a gun in his car.
In reality everyone is fitted up. It is the nature of the way the police investigate. Once they have failed to eliminate a suspect from their enquiries they have to make the case fit around their man. It works provided they have the right suspect in the first place.
The first visit was much different from what I had been used to. It was a small room adjacent to the wing. To get in an out of the wing a request through a microphone had to be made. Gazing down on either side of the heavy metal door was a camera supplying a visual to the operator of the door in another remote building. If the visit was strange for me it was disconcerting for my family when they came to visit. The first visitors were Mum, her sister Winnie and Cousin Maria. When they where redirected from where they would normally go it was understandable that they were concerned. They were being taken to the centre of the prison complex and I knew they would have felt the initial intimidation that everyone experiences when gates are locked behind them. "What's going on here?" asked Mum.
The screw reassured her, "It's alright love there's nothing to worry about."
When I entered the visiting room I detected a sigh of relief from them all. They had a little baby with them, dressed in a red and black hoop long sleeve polo shirt and black corduroy dungarees that contrasted with his curly white hair. He was busy crawling around with a dummy stuck in his mouth. "Is that Karl?" He was around eleven months old now.
A screw remained in the room and because of the smallness of the room was privy to all what was being said. But unlike my previous experiences there was no intimidation and he was not in your face. He and those subsequently were very discrete and courteous at all times to my visitors. On returning to the wing I was stripped search. I did not find it any big deal and the prison officers did not make it an issue either. There was give and take.
There was more opportunity for association as your cell door, for the best part of the day, was open giving access to the landing *cum* recreation centre. But beyond that you were well and truly

locked in. The cameras that oversaw everything you did were only initially intrusive. It was not long before they were hardly noticeable. The down side of having your door constantly open was that you were always open to visitors, which can be a distraction. Furthermore, remaining in your cell can be interpreted as being unsociable. On balance I preferred the privacy of the block but the Category A section was better than the wings.

It was partly due to the screws. They seemed to have more respect than those screws on the wing. That is not to say that there was deference or reverence on their part. They did not have to show much courtesy to be better than their contemporaries on the wings. Why that was I don't know. It may have been that the ratio of screws to prisoners was greater than the wings and therefore they had more time and less stress. Or was it because the prisoners they were dealing with were people who you don't fuck around with? I figured the truth lay someway in between.

It soon becomes rather mundane after a week or so. The conversations became rather repetitive. Still what was good about my new abode was the exercise period in the cage. It allowed for a kick about with a football that was not practicable in the other exercise yards because of the numbers. In addition, the wire roofing ensured there was no worry about the ball going over the fence.

It was after a few weeks when another prisoner, Keith Rose, came on the scene. He was charged with murder and kidnap. The finer details of the charge I was not aware of. However, it seemed like the screw in charge had it in for him. He was given a hard time from the moment he arrived. In one conversation I had with him he told me that he was a firearms expert as well as a pilot. Following the advice of Scoosh, my former cellmate, I treated both with deep scepticism but on further questioning established he knew more about guns than I. I knew that I was going to be presented as a gun fanatic because several books on guns had been found in a garage. I expressed my suspicion about the idea of the gun residue being restricted to the cuffs and the chest of the green jacket. It seemed too contrived. He dismissed it completely. He suggested that I get a firearm's expert on

board. We duly did.
After a couple of weeks I found I was being moved upstairs. I knew there was some alleged IRA guys up there and I thought about my time in the Marines and in Ireland in particular. It was going to be interesting to know how things would pan out. There were four new people to get acquainted with. Scott, Bob, Liam and Damian.
"Hi, I'm Liam welcome." I shook his outstretched hand.
"I'm Terry."
"This is Scott."
"Alright Tel mate."
"This is Bob."
"Alright." I said to Bob slightly nodding my head Bob reciprocated.
"And this is Damian."
“Hello." said Damian with a grin.
"Fucking liberty they’ve taken with you Tel,” said Scott breaking off the formalities. "I know Panay and Gill from the Phoenix."
Scott was the archetypal Essex boy and proud of it. We had mutual acquaintances; fortunately it did not include his accomplice. He had been involved in a robbery at a nightclub in Ilford Essex. It all went horribly wrong his accomplice accidentally shot him as well as badly wounding the manager. The escape entailed a police chase around the East London area that included hi-jackings and kidnapping. Scott played a passive role in most of this lying on the blooded back seat of the respective hi-jacked vehicles. He was able to evade immediate capture. A few years later, following a routine police check his name came up on a police computer as a suspect. It was simply a case of checking his DNA. He said it was his first time. I believed him.
Then there was Bob. As a Category A prisoner he was obviously charged with something heavy but I never found out what it was. I never asked and he never volunteered. However, the case against him must have been weak because the prosecution case fell at the committal stage. So I did not get to know him very well.
Liam was the eldest of the two Irish lads. He was a similar age to myself, single and a history graduate. He was both educated

and intelligent and a reader of the broadsheets. He was a native of Southern Ireland and wore a very full beard that I suspected had only been commissioned since his incarceration. His co-accused Damian was in his early to mid twenties. He was a married man with a young family from the Short Strand, Belfast that was a Republican enclave in an otherwise Loyalist area. Liam and Damian seemed poles apart socially but for being Irish and the co-accused of some alleged offence against the Crown.
The four prisoners were arranged around a scrabble board. Scott was the only non-participant. He was reading 'For Him Magazine' while the eight letter words were the focus of the other three's attention. Scott showed me an article in a back copy concerning an interviewing with Frank Warren. While in prison I had become a student of Frank Warren. The magazine quoted Frank as saying, "It was silly of Marsh to lie."
I recognised that article as libellous. Prior to my incarceration I was aware of the Law of Defamation but I did not really have a proper grasp. I remember on one occasion I had what I thought was a libel against me and contacted my local solicitor. We both made a visit to a Barrister whereupon he informed me that my claim was fraught with difficulties. I paid him £1500 pounds for the privilege. I did not actually worry about the difficulties I went to the solicitor to issue a writ. The fifteen hundred pounds I spent on the advice could have been spent on the writ. The ball would then be in the court of the Defendant. Then they could pay for the advice and be told it was fraught with difficulties. It was a combination of my ignorance of the law and my deference to legal people that caused the whole thing to be fudged.
Now I was wiser or more appropriately less ignorant and all deference had gone. I saw the libel laws as primarily responsible for putting me where I now was. Had Frank Warren not sued me, then the so-called motive, the police deluded themselves to believe in, would have not been there. They would have had to look for other motives like his debt recovery arrangements or his extra marital affair to name a couple of avenues.
Those numerous defamatory articles previously written against me were now all listed in my mind. When I get out of here I will start using the libel laws as a sword. I think the laws were designed to act as a shield to protect people. But it had failed to

protect me and now I would have to use it as an act of vengeance. But that was for the future.
For the moment it was the present that was causing me anxieties. It concerned my two Irish colleagues. It was nothing that either of them said or done. It stemmed from how I felt. I felt a tinge of embarrassment and a degree of remorse. My time in prison had made me see those at the sharp end of authority, the screws, in a light similar to the role my mates and I played, as soldiers, in Northern Ireland. We had been given a degree of authority, which meant, to a point, our will prevailed. Now when that will is the will of and the wish of the state so be it; the problem arises when you make it personal. It is no longer the will of the State that must be seen to prevail, but your own will in order to look clever, funny or hard in front of your colleagues. At the expense of those you have a duty to serve and protect. It is not the way. It is counter productive and I was able to make the causal link between my actions in 'active service' in Ireland and these two guys whom I now faced across a scrabble board.
In one sense what I had received, on occasions, from the screws was deserved from the time I abused my authority with things I had dished out or was complicit to when I was a squaddie in South Armagh. It made me feel better that I in some way got a taste of my own medicine.
When the moment was right I spoke up, "Look I feel that you should know that I served in the Marines in Ireland,"
"We've no problem with that." said Liam. Damian did not comment. It was no big deal, but it made me feel better and I was able to enjoy the scrabble much more. They were both vastly superior to me at the game. I would like to think it was because they had more practice than me, but I think intelligence was the contributory factor. Besides mastering the Italian, winning a game of scrabble became another ambition. As the games progressed so did our conversations about our experiences. In particular our shared experience of Northern Ireland although from different perspectives.
Damian took what came his way whereas Liam would make representation to the screws when issues arose. Liam saw himself as a prisoner of war. That is not to say that Damian lacked the political dimension that seemed to be more apparent

in Liam. It seemed a class thing. Damian told me about the time he got told off by his Mum for being an hour late bringing home the fish and chips from the local chippy. He got caught up in a gun battle between the Brits and Provos. The excuse was not good enough. It was like gun battles were an every day occurrence. Damian saw things and lived things that made him what he was.
We got talking one day about the three IRA volunteers that got shot by British agents in Gibraltar. Liam took the view that it was a fair killing since it was a war. His criticism of the government was that it would not recognise the dispute as a war. Portraying those involved as criminals. I made the point that the British played it all wrong. I referred to the subsequent funeral, at Miltown Cemetery, of the three killed in Gibraltar and the appearance of the Loyalist Michael Stone, who later claimed he was intent on killing either Gerry Adams or Martin McGuinness, with his guns and grenades. He failed and fled shooting dead three men in his effort to escape as some of the mourners pursued him. "The government should have made heroes of those mourners. Did you see how some of them chased after Stone as he was firing his guns? Now if I was in charge I would have given them medals praised them and want to shake their hands."
"Now you can, put it there pal." said Damian as he held out his hand.
"You're a braver man than me." I said.
We spoke about my fights and in particular my title fight. In that fight when the 'shit' was flying much was made of me being a former Marine Commando. Damian remembers watching the fight in his local club. Because of my military background everyone was cheering for the other guy. "We were really pissed off when you won."

Every week we were able to make orders for various items and a prison officer would come to collect the orders and deliver them a couple of days later. He always referred to me as Terry. It was amusing for my peers and mildly embarrassing for me. However, what became more amusing was the big cross in red ink written over 'Mr', which always preceded my name when I wrote the order. Some screw in the supply chain took exception to the prefix and crossed it out. It said so much about the system. We used to look forward to the delivery day in expectation. The red cross was always there. It gave us a feeling of superiority over those petty minds containing us.

The section was reduced to three when Scott having been convicted was sent to Maidstone Prison; he got a thirteen stretch. The scrabble became even more intense as I had managed a draw but the win still eluded me. Still my vocabulary improved, as did my overall knowledge. Liam and Damian gave me a history lesson of Ireland albeit with a Republican perspective. Perversely, in so many ways, I was seeing more of the world now I was in prison than when I was out.

Much was happening around the world. And I had both the time and information through Liam's and Damian's broadsheets in which to follow the events and have a better understanding of what was going on. Until then the only broadsheet I had read was the Sporting Life.

Nelson Mandela has been released from jail after more than 27 years. The Soviet Union began to fragment and the Cold war was declared over. I did not really understand about the cold war other than it was about the competing ideologies of Capitalism and Socialism. Yet I did not really know the difference. One explanation that stuck in my mind was 'Under Capitalism man exploits man whereas under Socialism the reverse is true'.

We had a new arrival in Paul Taylor. He had been described as the leader of the Strangeway's riot or protests. It had been put around in the newspapers that he was a rapist. It caused him no end of embarrassment and he was keen to show his depositions to anyone who would read them.

He cut a lonely figure. It was hardly surprising in view of his predicament. He was from up north and his incarceration in London could only have been an act of spite on the part of the authorities. As I understood it, he had completed his sentence and was now on remand awaiting trial for 'rioting' or some similar charge. He was well proportioned but as the time moved and the days went into weeks he noticeably became very rotund. A result, I think, of the inactivity and his daily consumption of several pot noodles from his canteen orders. He would pass his

time drawing and then colouring cartoon characters on envelopes. I would use them when writing to Kelly and Karl.
With regard to sending letters I had a little task that proved more difficult than I had imagined. It was early September and amongst Mister Marsh's usual request for long life milk, Alpen, Kit kats, teabags, baked beans, sweet corn and sardines there was an order for one hundred birthday cards and stamps. I got a visit from security wanting to know why. I showed them the poem:

September 20 is the day,
to celebrate in a special way
The cards that come they will be many,
from Auntie Trace and Uncle Kenny
A hundred cards came from his Dad,
who at that time will feel so sad
He cannot share the special day,
being locked up a long way away
The cards are a token of what he feels,
and hopes the gesture does appeal
To Karl, not now but when he's older,
for he can always cry on his Dad's shoulder.

They had to think about it. I got an answer a couple of days later. I was allowed fifty cards. You would think they were paying for them.
I was due a visit from my barrister who would be representing me at the trial It was pencilled in for late October. I was intrigued by how many barristers were keen to defend me. A bit of fame certainly has an advantage in such a position. Judith Nutt who represented me at the Committal proceedings was still on board but she would be taking a supportive role to a more senior barrister whom was a Queen's Counsel (QC) named Richard Ferguson. My QC was presently busy representing Ernest Saunders in a trial that involved matters during the Guinness take over of the Distillers Group. The plan was for him to see me on the conclusion of that trial. However, an adjournment allowed him the opportunity of paying an earlier visit. He was not hopeful for Ernest Saunders. "I told him not to

go into the witness box but he insisted... they kept him in there for a very long time. It was a mistake."
There was not much for me to say he was already well versed with the case. Henri had already supplied him with my history. There was little said it was eerie, this man was going to be representing me and he hardly knew me. At best pre-trial he would only be spending a few hours with me. But it was explained to me by Liam, "This was not about you but about the evidence in the depositions. The only people working on you are the Prosecution."
A new statement that had been submitted concerning the green hooded jacket unsettled me. The jacket had been taken to someone at the Royal Ordnance Corp who was asked to examine it. Upon examining it the person concerned noticed a small hole on the left breast. On being asked to give an opinion on this hole it was conceded that it could have come from a badge since discarded. The evidence had shown that the gunman wore a jacket with a badge and they were trying to make a case that this was the jacket. The point about the omission of the badge at the committal had caught the prosecution out.
This hole only seemed to appear retrospectively. It did worry me immensely. I had examined the jacket at the committal and saw no hole. I believed that the hole was made sometime between the Committal and the Royal Ordnance Officer examining the jacket. However, too many people would have had an opportunity to tamper with the jacket in order for the culprit to be identified.
As much as it unsettled me it was strangely reassuring. It highlighted the weakness of the case that some misguided person felt the need to tamper with evidence. I had given the police the benefit of the doubt with regard to my arrest and subsequent charge. The cellmate confession, I'd concluded, was more a case of opportunism on the part of the storyteller. However, I believed a rogue copper within the organisation was intent on fitting me up, but I did not know who it was.
The Jury found Mr Ernest Saunders guilty and the reviews of the case was that he should have remained silent and not gone into the witness box. At my next meeting with Richard Ferguson he did not make any further mention of this but all my visitors were telling me not to go in the witness box. I was hostile to the

suggestion because I wanted to fight back and that, I perceived, was my only available weapon.
I received a visit from Tina Weaver following some letters. I was hoping that a romance could flourish. There was a battle going on between my head and heart. I had to be strong. I knew following the trial and the acquittal a newspaper deal was on the cards. That was likely to be big money. Henri already had received approaches. Henri was not the only person approached. I had heard that the Daily Star had signed up Jacqui. The word in Fleet Street was she was theirs. I just hoped that the Star would not take advantage of her and paid her appropriately. Others associated with me had also been approached by various arms of the media, who seemed to be covering all bases.
Despite what the verdict was going to be I am the same person pre-trial as that post-trial. Yet, depending on the verdict I was going to be either a victim or villain. I was neither. The verdict had a life of its own and mattered more than the reality. It may be that the verdict is consistent with the reality but if that is so, is it through the thoroughness of the due process or simply by chance?
On the scrabble front I was getting there. I could taste the victory. I was left with the letters, U, R and D. Not high scoring letters but I put them on the exposed S to spell 'SURD' on a triple word score.
"Get off." said Damian.
"No such word." said Liam.
"Yes there is, it is a math's term"
"I'll get the dictionary, I'll show ya."
The cell doors were locked; I went to the screws' office. Our keeper was crashed out snoring heavily. I called over to Liam who joined me to witness the screw slumped in a chair, head back mouth wide open, the keys for the taking. We laughed at the situation but even our laughter did not wake him. I was overruled on 'SURD'.
I had another legal but Richard Ferguson was absent. It was with Judith Nutt and Henri. It was going to be Judith's task to cross-examine Jacqui. She had a pre-planned strategy she wanted to run by me and check for accuracy. She seemed really up for it. On hearing the bones of the presentation I began to feel

sorry for Jacqui anticipating that she would be left humiliated by my representative 'acting on my instructions'. It was not a true description of what was happening. More accurately Mr Ferguson was acting on my behalf. To say he was acting on my instruction would suggest that I was running the show. I thought I was in the initial stages but I was no longer under such delusions. I was not a player in this I was the prize.

The days of reckoning were closing in. A couple of suits, shirts and ties had been sent in to the prison for a good appearance at the Old Bailey. I remember as a kid my Dad making reference to the Old Bailey. He was referring to the statue that sat spire like above the building. In one hand it held the scales of justice while the other hand held the sword of truth. Dad had pointed out the statue faced the West End while its arse faced the East End. I made the observation that I was going to be the first person to top the bill at both the Old Bailey and the Royal Albert Hall.

CHAPTER TWENTY-SIX
THE QUEEN VERSUS TERRY MARSH

Come the first day of the trial I was transported in a Cat A prison van which I shared with Luke from the floor below. As we raced through the London traffic everything seemed to be moving so fast and I wondered how all these cars managed to avoid each other. I was not frightened but found the speed difficult to adjust to. It had been nearly 5 months since I had last seen the outside of a prison. I had adjusted to prison and now everyday life was an aberration.
I was placed in a large cell joining many others. Some were familiar faces from my times in the Scrubbs, Pentonville and C wing in Brixton. I sat and waited and watched the drama that was being played out in front of me. There was about twenty in the room. Purely on statistics there were both innocent and guilty. To what extent would the verdicts reflect the reality?
Before me was an array of emotions from outright bravado to complete bemusement. There was a French lad who was up for the stabbing of a young lady. He could barely speak English when I had first met him in the Scrubbs some eight months earlier, but now he had mastered English sufficiently to express how he feared he would never see his grandparents ever again. He had come to Britain for a holiday and ten months later he finds himself facing a life sentence. He appeared totally bemused by it all.
Then there was the security van driver who was accused of being the inside man on a robbery. He was dithering on what he should do. He was soliciting for advice. "Believe your innocent if you don't believe it how the fuck do you expect the jury to believe you." was the advice proffered by one prisoner who seemed sure that he was going to beat the rap.

"Do me a favour mate, it's the fucking day of your trial and you still haven't got your story." was the input of someone else. Also present was a few guys accused of involvement in the Brinks Matt robbery. There was Gordon Parry who I got to know at the Scrubbs and Pat and Steve Clark who were father and son. Pat had offered to make a statement contradicting the so-called confession statement against me but Richard Ferguson thought it would be prudent not to accept the offer. In fact I had many prisoners offering to make statements contradicting the statement of Peter Harris. Most had as little truth in them as that contained in the prosecution statement of Harris. Can two wrongs make a right?
My first entry to the dock was strange. I had an idea of where I was going and what it would look like but I had no idea as to when the moment would be. The cells were in the courts basement; in earlier times they would have been called dungeons. As I was escorted along the narrow passages and up various flights of stairs I was suddenly looking into a larger space. I was still looking upwards as I appeared in the dock to see the public gallery Mum, John, Dennis, Dartsy, Ambrose and Glen Murphy. Glen was now a well-known actor in the successful series London Burnings. We got on well before all this nonsense had occurred but he did not try to disassociate himself from me much to his credit. Perhaps the prudent thing to do would have been to keep a low profile with private support, but he went public with his support for me and to hell with the consequences.
I smiled and waved. Dressed in a blue serge suit with my Royal Marine tie, as an accessory, I did look smart. I did not particularly like dressing up for the occasion but I was under orders from John, Mum, & Dennis. I think they may have had instructions from Henri, who was seated forward and to my left behind Richard Ferguson and Judith Nutt. To their right were two other barristers who I rightly assumed were the prosecutors Anne Curnow and Nigel Sweeney. Seated behind them were the coppers. Opposite them and to my right was the section for the jury and the witness box - it looked inviting. Seeing the witness box and the opposition made me want to take up the challenge. 'Fools rush in...' Behind me was an equally large area as to my

fore that was packed out by others whom I could not then identify. I was later to learn that the mass behind were a mixture of reporters, lawyers, police cadets, court staff and anybody with a bit of influence on the legal circuit. The seating capacity compared to the public gallery was much greater. If only I could have packed them in like this when I was fighting. To my disappointment I was not topping the bill. I was in Court number two. Still it wasn't bad seeing I was a mere novice in the criminality department. It could hardly be referred to as the under-card. I was ordered to stand by the warder escorting me. I obliged.
"Terry Marsh you are charged with the attempted murder of Frank Warren and possession of ten 9 millimetre rounds of ammunition how do you plead?"
The show was on the road. It kicked off with a legal argument concerning the admissibility of some evidence and the relevance of both charges against me being put before the jury. The Crown wanted to have both charges presented together whilst, understandably, Mr Ferguson argued that the two alleged offences had no relevance to each other. It was 9mm rounds that hit Frank Warren and I was charged with being in possession of nine millimetre rounds but they were of a different make to the offending bullets. Our concern was if the jury had to make a verdict on both charges. Confusion could arise and there could be a difficulty in differentiating between the two charges.
Had Mr Warren been struck with a hammer then I would have had serious problems because there was a hammer in the house. Had he'd been stabbed, again I would have had problems since there were numerous knives in the house. As it was he was shot. I didn't have a gun but they did find a gun book, several in fact. It was also highly inconvenient that bullets were allegedly found. But the relevance of them was put into perspective by the judge's decision to let the charges run separately.
The other issue concerned evidence that was illegally seized by the police during the search of my parent's home. Documents, relating to communications between Henri and I, concerning the now postponed libel action were seized, contrary to what was specified in the search warrant. Amongst those documents was, at face value, a damming piece of evidence. I received advice

from my Counsel Mark Warby that suggested, I could not win the case and that I should settle out of court. He had given such advice on an incomplete submission. The error occurred through misunderstanding and omissions however, to a partisan audience, like the police, it would support any already biased theory.
It allowed me to run with the line that the police had acted illegally. It was by no means immoral but it did not stop me milking the fact. I told everyone who would listen. After all it was something that was in my favour and against them so you take it. What had happened was that they had seized the papers while doing their various searches and only later discovered that they were legal papers. However, the documents that had been seized illegally were admitted. The legal joust took all day and it was time to be escorted back to Brixton. Luke's spirits were up he was sure he would soon be walking.
The following day I still had not got used to the rush hour traffic and anticipated accidents at every junction. On arriving at the court in one piece I was back in the holding cell with many others for my morning's entertainment. It was also like watching a play when I was in the dock half an hour later. The dock was raised, on a similar elevation to the judge looking down at all the other participants. The jury was sworn in. I took the names of each with the intention of inviting them to a meal after the trial, subject to the verdict of course. The day started with the Prosecutor, Anne Curnow, addressing the jury. She talked through the Prosecution case. Guiding them through what they were going to hear in greater detail over the forthcoming days.
"There was a man who was identified as the gunman. Our case is that man was the defendant...There was no positive scientific evidence linking Marsh to the gunman...The Crown points to motive, the descriptions of the gunman, the coat recovered and his possession of similar calibre ammunition. One thing that is crystal clear is that the gunman intended to kill Mr Warren and only failed by a few centimetres." I was really annoyed, she referred to Frank as Mr Warren and me as simply 'Marsh'.
She went on, "During the course of evidence you will hear the evidence of William Hawes who identified the defendant on the night of the shooting. You will hear how they came face to face.

You will also hear about a confession, by Marsh, made to a cellmate...you will hear how Marsh had a keen interest in and a history of possessing guns." She went on and on. The motive? "Marsh feared the libel case. He would be exposed as a cheat and a liar. Bearing in mind Marsh's high media profile during his very successful boxing career, he was facing personal humiliation of a very high order." She was convincing, she even had me believing her. It was time to call their witnesses.
I did not know who was going to appear. There was now over a hundred statements. It became apparent to me that the Prosecution and the Defence teams had been in discussion. This I found unnerving, one of my side was fraternising with the enemy without, either, my knowledge or consent. This get together was merely a means of finding the common ground. If there is a witness with whom no issue is taken then it can be agreed that their statements may be read out in court rather than having to call the signatory to the witness box. Only, those 'contentious witnesses' would have to be called to allow for cross-examination.
The police had it in their heads that I still had possession of guns from my time that I had a firearms certificate. The Browning 9mm and Magnum revolver had long gone. The second firearm certificate that I had been granted I never received. A cock up at their end but according to their records it had been sent to me. They were trying to imply that I had bought guns on that licence and still had them. Notwithstanding that the certificate would have long expired. It was really frustrating listening to the Prosecution being selective with their questioning. I quickly discovered this was not about searching for the definitive truth but about presentation.
At the cross-examination stage Fergie was able to put our truth. It was revealed that the Essex police headquarters had records of issuing the licence but no proof that I had received it. That was good enough for me, I knew the reality, but had the jury grasped it?
Fergie spent less time on the questioning than the Prosecutor and I feared that it might go against me. The other side of the coin was that more was in fact less. They did not have anything and therefore had to pad out what little they had to justify the

case. I would swing to and fro on this line of thinking several times in as many minutes. I was trying to get inside the minds of the jury. I felt like shouting at the salient parts, did you get that, just to re-emphasise the point.
Next was Bob Burrows of ITV. He was another person with whom I had little real contact. He seemed as though he really did not want to be there. He talked his truth about the relationship between Frank Warren and myself and how things ended when I was informed that I would no longer be allowed to commentate on the boxing programme. A reference was made to the occasion when I was refused entry at the promotion in Wales. Ms Curnow interrupted Mr Burrows, "We will come to that later." I knew what she meant. It was the time I gained entry to Frank's promotion dressed as Father Christmas.
It had come to the attention of those close to me that this was going to be one of the press angles should I be convicted. 'Marsh master of disguises'. The News of the World had signed someone up for the exclusive. Had the gunman dressed up as Father Christmas I would have really been in the shit. 'Santa Claus is gunning' and 'Warren Sleighed, were two headlines that sprang to mind.
Whether the Prosecution was going with such a line I did not know. However, because of the 'rules of evidence' there was only one potential witness, Leslie McCarthy. Leslie's name had cropped up at the Committal hearing. The so-called eyewitness, Hawes, had referred to receiving fight tickets from one of the detectives who took the incriminating statement from him. "Where did the tickets come from?" was one of the questions we asked the detective Michael Carroll, "Leslie McCarthy." was the reply.
We knew of Leslie's conviction and imprisonment for attempting to pervert the course of justice of a trial at this very venue. Now we find that he is giving free tickets to a detective who passed them on to a witness who had just made an incriminating statement that contradicted his previous statements. It seemed as though Leslie McCarthy was going to be called. I was not aware of the finer details of Mr McCarthy's transgression so Henri contacted police boss Inspector Rees for details of the criminal history. While at it we asked for the record of Bob

Hawes' the so-called eyewitness. Rees came back with the report that there was 'no criminal trace' on either. Henri pushed the matter of McCarthy, the prosecution prevaricated and we never got a reply. But he was one witness who was not called and no further reference was made to the promotion in Wales.

One man who spent quiet a bit of time in the box was, Stephen Heffer, Warren's solicitor. He was there to put his truth about the alleged libel. He had a difficult task of telling his truth and also respecting the so-called client confidentiality. What became apparent to the Judge was that the so-called motive for me 'shooting Frank Warren' was eliminated. Fergie was good he had done his homework.

In fact it was Henri who was supplying the ammunition for Fergie to fire. It was a consequence of being a high profile case. Henri and my family were being inundated with information about the witnesses. It was effectively dishing dirt but we had loads of dirt to dish on most of the witnesses. Frank Warren in particular. When my former manager entered the witness box he was unusually wearing glasses. He was subsequently reported as giving me a stern stare that I had not noticed. I was probably distracted by his chin, which appeared to me to be quivering. During the prosecution questioning Frank came across as a compassionate, caring, selfless sort of person. Questions were put to him about his role as my manager and how we interacted. He spoke his truth. I was busy jotting down notes in preparation for Fergie's cross-examination. I had much to challenge him on. At the cross-examination Fergie did not use any of what I put. Only as the line of questioning developed did I recognise his strategy. Ms Curnow had shown Frank through her questioning as an angel that I am sure he is. How could I have any reason to shoot him? Unless of course there was tension between us. Fergie was not challenging anything concerning the Crown's case regarding the relationship between Frank Warren and Terry Marsh – there was no tension from me.

Frank spoke about the night he was shot. He got out of his car and got shot. He could not or did not add anything further.

As Miss Curnow sat down Fergie stood up. It was his turn. He started questioning Mr Warren on other relationships that he had with, his creditors of which there were many, his mistress,

and his relatives. My information about Frank's cash flow was bang on. Under questioning Frank admitted his company Rex Williams Leisure Ltd had gone into receivership with debts of £3 million pounds. A subsidiary of the Company, Silvertape had been wound up with debts of £2.5 million. His Company, Frank Warren Promotions, had not filed their accounts. It was also admitted that there was a personal loan with National Westminster Bank for £800,000. My arrest must have been a blessing in disguise. It had the effect of saving him from financing the libel action. His libel cost was a relatively meagre amount, but nonetheless a serious lump of money to find if you're strapped for cash. It leaves the question whether or not he could have afforded to have representation at the time. His debts amounted to around £4,000,000. To be fair he claimed he had assets to cover them.
There had been numerous stories in the press following the shooting and these stories gave us leads to pursue. Henri scrutinised all the news cuttings concerning the police investigation. A couple had stood out. One concerned a florist in Romford. A copper must have tipped off a journalist about a flower girl whom Warren was associated with. It came following a statement from the flower girl's mother, which we had sight of. According to the statement the daughter was Frank's mistress. Mrs Tarrant informed the police that the family received a phone call saying, "Nicola was next." Understandably she went to the police. Nicola had a daughter by an estranged boyfriend Andy Holt. I had met Holt in the Scrubbs, he worked on the hotplate at around the same time as Peter Harris. He did not hold Frank Warren in high regard, "Warren grassed me up." Holt was keen to tell me. He was clearly jealous and bitter about his ex-girlfriend's lover.
At Frank's post-shooting press conference, Frank, when asked if he knew a flower girl from Romford replied, "What kind of flower, Homepride or My Fair Lady?"
Fergie asked the same question, "Do you know a flower girl from Romford?"
The witness complained knowing where this was leading to, "I've come here today the victim of a shooting and now I am getting a character assassination." he complained further, "The purpose of

the defence is to throw as much mud as possible, hoping some will stick." Frank went on, "It has no relevance to the case whatsoever."
For the reasons explained it did have relevance. The flower girl's Mother had received a phone call that her daughter was next. It had to be pursued. Frank was ordered by the Judge to answer Fergie's questions.
"I do not propose to mention the girl's name unless you compel me to, but it is a fact that you did know a girl in Romford involved in running a flower business?"
"That's true."
"Not to put too fine a point on it, you have been conducting an affair with that Girl?"
There were giggles and gasps all around how I suppressed mine I do not know.
The judge intervened before the witness gave an answer. The jury was sent out. The judge wanted to know where the questioning was going. The point was that Frank had trodden on a few toes in his time and that it was possible that a number of vendettas existed. The judge allowed the line of questioning but warned Fergie to tread carefully. Although no names were mentioned it confirmed that Andy Holt was a protagonist in the affairs of Frank Warren's mistress. The court was adjourned before Fergie was finished. It meant Frank having to go home with something to think about. I didn't exactly go home but was transported back to Brixton.
Luke was buzzing. The prosecution case was falling apart. He was predicting being home at the end of the week. I figured I'll be out before him but did not want to gloat. Liam and Damian got the gist of what was happening from their radios. They were saying that the reports of the case suggested it was very weak.
The next day the questioning continued. It started with Fergie asking Frank if he had ever visited anyone in prison. "I don't remember?" was Frank's honest reply. It drew a few sniggers from the gallery the majority of which were either my friends or relatives. Fergie pushed him further and was able to remind him of one occasion when he made a visit to a prisoner. It was boxing related as Frank pointed out but he had to have his memory jogged. Fergie asked further questions to which Frank informed

the defence Counsel that he could not recollect. "It's like a game of poker Mr Warren. You don't know what cards I'm holding." was Fergie's passing remark before he pursued a different line of questioning but not before being rebuked by the Judge.
Questions now concerned Frank's relations. I did not think it was pertinent but who was I to question the approach of a top QC. After all this was only my first case notwithstanding the wheel clamp fiasco. "We can choose our friends but not our relatives Mr Warren." Fergie was laying the ground for Warren's Uncle Bob. He had been involved with some gangland battles in the 1950's for which he served time in prison. It did not necessarily make him a bad person. I had come to learn that there were a lot of good people in prison as there were many bad people outside the walls. Frank rightly pointed out he was three years old at the time. He could hardly be accused of aiding and abetting.
I was enjoying it. For me it was now a case of using the double-edged weapon to which I had been a victim for the past ten months. In this part of the game Frank was the ball that was being kicked around. It was not our job to be objective. The game dictated that anything and everything must be twisted into your favour. That seemed to me the way the police were approaching it. If it's black you argue its white: Its white really but you can't see that because its dark. Frank's brother, Robert, had recently been charged with an assault and he was also questioned about that. Frank was quick to make the point that he was acquitted.
Witness's came and went. There was Warren's partner John Botros he, like Frank was up to his eyes in debt. I suspect, financially, he had more to gain from his friend's death than I. I mean that as no slight on Mr Botros, a lawyer by trade, but it was just a way of putting matters into perspective. Had Frank died I would have no way of recovering the fifteen grand. I had spent defending the libel action. As much as the libel action was presented as a motive for wanting him dead it was also a reason to see him alive. Everything can be twisted. What chance have the jury got? However, Mr Botros was above suspicion, he had saved Frank's life by grappling with the gunman. In view of his dire financial position his selfless act made the deed even more heroic – I assume there existed a mutual life insurance policy.

Next was Frank's driver who gave his version. What both Botros and the driver emphasised was that the gunman was athletic and run away very fast. Well, I was known for running far but not fast. There was another matter of a broken neck that I was still recovering from, following the trampoline accident that occurred less than three months earlier.
A week before that accident I had taken a swim test at Dagenham swimming club. It was another discipline towards my stunt licence that I was trying to acquire. I got talking to some of the kids who were at the club. I remembered the occasion well. One of those kids, Bradley, was at the scene of the shooting when it was all happening. For a dare he had gone up to the suspected gunman and spoke to him. The gunman was a bit of a weirdo, which was unfortunate since it did not eliminate me from the enquiries. Bradley had made a statement to the police. A description of the gunman was given and Bradley informed the police that he asked the man the time. Looking at his watch the man gave the time. Bradley thought the watch was on his right wrist. It explained why the police was making a great deal about my watch being on the right wrist. I know us left-handers are in a minority but we are not a rarity. Still Bradley only thought it was the right wrist. There was no certainty about it.
Bradley was around thirteen years old. He entered the witness box and I thought this would clear things up. The Prosecution set the scene by asking Bradley the appropriate questions. Then came the killer question. "Did the man remind you of anybody?"
"Yes, Terry Marsh." was the teenagers reply.
I was gob-smacked. The seriousness of it all hit me. I had to take a reality check. This lad had no agenda he wasn't a plant or a grass or some low life trying to do a deal. How can I square what he said with what I know? I suspect that someone had unwittingly groomed him. How else could he come out with such a statement? There was no mention in his first statement about me. He had made a subsequent statement following my arrest because of our earlier meeting at the swimming baths. Bradley's mother, so I understand, had initiated it when she heard of my arrest. He had then said it could have been me but then again the description of the gunman was so vague it could have been anybody between twenty and thirty-five. One of the jury must

have been thinking along similar lines, he asked the judge to ask the question, "When was it that the gunman reminded him of Terry Marsh?" Bradley back tracked, "I only said he had a similar build when asked after the arrest." It was reassuring that the jury was paying attention and in this instance not tricked by the Prosecution's sophistry.

Yet it was too close for comfort. I began to worry. I now got nervous every time one of the coppers approached the prosecution Counsel thinking, 'What are they going to spring on me next'. I knew the evidence but I was suspicious of everything and everyone. I thought I was right to be so minded. I had just heard from Luke, he would not be walking after all. His co-defendant had done a deal dropping him in it.

While sitting in the cells during a recess I had a note passed to me by a screw. It was from a prisoner from another cell. I knew this guy vaguely, but had it not been for a conversation with the police earlier on in this saga I would not have been able to place him.

A couple of year's back I had put in an appearance at a wine bar on its opening night near Twickenham. The owner was a guy called Ant. He was rather young to be a wine bar owner and had just completed, despite his youth, a long stretch in the Scrubbs. Photos were taken, as was the case hundreds of other times. A photo surfaced with this wine bar owner, Ant. It was while the police were taking me to the Magistrates court in Barking, from the Scrubbs that this photo had cropped up in conversation. I assumed that it had some significance in the minds of the police but for the life of me I did not know what.

When I received this hand written letter from Ant, via a screw, I became suspicious. The screw intimated that I could change cells. I smelt a rat. I did not even finish reading the note. I declined the move. I tore up the paper thinking I may be searched while it was in my possession. Why tear it up unless it was incriminating? Its content seemed harmless but the circumstances seemed ominous. I ate it. Destroying evidence some might say. Destroying potentially fabricated evidence would be my view.

I was in front and approaching the final whistle. Had I been trailing I may have taken the note, as a possible lead to undermine the charge but my actions were now a risk aversion strategy. Was this guy genuine, had he done a deal with the police? Was his presence at the Old Bailey coincidence or conspiracy? Do I mention it to Henri? If I mention it, it suggests I consider it significant. If, I considered it significant, why was that? What do I know that I'm not telling? Had the coppers those many months back not mentioned him I would have been oblivious as to whom he was. Would that have created more cause for concern? Was I being paranoid? 'Paranoid is defined an irrational belief that you are being pursued'. Well, it was not an irrational belief I had the Metropolitan police on my arse and the Crown Prosecution service. Not to mention a man who went under the alias of Peter Harris.

It became apparent that other forces were also at work. Bill Hawes was the next witness. Mr Hawes was the witness that allegedly saw me running from the scene. Were it not for Hawes there would have been no arrest. Prior to this day's proceedings I again met up with my legal team. Henri showed me a statement that he had taken the previous evening from a Mr Jimmy Walker. I began to read the transcript. Jimmy Walker was a friend of Bill Hawes. He alleged many things about Mr Hawes but pertinent to my case was that he was paid to put my name in the frame.

When Hawes got into the witness box at the Old Bailey the scene was set. He spoke about his encounter with the gunman. He heard two loud bangs and then later saw a scuffle between John Botros and the gunman.

"This man came running towards me. He stopped two or three feet in front of me and he held his hands up, moving them from side to side excitedly." He then demonstrated the pose and raised his hands above his head 'Rocky style'. He went on, "The man bore a resemblance to Terry Marsh but I could not say it was definitely Marsh." He had not specifically identified me but had done damage. It was time for Ms Curnow to sit down as my man Fergie arose. Jimmy Walker, his friend hitherto was seated behind Fergie alongside Henri. It was not conventional and it may have had an unsettling effect upon the witness. I don't know what Fergie or Henri's take on this was but I thought that Mr Hawes had nothing to fear as long as he was telling the truth.

"Mr Hawes," asked Fergie, "did the Detective Sergeant who had interviewed you give you three £25 tickets for a Frank Warren boxing Promotion?"
"Yes," replied Mr Hawes.
"Had you suggested to a friend that he could make a few quid out of giving evidence?"
Hawes went apoplectic he pointed to Jimmy Walker seated behind Fergie and Judith Nutt, "That man is a lying bastard, he is evil, I never said anything of the kind." He then directed his rage at his now former friend Jimmy Walker. "You should be ashamed of yourself Jimmy you broke the oath." He was referring to the breach of trust and confidentiality expected from fellow members of Alcoholics Anonymous.
Hawes said that he was not answering any more questions even if it meant being sent down to the cells. The judge placated him and the questioning continued. He was asked about his past that revealed matters neither his wife nor daughter was aware of. It would have been interesting to see whether Hawes would have remained as placid if Fergie had pursued the line of questioning regarding 'earning a few quid'. But he didn't need to the witnesses reaction said it all.
It was looking good but I wasn't unscathed. As Frank Warren had said, about our defence strategy, throw enough mud and some sticks. It also applied to the prosecution. Some was sticking to me. The kid had said at one stage that the gunman reminded him of Terry Marsh. Hawes said the gunman looked like Terry Marsh and we also had the alias Peter Harris ready to tell the jury that Terry Marsh confessed to him. Would he be throwing any more mud?
The front row of the public gallery had been cordoned off with yellow tape. Why was this? What was different about this witness? As he approached the witness box he was wearing a hooded jacket with the hood placed firmly over his head. He wore sunglasses to hide his face. Perhaps he was the gunman. Having reached the witness box unmolested he climbed the steps and duly removed his hood and shades. Why was it necessary for the first row of the public gallery to be cleared? All my friends and family had already had a good look at the chief prosecution witness at the Committal hearing. Perhaps it was in case

someone took a shot at him or most likely simply for effect. So much of this trial was about presentation and effect. It contained very little substance, if any.

As with the others it was the turn of the Prosecution to bat first. I waited expectantly for him to give his evidence. The gist of what he said was that I had told him I had shot Frank Warren. He spoke of the shooting and how I, on seeing all the blood, thought I had killed Warren. He alleged I said, "He ties people up in legal documents and then stuffs them for cash." He mentioned that I had two guns. One illegal and one legal, a firearms certificate, and two boxes of ammunition, only one of which the police had found. The gun was going to be left at the scene of a robbery by a brother. He also quoted me as saying that the police had a footprint of the trainers I was wearing when arrested.

There was a ring of truth to much of this. He even had my autograph that I had addressed to his wife Jackie. I couldn't deny that. It was done in my own inimitable way, 'You're a cracker-Jack'. His wife never received it; it was given to the Crown Prosecution. What I found the most offensive, but was in fact the least incriminating, was the claim that I had said to him on the hotplate, "You look after me and I'll look after you." He explained that he worked at serving the food on the hotplate and that I asked for extra portions. Not withstanding that the food was appalling. It was not my style.

While I was banged up I had received a letter from an ex-marine, old opponent and mate Andy Gill. On leaving the Marines he became a prison officer, one of the few good ones. He had dropped me a line warning me about what I might say. "A lie surrounded by truth is difficult to find." The advice was too late the damage had already been done. What he was saying was a total fabrication and anyone who was familiar with prison, either as a screw or inmate, would recognise it.

I had, early in my remand, written a note to the prison Governor or one of them stating that I would not be talking about my case. Many who were aware of the potential pitfall suggested it. The problem was that my note came after the time that Mr Harris had alleged the conversation took place. Any half-decent prosecutor could twist my actions and argue that I had made the

statement as a retrospective measure to cover myself for being loose with the lip with Peter Harris. Or that's what I thought. So I remained silent on that matter fearing that it would be used against me.
Now it was time for Fergie. During the questioning with the Prosecution Harris revealed that he got a sentence of two and a half years imprisonment. "Did you expect to get two and a half years?" asked Fergie.
The judge who sentenced him had been made aware that he had helped police, but did not know of the specific details. Such occurrences are irregular the court was informed. The witness was aged 36 which was also the number of conviction he had to his name. His two and a half years were for fraud and deception.
Fergie read out the articles that were found in his possession 74 items in all, which included twenty credit cards, seventeen cash cards, seven driving licences, three cheque books, three vehicle registration documents, three club memberships, two P45s, two birth certificates, one AA membership, one British visitors passport. All that seemed to be missing was the partridge in a pear tree.
"All these items you were not entitled to," said Fergie, "you intended to deprive members of the public of their money."
"I was looking after them for someone else." Harris replied.
"Out of the kindness of your heart?"
Fergie seemed to make the witness a figure of fun. There was periodic sniggers and laughter during the cross-examination of the witness. He showed the guy as a complete incompetent rather than a calculating prisoner. He was a person not to be taken seriously. Would the jury take this man seriously? Fergie took him through his record of assorted transgressions. "You used Terry Marsh as a means of ingratiating yourself with the authorities and thereby reducing the sentence." said Fergie, "I would suggest that there is not a word of truth in what you said Terry Marsh said to you. You are a man, as demonstrated by your record, who is an inveterate, habitual liar." I did not know the meaning of inveterate but I was nodding my head in approval.
It was time for the prosecution to do their damage limitation. Miss Curnow rose to her feet ready to question Mr Harris. How

different the tone of questioning would be. The rare occasion the prosecution go easy on a criminal. It did not particularly achieve much but allowed this prosecution witness to finish on a higher note. The final question from Ms Curnow concerned what lay ahead for Harris now that he was in prison parlance, 'a grass'.
"It will be hell." were his final words.
It was time for the witness to leave the witness box donning sunglasses and hood. I felt that we should have been able to re-examine him. How the fuck was his present prison stay going to be hell when no one knew whom the fuck he was? He was under a false name.
Other than police officers there was only one other witness called, a middle aged lady. I recalled the name from a witness statement I had read but did not think much about it. She was smartly dressed and wore a wig that I assumed was for presentation. She spoke with a slight Geordie accent. She told the court that she had been driving home from work when she saw a man leap over some railings while she was stationary at a set of traffic lights. I considered it was a waste of time calling her. I relaxed what was otherwise a focussed approach listening to every word that came from the witness box. She then began to give a description of the man she saw, about 5 feet 10 inches. She went on to describe the person she saw as having tight curly hair, athletic, white and a long face. I had never examined the shape of my face before and now I was trying hard to remember images of my 'mug'. There were no mirrors in the dock. I asked, in a whisper, the escort next to me "Have I got a long face?"
He nodded his head. I was back in my concentrated mode, suspicious and distrusting.
I felt uneasy because there was nothing in her statement that was contentious from my point of view. Her statement could have and should have been agreed. The wig I now saw as a means of disguise. What was she hiding? Was this, what I would describe as, a utility witness? Meaning a witness whose statement was sufficiently vague that could be added to at the trial without contradiction. Why was the description of the man she saw not in her statement?
When it came to the cross examination, Fergie tried every trick to twist her words or discredit her testimony but she was wise to

it and was not thrown from her initial testimony. She was so sure of what she saw and said. There was no room for doubt at all. I had heard stories from inmates about police performing such tricks and I feared this was such a rouse. I passed notes to Henri asking if she would be able to prove who she was. She was not asked. Perhaps Fergie, thought it impertinent or against court etiquette. I was not happy with his reticence but kept my thoughts to myself. Should I be convicted I would know where the fault lay. I felt deeply uncomfortable about the whole manner of this witness. On more sober reflection I should have had nothing to worry about as her times were in complete contradiction to everyone else's. But such details can get easily lost. My reaction perhaps did not do me any favours as it brought attention to the witness which otherwise may have gone unnoticed by the jury. I was rattled. Earlier I had sat impassively listening to the other witnesses: Hawes, Warren, Harris and some coppers. I thought I understood each of their respective agendas. I understood why they were saying what they were saying. Mrs Bertt however, was different what was her *raison d'étre.*

We were then entertained with the various police witnesses who gave evidence about the arrest and exhibits found. References were made to the police's wild goose chase to Kings Cross in search of a left luggage locker containing an Uzi, an Ingram, 500 rounds of ammunition and a white phosphorus grenade - allegedly. The judge wasn't pleased. What I found fascinating about this was that when it came to the police statements concerning the alleged contents I was quoted as saying "There was an Ingram and Uzi 500 rounds of ammunition and a phosphorous flare gun." I found it intriguing how three coppers all misheard. I quite clearly said, 'a white phosphorous grenade'.

The presentation of the police interview was played out by Wiggins and Ms Curnow reading from the prepared script. It lacked the rawness and rhythm of the original. There is such a big difference between the written word and the spoken word and it was never more apparent to me. It raised a few laughs but not as many as I had expected or deserved. It's the way you tell 'em. That was the case for the Prosecution.

They would say that it was not the complete case. One witness was missing, Mrs Jacqueline Ann Marsh. The police wanted her badly to give evidence but since we were still officially husband and wife she was not a compellable witness. It was the main reason that I hastily signed the divorce papers earlier in my imprisonment to relieve her of that protection. We could have been divorced in weeks. However, Jacqui had contacted my family and said that she did not want to attend the court and so she was put in touch with solicitor John Marshall who had helped us before.

She with Mr Marshall turned up at the Old Bailey but was not called. Much to the disappointment of the prosecution and also parts of the defence namely Judith and I. Judith had prepared well for cross-examining the defendant's wife. We had tapes and bundles of ammunition, metaphorically speaking, to throw at her. Judith was going to be deprived of her moment. My feelings were mixed. I think Fergie and Henri were relieved. Not because what Mrs Marsh would say but how their client would react.

The prosecution had told a good story but they were guilty of adjusting the facts to fit the theory rather than the reverse. It was now my turn. There was an adjournment. Henri and Fergie joined me in the dock where we held an impromptu conference. Fergie was advising me not to go into the witness box and give evidence. I had been prepared for this strategy but it was dependent, I presumed, on how the prosecution case went. In view of Fergie's advice it must have gone as he had hoped or expected. This was his plan all along. I now realised why all those whom I trusted and valued in the preceding weeks were advising me, 'to shackle the cackle and zip the lip'. They were doing Fergie's bidding. I felt uneasy about it and felt I had to get in there. It would be my way of hitting back. There had been a number of matters that I wanted to correct. They had no great importance to the case but I did not want them to go unchallenged. On the other hand there were other factors to take into consideration. I was only too aware that there was a big pay-day should I be acquitted and the more exclusive the story the more the money. If I went into the witness box the press would get most of what they wanted for nothing.

The difficulty I had was if I was to give evidence and be convicted I would only have myself to blame. I could live with

that but to be passive and then be convicted would be very difficult to come to terms with. Better to have fought and lost than not have fought at all. It was finely balanced but what swung it was something Richard Ferguson had said regarding his former client, Ernest Saunders. Against advice he insisted on getting into the box and he talked his way into prison. Fergie was strongly urging me to remain silent I suspect in a similar manner to Mr Saunders. "Okay, if it goes wrong I will blame you." I said to Mr Ferguson.
"I will be happy to take the blame." he replied.
When the proceedings recommenced the jury took their seats. Fergie rose to his feet. "On behalf of the defendant I undertake to offer no evidence." Fergie made a submission that there was no case to answer and asked that the case been dismissed but it was his submission that was dismissed.
It was now the turn of prosecution and defence to make their closing speeches. It was now Thursday afternoon and the judge decided that Friday would be a day off so that the respective Barristers could prepare their speeches. I would be returning to Brixton for what I hoped would be my last weekend in prison. On my return I noticed the notice that had caught my eye when I first entered the system: *'Her Majesty's Prison Service serves the public by keeping in custody those committed by the courts. Our duty is to look after them with humanity and help them lead law-abiding and useful lives in custody and after release.'*
They failed in their duty to look after those committed by the courts with humanity and not many, if any, lead useful lives in custody.
It was good getting a visit from John and exchanging views on the trial. I still felt uneasy about the Geordie witness. John however, was able to confirm that she was a 'real person' having managed through a bit of detection and cross-referencing of the electoral register to locate her house. It would have been nice to speak to her but that probably was a step too far.
The Italian course I had not quite finished. I had covered every chapter without entirely mastering it. So if I were to get lumped off then I'll be able to give it my undivided attention. I also thought about further education. Prison showed me my ignorance. The various court hearings gave me a chance to listen

to barristers, solicitors, and judges and I was very impressed with their command of English. I wanted to have what they all had – higher education. That was to be my plan when I walked. But there were other distractions that first needed to be overcome. My children need rescuing, my wife needed ditching, a libel needed winning and there was the outstanding charge of possession of 9mm rounds.

Despite the uncertainty that lay ahead it was a relaxing weekend. We played scrabble and I claimed victory finishing with the word Oink. My two Irish opponents again denied me victory. Onomatopoeias were not accepted. What that meant I did not know.

I suspect that Ann Curnow's weekend was not as relaxed being busy preparing her closing speech. She had done a good job of it. Prior to her speech I thought I was well clear with nothing to worry about. Now I considered I was fucked and Fergie was my only hope to make up the deficit.

CHAPTER TWENTY-SEVEN
TO SUM UP

"Times had changed for all of us between now and November 1989, and they have changed for Terry Marsh even more in the last three years or so. On 4 March 1987 Terry Marsh stood proudly as light-welter weight champion of the World, a courageous but fair boxer, a respected master of his own destiny. Today, you will be the masters of his destiny and make the decision that will have the greatest possible influence on his life.
What is there? There is the evidence of a man who can't even stand before you in his own name. There is the evidence of a man who comes into court dressed like a fugitive. There is the evidence of a man whose criminal list of convictions fills six pages. You may think it is an insult to your intelligence, and a travesty of justice to ask you to convict anyone on the testimony of Peter Harris.
Harris told you Marsh told him that the gun was being used in a robbery or attempted robbery - that hasn't happened. He said Marsh thought he had killed him because of the blood and mess, when there is no way the gunman could have seen the blood and mess, because there wasn't any while the gunman was at the scene.
The consensus description of the gunman was meaningless and could apply to virtually anybody in his late 20s or early 30s. There was no identity parade, because the police did not have the courage of their convictions. The Defendant is presumed innocent and has to be proved guilty beyond all reasonable doubt.
Marsh was a man of good character, who had defended his country in Northern Ireland. Had seen live action, he was experienced with guns. Do the actions as described to you fit

someone who has seen service in the Royal Marines, who has been fired at and returned fire and shown his skills, courage and nerve in the boxing ring? Would an experienced gunman have wasted a cartridge? Marines are trained to shoot twice to the body and then once at their prostrate victim.
But there would have been no mess up, no fumbling... if a trained marine had done this shooting. This shooting has the hallmarks of someone who bungled it and panicked.
No one condones the shooting of Frank Warren, and hopefully one day the real culprit will be brought to justice but justice demands you should put a decisive end to the prosecution against this defendant. At the end of the day we say Terry Marsh is innocent, you will have the right and privilege in due course of proclaiming that to the world, and we hope you will do it."
I felt like breaking into applause. He was so right. He earlier had made representation to the judge that the matter should not go to a jury. Despite all the hype from the prosecution it rested on one piece of evidence the so-called confession. It was back to Brixton for the night and I watched through the bars the fireworks burning in the dark sky above. It was a time to remember.
The next day my analysis of the case was confirmed in the summing up of the judge. He went through the case addressing each witness and what was said. He was then pointing out what was and what wasn't relevant. "Ignore the defendant's police interview. It was not under oath." he told the jury. So even if I had made a confession to Harris shouldn't it have been ignored for the same reasons. It lasted the whole day and run into the following day. Despite the long summing up the case boiled down to one factor, the evidence of Harris. The rest of the case seemed to exist in order to give some support to what he claimed. "It is wise to look for independent support, because he has 36 previous convictions." the judge said.
I was now in the hands of the jury. I did not expect them to take too long in reaching a verdict but that was not to be the case. I had gone back down to the cells and was placed in a smaller cell. I shared it with the Brinks Matt boys. There was an adjournment in their hearing - a legal hitch.

They seemed to speak freely about their predicament and plan of action to each other despite my presence. It was fascinating stuff and kept my attention. It was just as well since the jury were making a meal of things. The 30 minutes went into an hour and then a little while longer until the door opened. The busy negotiating between the others stopped. The walk to the dock became like a journey to the ring and I began limbering up. There were no pre-fight nerves as such. Unless, limbering up is considered to be a nervous response. I think it was.
As always when under pressure, in fights or life, I wore a big grin. I knew there were people out there who would take pleasure in my suffering. I was not going to give them the added satisfaction of seeing me hurt. Then they win twice. Let them think I'm revelling in it.
As I surfaced into the court so everyone was informally positioned. I was a picture of optimism and joviality. A few words were exchanged between the visitor's gallery and me. Then the usher, anticipating the entrance of the judge, called us to order. The jurors were called. As they walked past taking their seats they seemed to go out of their way to avoid eye contact with me. That was not a good sign. I was no expert on these matters but I had been given a good briefing on the idiosyncrasies of the jury in the past week or so from various sources quoting empirical evidence. Anyway, I knew what reaction I would be displaying. Guilty meant I would smile. I even had a small matchbox in my hand with one of its contents attached as an appendage imitating an aerial. 'Beam me up Scotty', was going to be my first words uttered as a criminal.
Not guilty meant that I would be the coolest person in the Court. I did not want to be seen to gloat after all this was no victory. Defendants in court cases never win they merely, at best, hold their own. Damage is always done to some degree and it would be no different for me. The important thing was not to show your hurt otherwise, you've guessed it, they win twice.
Still victory or defeat for the prosecution was going to be delayed the jury could not reach a unanimous decision. I took comfort from that, ever the optimist. They were sent back by the Judge and allowed a majority verdict of 10 to 2. I went back into the hole in the dock and joined the Brinks Matt boys. They by now

had resolved their differences and the conversation focussed on my immediate scenario. I was back up again in next to no time, but informed that the jury wanted further direction regarding Harris. The court was still in its informal stage and Henri and I played the game of second guess the jury. "On the one hand...but then again on the other it might be." It was impossible to predict. The jury wanted to know if Harris's testimony could stand alone? The judge made the point that they should look for corroborative evidence. It really worried me and everyone associated with me. There was corroborative evidence in the sense that the evidence of the prosecution supported it but it did not follow that that prosecution evidence was true in the first place. As I was returned to the cells again I looked up to the gallery. "Exciting innit?" I exclaimed.

Over 4 hours had passed from the time the jury retired till they had reached a decision, albeit a majority. I was asked to stand up. I'd been there so many times before at the end of each of my fights. Any boxer will tell you about the uncertainties that go through your mind those few seconds before the verdict. We have all been victims of bad decisions. Waiting for this verdict, strangely, was no different. I seemed more preoccupied with how I was going to react to the verdict than the verdict itself.

The foreman of the jury was then asked whether they had reached a verdict. "Yes" replied the foreman. Get on with it and stop fucking about, I thought to myself. But I did not have to wait long. "How do you find the defendant, guilty or not guilty?"

"Not guilty." was the reply.

"I showed no emotion and felt no emotion. In the few seconds I had between the verdict and Henri running towards me I thought how disgusting the whole thing was. Ten months in prison un-convicted. And we as a nation have the audacity to sit in judgement of other countries. When Henri reached the box he grabbed me like I had just scored a goal for West Ham of which he was a dedicated follower. I reciprocated his joy. The gallery cheered and my old Navy pal Ned Rawlins shouted out. “Three cheers for the jury.” The judge seemed to allow the minor celebrations and did not make anything of it.

Of course there was another matter outstanding namely the charge of possessing ten 9mm rounds of ammunition. Fergie

rightly requested that I be bailed to appear the following day on the separate charge. I did not think that far ahead. If I did I would have preferred not to have bail. It would have shown the system up for what it was - a fucking joke. Without the request I would have gone back to Brixton for the night before facing the Court again. I would have refuted the charge strongly but even if found guilty I would have still been walking out of the court a free man because my time on remand far exceeded any sentence that I would have got. This even includes the remission I had lost for standing up for what was right both legally and morally in the prison. That was something those officials responsible have to live with. I regret not going back to Brixton and not saying good-bye to Liam and Damian and doing a bit of gloating.
I couldn't go too far as I had to be back at the court the next day. There was also a matter of a newspaper exclusive. From the very outset I had adopted a twin track approach and would now be able to utilise Henri's other skills. There was the trial and now the subsequent prostitution of my story.
My exit from the Old Bailey would be the picture on all the front pages. However, such promiscuousness with the photographers would diminish my bargaining power with the papers because they would all have the photo they wanted. So there was going to be no joyous exit from the front entrance. I was going to be leaving from the back with my head covered. I must have been the only acquitted defendant to leave the Central Criminal Court in such a fashion. John had a change of clothing ready for me. I got changed in one of the court's toilets. On leaving the toilet I was speaking to John when a lady said to me "I wondered what you sounded like." I did not recognise the lady at first without her wig and gown. "I would have liked to have questioned you."
"It would not have been fair, you're a professional I'm an amateur." I replied to Ann Curnow the Prosecutor. The conversation took place in the restricted confines of the court corridors. Once we reached the public parts I had to remain silent. Journalists asked how I felt. My lips remained sealed. Were I to speak then the quote would be enough to claim an exclusive. So as I did in the court I did outside the court - remained silent. One journalist I very much wanted to speak to was Tina Weaver. Our paths crossed in the court corridors but I

kept my silence despite the support and comfort she had given me with her visits and letters in the preceding 10 months. Business had to come before pleasure. I really wanted to reach out to her and give her a big hug.
A statement had been prepared and while Henri was reading it outside the front of the Court I was trying to sneak out of the rear exit, rather unsuccessfully. The media had all bases covered. With my head covered dodging those photographers eager to get a shot of me I was led to a waiting minibus with World Sports Corporation posters emblazoned on every panel. Inside the minibus it sped off. A number of motorcyclists followed in pursuit with photographers riding pillion. I lay flat on the floor to avoid the photographers and when it was safe the cloak was removed from my head. I felt like I played a part in a sting and now it was time to collect the bounty. There was laughter from everyone in the bus. A few were singing, 'We're the self preservation society'. The photographers were still in pursuit but that added to the fun of it all. Panay and Gill the owners of the Phoenix were expecting us.
The Phoenix had been the scene of a number of press conferences for the Mendy, Maloney and Marsh promotions but now it would be a press conference with a difference. The only press allowed would be the one with the biggest cheque. The others would remain outside on the pavement. Predictably it was the Sun newspaper that gained entry. I had made big mistakes with the first Sun exclusive and it was not going to happen again. They came in with an offer of £130,000. John advised me not to take the offer, reminding me about an earlier article printed in the Sun. I said that they could have the story but there was a matter of a newspaper article printed by them that was libellous. "My hell with Tel" was the headline and was claimed to have come from Jacqui. I wanted a settlement. The settlement was quickly reached at £120,000. There was some irony because the Star had done an article during my incarceration quoting Jacqui and they run with the headline 'Its hell without Tel'. It wasn't libellous but fundamentally fictitious.
I must admit I did have some reservations about this story. Neil Wallis was one of the Sun's representatives. It was Neil who penned the story about the epilepsy. Whenever he spoke to me I

was guarded with my reply not wanting to be misquoted again. I expressed my concerns to Neil to put him on notice. The clock was ticking away and the deadline for the first print run was fast approaching. A picture was needed and I duly obliged wearing a tee-shirt John had printed up. It displayed a cartoon character and the words, 'Who framed Terry Marsh?' As one Sunday newspaper journalist rather snidely later remarked in answer to the question - The Sun.

It was the photo they wanted for the front page. It was going to be the only paper with my post prison mug splashed on it.

The follow up was going to be my jail diaries. Part of the deal was that Jacqui was on board as well. The Daily Star believed they had Jacqui signed up but the Sun gave an undertaking to pay any legal costs should the Star make an issue of it.

I stayed at the Phoenix that night it prevented anyone else from getting photos. There was a bit of sour grapes on the part of the other papers not getting the scoop. Still I was prepared for a backlash. It was par for the course. It was something I did not anticipate on the epilepsy exclusive and came as something of a shock. But now I was not surprised or for that matter bothered. Unlike the epilepsy story this exclusive was totally mercenary.

Yesterday I had left the old Bailey with a cloak over my head this morning I was back. Nothing had changed except my direction of travel. Minders accompanied by the Sun reporter kept the rival photographers at bay as I was guided into the Court. I met with Fergie and Henri for the pre-trial brief. "The Prosecution wants to do a deal. They are offering not to have a hearing but to leave the charge on file."

It meant that I would be walking without a stain on my character. I would not be running the risk of being found guilty and getting a criminal record. By going for the trial there was a down side but no upside. Remember, Defendants never win. I opted for the non-confrontational approach and accepted the prosecution offer. I don't know whether it was the right thing to do or not. It seemed to be the wisest choice but nonetheless I felt it entailed a degree of capitulation on my part. Similarly to my declining not to give evidence. It seemed that I was adopting a risk aversion strategy. I hope I was not setting a trend.

Out of the Court and under the cloak I was led into the waiting car. The driver doubled up as the photographer. The reporter Ian Hepburn was busily penning my jail diaries while I dictated from the back seat squeezed between the two minders. We drove around London looking for photo opportunities. One that did go well was a photo of me standing outside the Scrubbs with the twin towers behind. A screw appeared trying to move me on: I was trespassing on prison property. What a difference a day makes.

Later that day the Sun's Neil Wallis asked me about Jacqui. I ducked the question but it did not stop him reporting in the paper, the next day, that I loved her. I suppose he just couldn't help it.

I stayed at the Chelsea Harbour hotel that evening and met up with Jacqui and the kids and shared a suite. We slept in the same bed but I knew there was no future. I only returned out of concern for the kids. If I was sure that she could look after them I would have not have gone back at all. But regrettably she wasn't able to, in the medium term, so I had to be around. The next morning I was invited into the journalists' room. They wanted to ask me a question. It was a sombre atmosphere and rather disconcerting, "Tel do you mind if we ask you a personal question?"

When someone says that you know it's going to be near the knuckle. My mind raced thinking what could it be. "Go on hit me with it."

"What would you say if we told you Jacqui was seeing one of John Conteh's brothers?"

It never went any further and never made the print. I presumed it was the boyfriend the police had alluded to. There was a further police statement that suggested that the tryst was before I was arrested. It was not a problem for me since we had parted some 18 months earlier. The only reason that she was in my life was because of the children. It was no good going for custody of the children because the social workers always seemed to favour the mother and with me being a boxer, gratuitous violence is assumed as an integral part of the psyche. Now I had been in prison for 10 months charged with attempted murder what chance would I have? The fact that I was acquitted would not go in my favour. Through their 'warped' view it would suggest that

I was not only violent but also cunning with it. I'd already had a taste of social workers putting the blame at my door, when Jacqui could not cope, instead of blaming the alcohol. But you could not win. They would argue she was driven to drink - I'm the one who should have been hitting the bottle.
Later Mum, Winnie and Maria paid a visit along with John to my temporary five star accommodation. The Terry Marsh story still had legs and so stories with new angles were being written. One that made front page on a couple of papers was that I was under investigation for a mortgage fraud for £120,000. Having been questioned about this at the Scrubbs a month into my imprisonment I'm sure nine months later if the police had any real evidence then I would have been charged the moment I left the court. This was a story that was at least six months old. However, it did not stop one of the coppers giving the information to the papers. When I was interviewed regarding this alleged fraud I had been cautioned by the police "...anything you do say may be taken down and used against you." It should include the addendum, 'and passed over to the press'.
When Mum arrived I tried to explain to her about the media 'backlash'. "While I'm in the news they need stories about me so they have to go digging. Don't worry about it its part of the game."
"We know." said John as he produced a copy of the Daily Star. The headlines read 'Terry's kinky secrets'. It was an 'exclusive' interview with Jacqui telling of the time her husband wore women's clothes. It was a bit of a conversation stopper. Jacqui looked mildly embarrassed and denied the story. This must be the exclusive the Star was trying to protect. How could they take anything she said seriously particularly at the time in question.
We were kept under wraps at the Chelsea Harbour hotel until the weekend when the Sun's sister paper the News of the World did their bit. There were some blinding articles in the Sunday broadsheets and they all brought laughter for different reasons. There was the partisan articles by Nick Pitt and Kevin Mitchell of the Sunday Times and Observer respectably. Their bitchiness was so naked that it was funny. Then there were the other reporters who were in awe at the way I treated the whole affair as a joke and appeared to be oblivious to the seriousness of the

matter. I was described as having an insane courage probably due to taking one punch too many in the ring.
Out of the confines of prison and the Chelsea Harbour hotel it was time to walk the real streets. I had adjusted to some degree to the speed of the traffic but it was still mildly disconcerting. Another thing I found strange was opening doors. It takes getting used to after having doors opened for you for the past 10 months. My first venture to the shops meant having to deal with money. My fingers had lost some of their dexterity when it came to handling cash.
Legal matters were still outstanding. The HM Customs and Excise liquidated my Company for non-payment of VAT, £22,000.05 was the amount. I told them I'd give it to them when I received it. The company still had baggage and I was going to put some more of my own money in it but not so the Customs could take it so the liquidation of the Company drew a line under everything. Creditors lost money I would have otherwise paid. The Customs did me a favour. It always feels good when something bad happens which you are then able to turn around to your advantage.
I tried and failed to make a comeback in the States. I got a licence from the Nevada State Commission having passed the medical. I had an arrangement with top promoter Bob Arum but British television were not interested in the proposed contests and so it was the end of the road.

CHAPTER TWENTY-EIGHT
TERRY, FRANK & ERNEST

I now truly was an ex fighter. Yet I'd like to think I was different. I was undefeated. An undefeated ex-fighter, some would say, is incongruous. But in many ways I was only undefeated because I had not gone the full trip. Perhaps I should have had the mandatory defence against Frankie Warren the American boxer who I signed a contract to fight. The sharing of the name with my former manager had confusion and an irony about it. It seemed, one way or another, I was destined to have that fight with a Frankie Warren. Not in the ring but in the libel court where Frank Warren claimed he was undefeated.

I was eagerly anticipating the libel proceedings to be continued but there appeared to be no action on the part of the Plaintiff. Comments in the newspapers attributed to Frank Warren gave me the impression the matter would be rigorously pursued. However, it looked like it was going to wither. That itself was not a problem to me. It was not a fight of my choosing and the timing was also a massive inconvenience I was now a single parent and an undergraduate studying Politics and Government. The libel soaked up a lot of cash that could have been put to better use. If Frank wanted to drop the action that would be fine by me but I wanted my costs. It was around £15,000 at that time.

I went to Court asking that either the proceeding be continued or I am awarded my costs. The judge made the comment that it was the first time he had come across a defendant who was pushing for the commencement of an action. The Court made a direction that adhered to my request. The action was to be re-instated. As well as the matter of costs there was also the suggestion, by the Crown Prosecution, that the avoidance of the libel action was a motive for the shooting of Frank Warren. I was keen to

demonstrate that was not the case and sought vindication.
The hearing was now only weeks away. Henri received a letter from Frank's solicitors asking how an impecunious student can afford to finance a defence. We replied to them knowing only too well that Frank himself was to use their phrase impecunious. We turned the question back to them concerning the liquidity of their client. The solicitors responded saying we had no grounds for asking such a question. They too, it seems, were taken in. The Rolls Royce and the apparent opulence can get you far. All that glitters is not gold, as Mum would say. I have found that those who flaunt wealth invariably do not have it. Lets be honest if you have money and you broadcast it you have the world and his brother wanting to borrow some.
This was going to be my toughest fight. Ernie Fossey my former trainer, an employee of Franks, was now in his boss's corner giving evidence for the Plaintiff. Ernie's wife, Pat, was also giving evidence supporting her husband's testimony. The only person I could call as a witness was my estranged wife Jacqui. However, I never believed half of what she said so how could I expect a jury to believe her? I was on my own. I of course had Henri supporting with Mark Warby as my Barrister and John, now reading Law at University, was ever present, but evidentially it was three against one. The libel hearing coincided with the school half term holidays. It was fortuitous that Kelly was away for that week with the Brownies and my own studying was not disturbed. John and I met up with Henri and Barrister Mark Warby and we walked the short distance from Mark's chambers to the Royal Courts of Justice near the Strand. They were both encouraging me to get into the habit or talking very slowly and deliberately. On seeing Frank I said, "Hello." as I did on the subsequent days. He did not respond verbally, but his chin appeared to quiver. I had seen his chin react in a similar fashion when he was annoyed. Was it his sub conscious equivalent of sucking teeth?
Both sides knew what the other was going to say. We had sight of each other's statements in the pre-trial disclosures. It was a matter of playing it out to the jury. In court hearings libels are different to other cases since the onus is on the defendant to prove their case. Furthermore, this being a Civil action meant

that the burden of proof was on the 'balance of probability' rather than 'beyond reasonable doubt' required for criminal matters. Frank claimed, I had said or implied something defamatory about him; I had to prove what I was alleged to have said – otherwise I lose.

It was first the turn of the Plaintiff to address the court. Frank went into the witness box. I expected there to be several journalists because of our history, but there was only one such person in the press gallery. John and I could not help notice how he was not doing a great deal of note taking, if any. Frank played it with a straight bat and handled the questioning competently. As you would expect from someone promising to tell the truth the whole truth and nothing but the truth. He said, under oath, that he had not known that I was suffering from epilepsy prior to the story in the Sun newspaper.

It was now the turn of Ernie Fossey. I was looking forward to Ernie's testimony I thought it would be interesting to see how the man delivers his testimony comparative to his boss. Frank after all had previous experience in the witness box. Ernie performed above and beyond his public duty. He had promised to tell the truth the whole truth and nothing but the truth. He went further than required; he began to verbally attack me across the court as he stood in the witness box while I sat on the benches behind my legal team.

I thought it was a free shot, but at the same time effective. Had it been Frank Warren who had done it then the jury could either be persuaded or not about the outburst and draw either a favourable or unfavourable inference. As it was it did not really matter what the jury thought about Fossey but it did matter what they thought of Marsh. It must have been a unilateral attempt by Ernie to ingratiate himself with his boss.

It would have undoubtedly damaged my standing with the jury but to what extent? Only they would know. The general consensus on my team was that it was damaging.

It was now time for me to put my side. To win comprehensively I needed to convince the jury that my statement was, on the balance of probability, true. The initial questioning from my Barrister was gentle as expected but the Plaintiff's representative didn't give me such an easy time. Frank and I

had conflicting accounts and it was very much a matter of credibility. My credibility was now to be tested under oath. The worst part of all was when I was taken through the Sun article regarding the epilepsy. I had up until then not gone through the article in its entirety in one go. It had been quite a few years since the article was published. I still found it difficult and embarrassing even after a number of years had elapsed. However, I now had to face up to it. "Did you say this Mister Marsh?" asked Frank's barrister, Tom Shields, referring to a part of the article. "No." was my reply.
Another quote attributed to me was read out. "Did you say this Mister Marsh?" I was sceptically asked again.
"No." was the reply.
It was becoming repetitive but from the other sides' position very effective. There was an exclusive story by me for which I was given a decent sum of money and I was saying that I had never said anything that was attributed to me despite taking the money. I was taken through the story line by line.
Frank must have been revelling in my discomfort. The roles were now reversed. I watched him squirm at the Old Bailey now it was his turn to watch me squirm. Meanwhile the solitary journalist was busy scribing my every word. This guy was more interested in Terry Marsh than Frank Warren.
The Sun line of questioning was now over. I was wild with anger not with the Barrister but the presentation of the epilepsy story that occurred years ago. I did not remember much about the questioning. My head was in a daze regarding the article. It was like I was in a fight taking a volley of punches. Before I could adequately respond to a punch I received another then another to the point I was reeling. I don't know if it looked like that to the jury but it certainly felt like it.
I still felt fazed by it all when asked about Jacqui. She was the one person who could partially support my story but she was absent. How could I call her? She was more of a liability. Mr Shields asked, "Mrs Marsh, is she alive and well?"
"Alive yes." I responded.
Mr Shields began to wind up his cross examination gradually building up to a crescendo, "So you are alleging Frank Warren is lying, Mrs Fossey is lying, and Ernie Fossey is lying.. "

“.. And I have proof that Ernie is lying.” I then produced a video tape from my jacket pocket, "Mr Shields, I am under oath I challenge you to play it."
My interruption had the effect of taking the wind from his sails: that had not been my intention. The now reticent Barrister sat down.
"Well," said the judge looking at Mr Shields, "What do you intend to do with the video?"
"I have not seen it my Lord. It could be anything.” replied Mr Shields rising to his feet again. The jury were dismissed while the pertinent part of the tape was played.
The jury was allowed to see the tape, which contradicted part of Ernie’s testimony and I was allowed to make my point. I don't think forcibly enough. The introduction was much better than the presentation. It was something of an anti-climax. Still it would have been even more frustrating had I not been able to show the evidence. The whole thing was getting to me. In the attempt to discredit the best they could do was reveal that I continued to drive my car despite the epilepsy diagnosis. I figured that I had early signs and symptoms that I could now recognise and therefore did not consider myself to be a risk to anyone although the doctor told me that I should not drive.
The re-examination by my Barrister was going to be a predictably calm affair just to put a few misapprehensions right, "Are you and Mrs Marsh living together?"
"No the families split." I replied, barely completing the sentence before being overcome with emotion. I felt hugely embarrassed being brought to tears in the witness box. I tried to remain composed but it was clear that I was loosing the emotional battle within. The judge interjected "Would you like a break Mr Marsh."
"No." I said, taking up such an offer would have been tantamount to a personal defeat. I may have been down but I was not going to quit. I can't explain my state. The question was harmless and I had no regrets about the separation. The other side could have seen it as a rouse to excuse Jacqui appearing and that was implied in their earlier questioning.
While I was blubbering I noticed out of the corner of my eye the reaction of Ernie Fossey. He was now sitting at the back of the

court in the public seating. He was gesticulating in a manner that made me think; he thought I had turned the tears on. The questioning over I was allowed to leave the witness box and it was now the turn of Consultant Neurologist, Leslie Findley.
It was an awkward situation for me and perhaps for the Consultant. He made the original diagnosis and now I was questioning this diagnosis in a very public manner, I might add at the same time he, bound by medical confidentiality, remained admirably quiet.
I missed the first part of his testimony as I left the court to compose myself and give myself a good talking to for showing such weakness - that's how I saw it. His input, I suspect, was of great benefit to the jury. It helped explain how the diagnosis came about and my reaction to it.
The other issues were whether or not Frank Warren had given permission for the broadcast to go ahead and whether the words spoken were defamatory. On the latter they had made their case but on the former it was not so clear-cut.
I always had suspicions about the Thames television interview. It seemed, to me, that something sinister was at work. I was not aware that the programme was going to include Frank Warren and Adrian Whiteson. I would have had no problem being engaged in a debate with either of them. But I went into the studio believing there was no hidden agenda on the part of the Television Company. I was not aware that Frank Warren was in the studios monitoring my interview with Nick Owen.
The programme that was broadcast was a pastiche of interviews with Marsh, Warren and Whiteson. Earlier, Trevor East, a Thames' Executive, was warned by the Thames', in-house Barrister, Peter Smith that, in his opinion, the broadcast was defamatory to Frank Warren. He insisted that the broadcast could not be allowed without the permission of Frank Warren. It would otherwise leave Thames Television open to a libel action by Warren. At the Barrister's insistence Trevor East contacted Warren by phone. East claimed that that he phoned Warren that evening at Warren's home in Hertfordshire at between 9 o'clock and 9.30. Frank earlier that evening was at his promotion in East London. The main fight was shown on the television programme later that evening. Frank could be seen sitting at the

ringside watching his fighter, my mate Shoey, getting bashed up. The Barrister listened to Trevor East explaining to Frank that his permission was required before the interviews could be broadcast. Trevor East claimed that Frank gave permission and so the broadcast went ahead. The consequences of Frank giving permission allowed us to offer a defence of *volenti*. This meant Frank was the author of his own misfortune and therefore would not be able to claim libel. Frank acknowledged the phone conversation at his home in Hertfordshire but claimed that he did not give permission saying to Trevor East, "You do what you want but I'm suing Terry Marsh."

We became aware of this because Peter Smith, the Thames Television in house lawyer, a friend of the truth, contacted Henri informing him of this matter. Sadly Mister Smith's actions did nothing to enhance his career at Thames. He was called as a witness for the defence as was Trevor East. It would be for the jury to decide whether that meant permission was given or not.

When it came to the judges summing up he instructed the jury, now only eleven due to an illness, on the three points. Was the defendants case proven, was permission given and were the words complained of defamatory? The Judge explained Frank needed all three in his favour. I only required one. The machinations were in many ways irrelevant but we requested that the jury return verdicts on all three, much to the surprise of the judge, who allowed our request. I did not want to hide behind the defence of consent I wanted a definitive decision on the matter of justification.

When the jury returned they agreed that my words were defamatory, but were split regarding the other matters; it was neither accepted nor rejected. The judge sent them back prepared to accept a majority verdict of 10 to 1. They returned a verdict that Frank had given consent for the broadcast. However, they still couldn't decide on whether my allegation was true or false. Frank was the loser but I was not the winner; I just held my own. I was both pleased and disappointed. I would have liked for the jury to have gone in my favour regarding the justification but it wasn't to be. It was my word against the word of Frank Warren, Ernie Fossey and his wife. It was a tall order.

Frank was first to leave the court. On my exit I saw him

surrounded by the posse of press. Henri suggested I delay my exit, he being more familiar with such matters of protocol. After all, my last exit from court was from the back entrance. In this instance the rear entrance led out to Carey Street. I remember Mum using the phrase when I was a kid "Carry on like that you'll end up in Carey street." I now knew what she meant.

"Fuck it." I said to Henri I'm going out now. As I appeared from the Royal Courts of Justice so the pack surrounding Frank peeled off to get the view of the 'winner'. Frank no longer had an undefeated record in the libel courts. The only one he could not beat was this 'impecunious' student Terry Marsh.

I made my comments to the awaiting assembled press. "I thought the jury's verdict was a vindication of earlier accusations that had been made against me." The main press reports focused on Mr Warren losing an estimated £100,000 the combined costs of the Plaintiff and Defendant. The one exception was Nick Pitt. He was the scribe who was eagerly scribbling down my testimony in the court. He later wrote that my post trial statement was something of an exaggeration and that this was not the end of the matter. I don't know whether he knew something I didn't.

The legal team, Henri and Mark along with John and myself went for a celebratory drink. Mark paid for the champagne. I explained I could not pick up the tab as the crunched up five pound note in my pocket was my one and only. I had almost spent every penny I had defending my name because that was all I had to defend. Was it worth it? It certainly was. It cost me around fifty grand but it was the price I had to pay to be true to myself. My love of money is only exceeded by my hate of hypocrisy.

As John and I made a leisurely walk down the Strand, through Fleet Street passing the Old Bailey then St Paul's Cathedral towards Fenchurch Street station it felt good - still undefeated.

The End